FOR LESBIAN PARENTS

For Lesbian Parents

♦

Your Guide to Helping Your Family Grow Up Happy, Healthy, and Proud

Suzanne M. Johnson, PhD
Elizabeth O'Connor, PhD

The Guilford Press

NEW YORK LONDON

© 2001 The Guilford Press
A Division of Guilford Publications, Inc.
72 Spring Street, New York, NY 10012
www.guilford.com

Printed in the United States of America

This book is printed on acid-free paper.

Last digit is print number: 9   8   7   6   5   4   3

Library of Congress Cataloging-in-Publication Data available
from the Publisher

ISBN 1-57230-663-7 (pbk.)

To our daughters
Bailey Suzanne Johnson O'Connor
Rowan Morgan Johnson O'Connor

Acknowledgments

We want to thank a number of people who have helped us as we worked on this book. First and most important, Kitty Moore, Senior Editor at The Guilford Press, who literally supported our work from day one and whose encouragement helped us get this project off the ground. We were also lucky enough to have had the assistance of editor Chris Benton at Guilford, whose suggestions and insights improved the book dramatically. An anonymous reviewer gave us feedback and comments at different stages of this project and each time added valuable advice. Many thanks to Kathy Martin, the world's most amazing transcriber, friend, and frequent childcare provider for our children. Our research assistant, Nanette Silverman, maintained a level of energy and enthusiasm that often exceeded our own. Her thoroughness is commended. Suzanne's colleagues and the administration at Dowling College graciously granted her released time from a full teaching load in order to work on this book. Last but not least, *Alternative Family Magazine*'s assistance helped us get into contact with many of the women we interviewed.

We want to offer our most sincere thanks and appreciation to those women who consented to be interviewed for this project. In sharing their stories, they illuminated our understanding of what it means to be a lesbian mother. Their openness, courage, and willingness to give of their time humbled us and made us proud to be members of the lesbian community.

Finally, we want to thank our daughters: Bailey, whose arrival turned us into a family and who is unfailingly delighted at the thought that her mothers are writing a book; and Rowan, whose joy for life is a constant inspiration and who did not give up her afternoon naps until we were almost finished with this book.

SUZANNE AND BETH

Contents

◆ PART IV ◆ Special Circumstances

◆ PART V ◆ Conclusion

◆ PART I ◆

Introduction and Overview

Introduction:
Why Write This Book?

Just like all expectant parents, we embarked on our journey to parenthood with our eyes opened wide, our hearts overflowing with love, and our minds filled with the belief that we knew what it would be like to have a child. We completely transformed our adult, academic-filled house into one with every state-of-the-art, developmentally appropriate infant toy and accessory. We planned how we would juggle our teaching and research responsibilities with childcare. We discussed the challenges we would face as a family marked as "different" but had complete confidence in our ability to meet them. We fantasized about what our children would be like. And thrown in for good measure, we relied on the fact that we both had our PhDs in developmental psychology. So what could we possibly need to learn that we didn't already know?

As it turned out, a lot. In truth we had absolutely no idea what parenthood would be like, although we would have vehemently challenged anyone who said differently. The fact is, no training, education, or fantasizing can truly prepare you for parenthood. It is something that you make happen and happens to you at the same time. It is overwhelming, exhausting, terrifying, thrilling, and joyous, all at once. It requires more stamina than a marathon. It demands more energy and attention than you knew you had.

In addition to the adjustments that any new parent must make, we had another factor to contend with: We are lesbians. Our child (and later our younger daughter as well) would be raised by two women. We quickly realized that we were setting sail in uncharted waters. We did not personally know any other lesbian or gay couples who had decided to become parents. There was not much written about families like ours. Of course we had read April Martin's *The Lesbian and Gay Parenting Handbook* and Suzanne Slater's *The Lesbian Family Life Cycle*. We loved Audre Lord's writings about raising her children. These authors were important to us, in showing us that others had gone where we were about to go. But living in our nice little suburban town in Long Island, we still felt a bit apprehensive.

We remember our first evening at Lamaze class with Beth weeks away from delivering our first daughter. We sat in the rec room with nine first-time heterosexual parents, all staring at each other as the Lamaze teacher went around the room asking each of us to introduce ourselves. When she got to us, Beth spoke first.

"My name is Beth and I'm about seven months along."

Lori, the Lamaze teacher, followed up. "And do you know what you're having?"

"Yes, we do. It's a girl," Beth said.

Then Lori turned to Suzanne. "And who are you?"

Suzanne smiled slightly, glanced around the room, and began. "My name is Suzanne. I'm Beth's partner of ten years. She really wants to go through natural childbirth, which I think is an oxymoron, but that's beside the point. I'm here to support her and hopefully be able to get through the birthing process without needing major medical intervention."

Lori looked confused for a moment and asked, "Medical intervention for Beth?"

Suzanne shook her head. "No, for me."

Lori smiled and nodded awkwardly. The other nine couples did the same. So much for attempts at humor.

There have always been children who have been raised by gay or lesbian parents, but it is only recently that so many families have been created by openly gay parents. The "gay baby boom," as it has been called, has come about as a result of a number of phenomena. The gay liberation movement of the 1970s empowered gay men and lesbians to be more open about their lives and to reject living in isolation and secrecy. Increased tolerance in much of society toward homosexuality followed, leading to a loosening of legal barriers against homosexual parenting. Advances in medicine also played a role, with various forms of alternative reproduction allowing lesbians to bear children. It is impossible to know for certain how many families there are today that are headed by gay men or lesbians; no one keeps records, and many parents keep their sexuality secret. While there are no definitive numbers, it is estimated that between six and fourteen million children are being raised by at least one gay or lesbian parent in the United States today (*Time*, 26 October 1998). While at times we may feel we are alone, we are not. We are growing in number, and our families are becoming part of the fabric of our schools and communities.

There is great diversity within the community of gay- and lesbian-headed families. Our families originated in various ways, including alternative reproduction techniques, adoption, and re-creating a family after a divorce. Some parents are "out" in their communities in all possible ways, while others maintain privacy. We come from different cultural, religious, and educational backgrounds, yet we are united in our desire to raise happy, healthy children.

The idea of having two mommies or two daddies needs clarification and definition, not just for people in the outside world but also within families headed by same-sex parents. One night, when our daughters were four and two years old, they were having a bath when our older daughter asked, "What's the difference between a mommy and a mama?"

We looked at each other. Buying a little time, Suzanne repeated, "What's the difference between a mommy and a mama?"

Our daughter replied, "Yeah, what's the difference? I know the difference between a mommy and a daddy. So what's the difference between a mommy and a mama?"

We could have said that Mommy (Beth) was the brave one who didn't fear pain and hormonal rages and breastfeeding and the dreaded episiotomy and that Mama (Suzanne) was the cowardly one that held Beth's hand and said "push" when it seemed appropriate. But we didn't. After all, she was only four. So Suzanne said something that would work for a four-year-old. "Mommy has brown hair and I have blond hair." Happy with the answer, she played on in the bathtub. Ultimately, the notion of biological and adoptive parent would have to come into the discussion. But for now she was satisfied.

Experiences construct one's reality, and children growing up with lesbian mothers are certainly having experiences that shape their reality.

These unique experiences will demonstrate themselves in some amusing ways. When our older daughter was three, Santa had delivered a dollhouse complete with two families so that we could assure her of two mommies or any other combination of parents that she wanted to use in her play. She had just begun playing when she turned around with the two male dolls and asked, "What are these guys for?"

Suzanne thought for a moment and said, "Well, they can be for whatever you want."

"Oh, okay. They can be the lawn guys that come and cut the grass every week."

Suzanne held back her laughter and nodded her head seriously. "Okay, they can be the lawn guys."

How different our daughters' experiences truly are. Parents tend to raise their children in households that resemble the ones in which they grew up. Most gays and lesbians with children were not raised in households with gay parents. We were raised in families with parents and siblings who are heterosexual, and the world still is and always will be predominantly heterosexual. Even as adults this assumption of heterosexuality persists in our minds. It never occurred to us that our daughter would ask about the two male dolls. Most of our friends who are also parents are heterosexual. She plays at their houses and interacts with her friends' mommies and daddies. Nonetheless, when it came to her pretend play, and the construction of a family, she immediately went for categories with which she was familiar. A family, by her definition, has two mommies. Actually, to be specific, one mommy and one mama. That's just what preschoolers do. But the effects will be profound culturally. The definition of what a family is and can be will truly be broadened by the generation that we, as gay and lesbian parents, are raising. Just as divorced families and stepfamilies became accepted and single parenting is becoming accepted, parenting by families headed by gays and lesbians will also become accepted. It will happen, not by writing about it, but by doing it, and doing it in an open and public way. Experiences do construct one's reality.

None of us has only one identity. In addition to being lesbian mothers, we all have different cultural identities, racial backgrounds, and religious affiliations. Many of the families in our community are multiracial. Our personal identities influence our childrearing decisions in countless ways. What makes each of our families unique is the particular mixture of identities and personalities of the family members. In this book, it is our intention to focus upon the one quality that all of us share: We are lesbians raising children.

For all our differences, our families are like other families in most ways. Parenting is universal. We worry about the things that all parents worry about—how our children are doing academically, how we should handle discipline, how they are getting along with their peers. There are many excellent parenting books that address these topics. But the day-to-day experiences that our family, and yours, encounter can be unique. The homophobia that surrounds us affects our families in subtle and not so subtle ways. Those issues are the ones that we address in this book. There is a need for lesbian mothers to have a parenting book that speaks to our unique concerns.

Throughout the book, we have quoted from a group of lesbian mothers about their own experiences and perspectives. In Chapter 1, we introduce these remarkable women and their families. They are a very diverse group, from all different parts of the country, and they have come to be lesbian mothers in a variety of ways. Some are the mothers of infants, and some are parents of young adults. Some live in large cities, while others have lived all their lives in small rural towns. Some have lived all of their adult lives openly as lesbians. Some lived for years in heterosexual relationships, only coming to identify as lesbians later in life. These women differ in their educational and occupational backgrounds. Some have advanced degrees. Others have never attended college. We interviewed women who are physicians, sales clerks, and stay-at-home mothers. You may recognize yourself in some of them, while others may not resemble anyone you have encountered. What they all share is the common experience of raising children in lesbian-headed families. They are the true experts on what it is like being a lesbian mother, and their stories will inspire you.

We were struck by the eagerness of these lesbian mothers to talk about their lives and their openness while doing so. While almost all of them were quite willing to be identified in the book by their real names, we made the decision to use pseudonyms to protect their privacy and that of their children. While we changed some details to ensure their anonymity, all of their stories are real. The direct quotations throughout the book are taken directly from their interview remarks.

Chapter 2, "Dos and Don'ts for Lesbian Mothers," contains an overview of the types of issues that becoming a mother presents to lesbians.

These are overriding lessons from the experience of lesbian motherhood that we have gathered from the women we interviewed as well as from our own experience.

We have divided the rest of the book into three sections. The chapters in the first section, "The Lesbian Family in Interpersonal Relationships," focus on the relations between lesbian parents and on their relations with the outside world. Chapter 3, "From Couple to Family," focuses on the transition to parenthood and how becoming parents affects partners. Bringing a child into a relationship involves legalities, of one form or another. It also changes the relationship between partners, who now have to negotiate a whole host of new issues, including changing family relationships, dividing childcare responsibilities, and dealing with jealousy.

Chapter 4, "How to Help Our Children Better Understand Our Family," deals with explaining your lesbianism to your children. This is obviously a topic of great importance to women who have come out after having children. But it is also relevant to those women who came out as lesbian before having a child. Children's capacity to think and understand changes drastically as they develop, and our manner of talking to them about this topic must change as well.

Once a child enters a lesbian family, a whole new collection of people—the child's physician, childcare provider, and parents of playmates—become privy to the parents' sexuality. In Chapter 5, "Dealing with Others: Family, Professionals, and People in Our Children's Lives," we talk about how to handle the other people in our lives and our children's lives. We will discuss how to deal with many people—professional and nonprofessional alike—who come into our lives because of our children.

Children can be very sensitive about being different from their peers. Children being raised by lesbian mothers are undeniably different from most of their peers in an important way. Even under the best of circumstances, children may fear being teased (or may be teased), feel embarrassed, or wish to keep their family makeup a secret. In Chapter 6, "Helping Our Children Deal with Others," we discuss how mothers can be prepared for the possibility that these issues will arise and how to deal with them if they do.

One very important person in a child's life is his or her teacher. We devote Chapter 7, "Dealing with Schools," to our children's teachers and schools. We discuss how gay and lesbian parents can introduce themselves to their children's teachers; how to encourage the teacher to be sensitive to your child's family; how to offer advice to a receptive teacher on teaching the class about diversity; how to deal constructively with a homophobic teacher; and what to do about a hostile teacher.

Showing an aspect of our diversity, Chapter 8, "Religion and Spirituality," explores how gay and lesbian parents deal with the issue of religion. Some choose not to get their children involved in formal religious practice, either because they do not feel the need for it in their lives or because they fear their children will be exposed to messages equating homosexuality with sin. Other families do participate in mainstream religion, supplementing the teachings with discussions about tolerance. Still others have found churches or synagogues that specifically minister to homosexuals and their families. We discuss the different choices that lesbian mothers have regarding religious training for their children.

The second section deals with child development and social issues specifically relevant to lesbian mothers. As our children grow up they will encounter the same stages of growth and maturation as other children. Some of these stages, however, are of more concern to lesbian parents than they may be to heterosexual parents. For example, all children learn about gender roles, come to understand the differences between male and female, and begin to identify as one or the other. Lesbian mothers may be particularly concerned about gender stereotypes, providing their children with male role models, and dealing with gender identity. Chapter 9, "Gender Development, Boys Will Be Boys, Girls Will Be Girls, and Men in Our Children's Lives," takes a look at these topics.

Our children, fortunately and unfortunately, will not be children forever. As our children move into adolescence their own sexuality comes into play. Lesbian parents face the difficult task of providing an environment that most of us never experienced ourselves growing up: one that is open to and accepting of their child's sexuality. Parents must be prepared to help their adolescents grow into mature sexual beings, even if (as in most cases) the child's sexuality is different from that of the parents. It is also possible that our own children may grow up to be gay or lesbian themselves. Chapter 10, "Sexuality and Our Children," addresses these issues.

Despite increased tolerance from much of society in recent decades, bigotry and hate crimes against gays and lesbians are still an unfortunate reality. The October 1998 murder of college student Matthew Shepard brought the issue into focus for much of the nation. Children of gays and lesbians are not unaware of incidents like the one involving Shepard. Parents are in the position of having to allay their child's fears about their safety while acknowledging that danger does exist. Children are also exposed to less extreme examples of gay bashing, such as homophobic jokes and remarks. Chapter 11, "Homophobia and Diversity," helps parents become prepared to help their children with these difficult issues.

The third section of the book, "Special Circumstances," examines unique issues that lesbian mothers may face at some point. Chapter 12, "Divorce and Lesbian Breakup," talks about the transformations some families undergo during the years their children are growing up. Heterosexual marriages and lesbian relationships sometimes end, with profound effects on the entire family. This chapter discusses how to handle this transition with children of different ages and how to deal with the former spouse or partner.

There are many types of stepfamilies in the lesbian community. The most common is formed when a woman ends a heterosexual relationship and begins a lesbian one. There are also stepfamilies that come about from the ending of one lesbian relationship and the beginning of another. Stepfamilies, no matter how they are created, pose special problems and opportunities. These will be addressed in Chapter 13, "Lesbian Stepfamilies."

Increasingly, gays and lesbians are creating their families via donor insemination, surrogate parenting, or adoption. Children who have biological parents whom they have never met sometimes have conflicted feelings about this. Their feelings, which may change over time, need to be dealt with respectfully and openly. We will discuss how to do this with children of different ages in Chapter 14, "Alternative Insemination and Adoption."

In the final chapter, Chapter 15, "Future Directions and Concluding Thoughts," we talk about the prospects for our families in future years. We also reflect on the impact our families will have upon the greater society.

Included in the appendix is a listing of parenting titles we have found to be the most helpful in answering general questions about childrearing, as well as resources of general interest to lesbian mothers and our children.

With the writing of this book we hope to provide helpful guidelines and advice for families like our own who are forging a new path in what it means to be a family. We have written this book to address those topics that are particular to families headed by lesbians. There are other people who may find this book of use as well. Lesbians who are considering parenthood may find it helpful, to get a glimpse of what they will be facing if they decide to have children. Gay fathers face many of the same issues as lesbian mothers and may benefit from this book. Professionals who deal with children of lesbians, be they therapists, teachers, or health-care workers, will find it helpful to learn about the experiences of lesbian mothers.

What we can provide as two developmental psychologists, mothers of two daughters, and a couple of sixteen years is a collection of childrearing information, facts, and experiences that we hope will be of value to you and to your family.

A note about pronouns: We wanted to show respect for families with both male and female children, but we also wanted to avoid using the awkward "he/she" throughout the book. We chose to use "he" in some chapters and "she" in others, when talking about your child. We are, of course, referring to both male and female children in all our discussions.

◆ CHAPTER 1 ◆

Lesbian Mothers:
Who We Are

In preparing to write this book, we interviewed a number of lesbian mothers about their experiences. We asked them about their family background; their decision to become lesbian parents (or to come out as lesbians after becoming parents); about their children's experiences, inside and outside the family; and about their concerns and hopes as lesbian mothers. We talked with women in different areas of the country, who had come to be parents in many different ways. Their experiences as lesbian mothers vary greatly. You will probably see yourself in one or several of these women. You may recognize their situation as similar to your own, or you may read about a particular incident and think, "Oh, that happened to me too!" We hope that you will begin to feel a sense of community with this group of women and realize that there are a lot of mothers out there just like you.

While statistics in this area are hard to come by, it is probably safe to say that, historically at least, most lesbian mothers started out as heterosexual mothers. Sometime after their children were born they ended their heterosexual relationships and began lesbian relationships. Diane is one example of a woman who followed this path. Diane has one child, Alyson, who is twelve years old. Diane and her husband divorced when Alyson was two. Diane entered her first lesbian relationship three years later. That relationship lasted for five years. Currently, Diane is single. Alyson maintains ties with her father and her mother's former partner, both of whom live nearby. Diane is very involved with the local gay and lesbian community, and she and Alyson regularly attend functions and marches. Alyson attends a small private school, where the teachers actively promote awareness of diversity. Diane works as a college professor in Massachusetts.

Another family that had its start within a heterosexual relationship is Gina's family. Gina works behind the counter of a deli and has a seventeen-year-old daughter, Carla. Carla's father was only briefly involved with Gina and has never been part of Carla's life. Gina first became involved with another woman while pregnant. She dated a few different women when Carla was a child. She has been with her current partner, Kathy, for seven years. Gina, Kathy, and Carla live together in New York, where they moved three years ago. Currently, Gina is not out to her co-workers and employer. She fears that she would lose her job. Carla has told only a few close friends that her mother is a lesbian. While Carla and Kathy have a friendly relationship, it is not parental.

Often, when a woman leaves her husband and falls in love with another woman, she is fearful that her lesbian relationship may cost her custody of her children. Several of the women we spoke with had this experience. Tess has three children: Evan is thirteen, Caitlin is nine, and Sean is eight. She and her husband divorced four years ago. Shortly after that she began her relationship with Barbara. Tess's ex-husband tried to get custody of the children, claiming in court that Tess's relationship with Barbara made her an unfit parent. He lost; the judge did not consider Tess's sexuality a relevant issue. The children now live with Tess and Barbara and visit their father and his new wife. Tess's ex-husband has mellowed since the custody battle and no longer criticizes Tess and Barbara's relationship. Tess and Barbara work in the publishing field in Washington.

Not only do custody issues arise; so do the tensions surrounding stepparenting and what role the mother's partner will play with the children. Irene and her partner, Kitty, have been together for two years. They both work as salesclerks in department stores in Missouri. Irene has two children, Bradley, age ten, and Brittney, age nine. There is a joint custody arrangement for the children, who live with Irene and Kitty for one week and with their father, Mike, for the next week. Mike reacted quite negatively to Irene's involvement in a lesbian relationship. He tried to use that fact to deny her custody and made a number of disapproving remarks to the children about Irene and Kitty. Since the judge's decision to award joint custody, things have improved. Mike has stopped making homophobic remarks to the children. Bradley, who initially blamed Kitty for his parents' divorce, is becoming more comfortable with her.

Not all lesbian mothers are in a position where they feel they can be open about their relationship. Marie and Shirley have been together for twenty-four years and have raised eight children together in Utah. When they met, both women were in heterosexual marriages. Marie had five children and Shirley had three. After becoming friends, they realized that they were in love and that they could not deny that and remain unhappily married to their husbands. Both women divorced, and they and the children moved in together. Marie and Shirley were not open about the fact that they were lesbians, to their children or anyone else. The kids told their friends that their mothers were like the ones on the television show *Kate and Allie,* in which two divorced mothers move in together. Marie and Shirley finally "came out" to their now grown children four years ago. The children all said they already knew. Marie and Shirley now have fourteen grandchildren.

A relatively recent means for lesbians to become mothers is through the use of alternative insemination. Since the 1980s, lesbians have created their own baby boom using donor insemination (see *Considering Parenthood,* by Cheri Pies, for example). Some women choose to use unknown donors, preferring anonymity and no ties to a father figure. Others choose someone they know. In some cases this is because they want the donor to play an active part in the child's life. Sometimes it is a relative of the nonbiological mother, whose service as a donor ensures that the child will be genetically linked to both parents. Some women are just not comfortable with the idea of an anonymous donor. Clearly, women who choose donor insemination represent a diverse group.

Most of the women we spoke with who chose an anonymous donor were in a relationship when they became pregnant and did not wish for a third parent to be involved. Rosita and Gabriella have two daughters, Katya, who is six, and Sofia, who is four. Gabriella is the biological mother of both girls, who were conceived with the same anonymous donor. Rosita has adopted both children. Rosita is a school guidance counselor and she also works part time as a photographer. Gabriella is an admissions clerk at a local hospital. Rosita and Gabriella first started seeing each other while they were in high school. They broke up for a few years, but then got back together as adults. They had known each other for sixteen years when Katya was born. Their family lives in New York.

Susan and Andrea have been together for eight years and have seven-month-old twin boys. Susan gave birth to the boys, who were conceived via an anonymous donor. She is currently a stay-at-home mother. Andrea is employed full time as a nurse. They live in a state where second-parent adoptions are not legally recognized, so only Susan is a legal parent. Once the twins were born, Susan and Andrea felt that they wanted their family to have regular contact with other families like their own. They started the first lesbian mothers' group in their area. The members of the group get together regularly for play dates.

In some cases, both mothers wish to have the experience of pregnancy and childbirth. Deirdre and her partner, Meredith, have two children: Kelsey is five and Tyler is eighteen months. Deirdre is Kelsey's biological mother and Meredith is Tyler's biological mother. Both children were conceived with the same anonymous donor. Deirdre and Meredith went through a second-parent adoption for each child, so they are both legal parents for both children. Deirdre works full time as a psychologist, and Meredith works part time as a graphic artist. Their family lives in Illinois.

Not all couples who have children together manage to stay together. Joanne's fourteen-year-old son, Will, is being raised by four women: Joanne (his biological mother by an anonymous donor); her partner, Denise; Joanne's former partner, Rebecca; and her partner, Elaine. Joanne and Rebecca split up when Will was four years old. They worked out the custody arrangement between themselves. Will spends most of his time with Joanne and Denise. Both Joanne and Rebecca are therapists. They live in California.

For women who do not wish to use an anonymous donor, asking a friend to fill that role can be the solution. Cheryl and Jeanine have been together for seventeen years and have a two-and-a-half-year-old son, Adam. Jeanine is Adam's biological mother. He was conceived through alternative insemination with a known donor, a friend of theirs. The donor is one of Adam's godfathers and sees him on a regular basis, although he does not function in the role of a parent. Cheryl has full legal custody of Adam, as second-parent adoptions are not legal where they live. Cheryl has been a stay-at-home mother since Adam was born and plans to return to work part time within the next year. Both Cheryl and Jeanine have master's degrees in special education.

Not all known donors have, or wish to have, a special relationship with the child they helped conceive. Tara has one daughter, eleven-year-old Tracy. Tara and her ex-partner, Wendy, who live in Ohio, broke up six years ago. Wendy has a new partner with whom she has another child. Tara and Wendy share custody of Tracy. Wendy used a known donor to have Tracy. Tracy sees her biological father, who lives in another state, about once a year. Tara also has a new partner, but they do not live together and do not plan to do so anytime soon. Tara's new partner has a very friendly relationship with Tracy, but it is not a parental one.

It is not uncommon to find children in our community who were conceived by a lesbian mother and a gay father. Lauren and Julie have a two-year-old son, Nathaniel. Julie met Lauren four years ago. At that time, Lauren was trying to become pregnant with her friend Simon, a gay man. Lauren and Simon intended to share parenting responsibilities. Julie understood this and was happy to take part in parenting as well. After some difficulties, Lauren became pregnant and Nathaniel was born. Nathaniel spends one evening during the week and half of each weekend with his father. Julie, who is retired from the military, stays home to take care of Nathaniel during the week. Lauren is employed full time as a physician in Pennsylvania.

For some couples, genetic links are extremely important. Some have found ways to have a child who is biologically related to both her mothers. Becky and Anne have a six-year-old daughter, Samantha. Samantha was conceived via a known donor—one of her uncles. Becky and Anne do not typically tell people which one of them is Samantha's biological mother. Their daughter is biologically related to both of them and looks like both of them. When Samantha is older, they will tell her that her uncle was the one who helped her mothers have her. Becky is a therapist and Anne is a computer technician. Their family lives in Illinois.

Not all cases of known donors work out happily. Karen is a physician's assistant and lives in California. Her daughter, Jessica, is in kindergarten. Karen used a known donor to become pregnant. She and the donor had a written agreement stipulating the amount of contact he would have with the child once she was born. When Jessica was four months old he decided he wanted more contact and rights as a father. Karen wanted to stick to their original agreement. After several years of court battles, Jessica now spends almost half her time with her father and his partner, and half her time with Karen. Karen is not happy with this arrangement. Although Karen was in a relationship with another woman when Jessica was born, that relationship ended shortly before Jessica's first birthday. Jessica has no contact with Karen's ex-partner. Currently, Karen is single.

Lesbians also form their families through adoption, although they are not always able to do so openly as lesbians. They may have to pretend to be single, presumably heterosexual, women to some or all of the staff involved in the adoption. This was the case for Margaret and Sarah. Margaret and Sarah have been together for nine years. They adopted their daughter Alexa from Russia two years ago. They are currently awaiting approval to go to Russia to adopt a second baby. Because authorities in Russia would not allow a child to be adopted by a lesbian, Margaret officially adopted Alexa as a single parent. Once she was in this country Sarah adopted her as a second parent. Sarah is employed full time as a paralegal. Margaret works part time as a physical therapist. Their family lives on a small farm in California, close to many members of their extended family.

Lisa and Robin, who formed their family through domestic adoption, went through a similar process. Lisa and her former partner, Robin, have two sons: Rafael is seventeen and Joshua is eleven. Both boys were adopted as infants. Lisa adopted Rafael and Robin adopted Joshua, and later they did second-parent adoptions. Before they adopted their older son, Lisa and Robin drew up a contract specifying what would happen in the event that their relationship ended. Lisa and Robin broke up when the boys were eleven and five. As they had specified in their contract, Lisa and Robin now share joint custody. Each parent contributes equally to the financial care of the children, and the boys spend half their time with each. The family lives in New York.

Not all families fit neatly into one category or another. Some have been formed by a combination of methods, with different children entering the family in different ways. Paula and Nancy, for example, have been together for twenty years. They have four sons: Richard and Fred, who are now in their early twenties and were Nancy's sons from a previous marriage; Thomas, who is sixteen and is Paula's biological son conceived with a known donor; and C. J., who is ten and whom Paula and Nancy adopted as an infant. When they were children, Richard and Fred spent half their time with Paula and Nancy and the other half with their father and his second wife. Thomas has regular contact with his biological father and his partner. Over the years, Paula and Nancy have had foreign exchange students living with them, some for several years at a time, and they consider these young people to be part of their family as well. When the children were young, Paula worked only part time and assumed the bulk of the childcare. About six years ago, Nancy decided to stay at home and Paula returned to full-time work. (Both women are lawyers.) Gradually, as the boys have gotten older, Nancy has been taking on more work outside the home. This family lives in Washington state.

Yvonne is in the process of expanding her family. Yvonne is currently a single mother of one son, seven-year-old Enrique. Yvonne was Enrique's foster mother from the time he was four days old and has since adopted him. Yvonne is currently pregnant with another child, who was conceived with an anonymous donor. Yvonne, who is white, chose a Hispanic donor, so that the baby would look like Enrique. Yvonne has been single throughout all of her son's life. She has a close circle of friends who spend a great deal of time with her and Enrique. Yvonne is a social worker. She and Enrique live in Massachusetts.

These women came to motherhood from different paths, and they differ in other ways as well. They live in different areas of the country. Some are in large cities, some live in the suburbs, and some are in rural America. Some practice traditional religions, while others are devoutly antireligious. Some are very involved in lesbian and gay politics, while others are not even out to their friends or people they work with. What they all have in common is their concern for their children and their mindfulness of how their lesbianism may affect their children.

◆ CHAPTER 2 ◆

Dos and Don'ts
for Lesbian Mothers

Lesbian mothers, no matter how they came to be raising children, share some universal experiences. In our discussions with the lesbian mothers described in Chapter 1, we found many shared themes. We thought it would be helpful to talk about these common experiences right up front. Women who are planning on having children, or weighing the pros and cons of parenthood, will want to read this chapter to get an idea of what being a lesbian mother is like. Those who already have children may find it helpful to reconsider the experiences we have that are so common that we don't think about them anymore. You may even find yourself recognizing some situations that you thought were unique to you. We will return to these themes again in more detail in later chapters, but these "Dos and Don'ts" represent the most common experiences of lesbian mothers.

Dos for Lesbian Mothers

1. DO expect to be outed frequently.

If you were a lesbian before you had children, you probably were open about your lesbianism, to one extent or another, in different areas of your life. Your family probably knew, perhaps some of the people at work, certainly your friends. But now you have a child, and your understanding of "openness" is about to undergo a radical change. Not only will you need to explain your family situation to people important in your child's life (like teachers and doctors) but you will find yourself talking about your family to casual acquaintances and even strangers. We remember being at a park with Bailey when she was a baby and chatting with another mother about babies and baby things. After a few minutes she smiled at us and said, "So, which one of you is the mother?" We were a bit startled (we were still new at the parenting business and not used to handling these kinds of questions yet), but then Suzanne just said, "We both are." The woman looked slightly confused for a moment, then just said, "Oh, that's great," and we went back to our discussion of disposable versus cloth diapers.

The point is that "coming out" is now something you will do with more and more frequency. As your child gets older, he or she will often come out for you. Your child will probably feel comfortable talking about having two moms, or a mom who has a girlfriend, to friends in school, to grocery store cashiers, to ballet teachers—you name it. You are out of the closet now on all fronts, and who knows about your life is not always in your control.

2. DO show your child that you are comfortable with who you are.

Your child is being raised in a lesbian-headed family. Whether your child will feel proud of that fact, comfortable with it, or embarrassed and ashamed by it will depend in great part on you. The openness you show to others, the ease with which you talk about yourself, and the degree to which you feel comfortable about your life all send very powerful messages to your child. It is critically important that you show your child that you are not ashamed of who you are; in fact, you are proud of yourself and your family. How do you do that?

First, don't hide who you are. Let people know your child has two mothers, if this is the case. If your child sees you avoiding all discussion of family makeup, or sees you become flustered and embarrassed at personal questions, he or she will get the message that your family is something to be ashamed of. If you need to, practice saying things like, "My son has two mothers"; "My daughter's other mother will be picking her up today"; "No, my son doesn't have a father." The more practice you get saying things like this (and you will get plenty of practice) the more comfortable you will be in doing so.

You may need to work on your own self-concept a bit. It is not unusual for lesbians to have unresolved feelings related to their sexuality and identity. Sometimes feelings of guilt, inadequacy, or shame may linger, even years after you think you have dealt with them. Having children will bring these issues, and many others, to the forefront. If you do have any residual negative feelings about being a lesbian, you need to work them out as best you can. You owe it to yourself; but you certainly owe it to your children.

3. DO get used to the idea that you will often be assumed to be heterosexual.

The world looks at a woman with a child and automatically assumes "straight, probably married woman." Particularly when you are alone in public with your child, you will be assumed by others to be straight. How does this prejudice show itself? Well, we have found that whenever either one of us takes our children to the pediatrician, the receptionist calls us "Mrs. O'Connor." Now, we are out to our children's pediatrician, and he never makes that mistake himself, but somehow the receptionist can't quite get it that neither one of us is "Mrs. O'Connor." It's not that this is a big deal; it's just that it's jarring to hear yourself addressed in a way that you're not expecting. And it does underscore the fact that the world assumes everyone is straight.

When Beth was pregnant with Rowan, she went to have an ultrasound. Everything was fine, and the technician printed out a couple of pictures for us to keep. This ultrasound machine had the capacity to print captions on the pictures, so the technician helpfully printed out "Hi Mom and Dad" on our ultrasound picture of Rowan. Beth could have made a fuss and asked her to reprint the photograph, but she chose not to (probably due to the presence of those happy pregnancy hormones as well as the relief of being told the baby was fine). Some situations are worth making a fuss about; others are not. You have to make the call. But know that these situations will arise.

4. DO ensure, as much as you can, that the people in your child's life are respectful of your family.

Very few people would do something deliberately to hurt your child or make your child feel left out. However, sometimes people can do hurtful things unintentionally. It is your job to insure that your child is not spending time with people who do not respect your family. This means talking not only to your child's school principal or director, but also to the teacher. It means making sure that your child will not be exposed to anti-gay rhetoric at church or in religious education. It means talking to your child's friends' parents before your child spends time at their home. It may mean limiting, or even eliminating, contact with some extremely homophobic individuals.

5. DO provide your daughters and sons with male role models.

Some lesbians' children have fathers who play an active role in their lives. The mothers of children in this situation do not necessarily have to go out of their way to provide male role models for them. Others of us have male relatives—our children's grandfathers, uncles, and cousins—who are regularly involved in our children's lives. Again, other than making sure our children get to see their relatives frequently, we do not need to go out of our way for male role models.

If you are not in either of those situations, however, you will need to make special arrangements for your children to spend time with adult men. This is not usually difficult to do. Many team coaches and children's activity group leaders are male. Your child will undoubtedly have friends with fathers, and they can be wonderful role models for them. We usually think of the importance of male role models in relation to our sons, but daughters need them just as much.

Don'ts for Lesbian Mothers

1. DON'T expect universal acceptance of lesbian motherhood, from either your straight or lesbian friends.

We have found that some liberal, generally open-minded straight people, who have no problem accepting their gay and lesbian friends, do have a problem when their gay or lesbian friends become parents. They generally couch their concerns in seemingly supportive ways, suggesting that it might not "be fair" to bring a child into a situation that will inevitably lead to teasing, ostracism, and so on. Or they say they worry about what kind of responses you will get from others as a result of being a lesbian with children. Whatever the form the "concern" takes, it still shows a striking lack of support for your choice.

Those women who had children prior to becoming lesbian may face a similar challenge from their straight friends. Most of the time the friends say they want you to be happy, but some of them most assuredly did not mean they wanted you to be happy WITH ANOTHER WOMAN! These friends, too, may say they have concerns about your child's well-being; this may in part be true. But their main concern is that you have announced you are a lesbian, and they do not like it. Some of your friends will come around; they just need time. Some, unfortunately, will not come around, and that will mean a loss for you and them.

We expect our lesbian friends to be whole-heartedly on our side when we become parents. We often have a romantic, idealized image of how our friends will draw together and celebrate our family (remember in the comic strip "Dykes to Watch Out For" when the whole community gathered to witness the birth of Toni and Clarice's son?). Reality does not always match our fantasies. Lesbians can be just as nonsupportive as those straight friends we talked about. They may even cite similar concerns, suggesting that it's not fair to the child. Lesbians are not immune to internalized homophobia, as these remarks demonstrate. Some just plain can't understand why any lesbian would want to have a child. They may feel that being childless is one of the advantages of being lesbian: We get to avoid the "drudgery" of motherhood. They may resent the time and attention that a child will take.

So, beware. You may not find the encouragement and support from your friends that you thought you would.

2. DON'T pressure yourself to be the perfect mother, or your family to be the perfect family.

Some lesbian mothers feel that they have something to prove to their friends and to the world about themselves. They feel that they can prove their worth as mothers by being not only the best mothers they possibly can be but the best mothers that possibly could be. Being "Super-Mom," they figure, will dispel any doubts about whether lesbians can be good parents. Having "Super-Kids" will demonstrate that being raised by lesbians is not only not detrimental to children but actually beneficial. In short, all we have to do is be perfect.

Well, not a single one of us is a perfect mother, and even our children, wonderful as they are, are not without fault. This is not a problem. The problem comes when we expect ourselves or our children to be perfect, to prove a point or to make ourselves feel worthy. We can't help but fall short of our goal, if our goal is perfection. Falling short of our goals leads to feelings of disappointment and inadequacy. So don't go down that road. Don't put unnecessary pressure on yourself.

3. DON'T assume that your sexuality is going to be a major problem for your child at some point.

Children of lesbian mothers are at risk for teasing and harassment from their peers. This is a valid concern and one that many lesbian mothers share. We worry that our children may suffer because of who we are. It is right for us to be concerned and to be prepared to help our children deal with potential problems. However, it would be a mistake for us to assume that teasing and harassment are inevitable consequences for our children. The fact that our children have two mothers, or one mother who goes out with women, is not necessarily going to cause them to be singled out and ridiculed by other children. Your child may not be the only one in the crowd with a lesbian or gay parent. Your child will absolutely not be the only one without a father in the house. And children today are much more likely than children of twenty or thirty years ago to know gay people or at least understand that there are gay people in the world. So don't assume that having a lesbian mom just has to lead to some sort of social difficulties for your child.

4. DON'T assume that your child will NEVER experience any social difficulties due to your lesbianism.

As we just discussed, problems with teasing and harassment are not inevitable: Unfortunately, neither are they impossible. Many of us, especially those who live in liberal, progressive areas where people are generally accepting of different lifestyles, would like to think that OUR children wouldn't have any problems like that. We think that, since we've been completely out and open about our lives and have never encountered a problem, the same will hold true for our children. After all, our children go to the most progressive schools, they know lots of gay men and lesbians, how could this be an issue for them?

Homophobia still exists, even in the most seemingly enlightened areas. Even if your child is in an idyllic environment, there still may appear an individual child or adult who will make hurtful, disparaging remarks. We cannot control everything that happens to our children. We cannot prevent people from saying unkind things to our children. What we can do is be aware that this could happen.

5. DON'T overlook the advantages that being raised by a
   lesbian mother will have for your child.

Your child is, in many ways, very lucky to have a lesbian mother. Children of lesbian mothers will have a different set of experiences, values, and expectations than most other children. Your child will grow up knowing that women can do anything; that there are many kinds of people in the world; that being different is okay; that love is the most important thing there is. Your child will have, as a mother, someone who is true to herself, regardless of what others think. Your child will see you demand respect from others. You can, and should, be proud of what you are doing, and the lessons you are teaching your child.

◆ PART II ◆

The Lesbian Family in Interpersonal Relationships

♦ CHAPTER 3 ♦

From Couple to Family

The transition from being a childless couple to being parents is an enormous one. Of course you thought a lot about having a child. As lesbian parents you have been preparing to become parents for much longer than nine months. There are no "accident" babies in our community. We typically plan for a long time, sometimes for years, before we even begin trying to conceive a child. Adoptions can take even longer, and require more effort, than having a biological child. Lesbians spend more time and money in achieving parenthood than the typical heterosexual couple. In short, we lesbians undertake parenthood with all the casualness of an armed invasion.

Then it actually happens. You are a family. This chapter is about the transition from being a couple to being a family. (For more on the methods by which many of us get there, turn to Chapter 14.) There are many important aspects of this transition period, from legalities for our families to our own emotional responses, that need to be addressed. If you are a single mother, most issues apply to you as well. In addition, single mothers have their own unique challenges, which we will also discuss.

The Impact on Your Relationship

Strengthening Your Relationship

Prospective parents often expect that having a child will bring them closer together. Often this is the case. Sarah feels that "what Margaret went through to go to Russia, to go to the orphanage and deal with the actual trip and bring Alexa home, made me feel ten times more strongly than I ever thought I could feel about her. I have so much respect and love and awe at all these things she could actually do. I think my reaction was probably similar to how a partner feels when somebody gives birth. Knowing that the person you love just endured all this, you know, partly for themselves, and partly for this child, but also partly for you. And I felt the same way about Margaret's parents. They went to Russia and went through all this, so my whole feeling about them totally expanded." Margaret adds, "When I was working full time, our lives had a lot of demands on them outside of the home. Our lives can be very demanding now, but they're inside the home, and we're together. Before Alexa came, if there was one thing that I wanted to improve about my life it was that I wanted to spend more time at home. I was involved in all these different things, and I was doing this and I was doing that, not related to Sarah and me, not related to a common goal, not related to our family or our home. Alexa has caused us to stop and be together and just do things as a family. So our relationship has been strengthened, because more energy is put into the relationship and our family."

Lauren feels that having Nathaniel has made her relationship with Julie "stronger in many ways. It's forced us to communicate better than we might naturally have done. Sometimes it shifts the focus more off of us and more on Nathaniel, which is sometimes good and sometimes bad."

Cheryl talks about how having Adam brought her and Jeanine "closer, because we're even more of a family, in a lot of ways. The decision making that we share has added a level. Before, the decisions that we made as a family were 'When do you want to eat dinner and what do you want to have? Is it okay with you if I go to school?' Now we really have to struggle through, and read, and think, and consider how to best make decisions for our family on Adam's behalf."

The Downside: Jealousy, Feeling Neglected

Not all the effects on your relationship of becoming parents are positive. It is common for one partner to have feelings of jealousy over the amount of time her partner spends with the child. This is particularly likely in stepfamilies or blended families, where the new partner walks into a relationship with a woman who is already a mother. Jealousy and feelings of neglect can occur in families where the child is brought into the couple relationship as well. A child takes an enormous amount of time and attention, and we all have limited amounts of both of those things. Something has to give, and it is often the adult relationship, at least for a while. "There's no doubt that the time that we spend on our relationship, the intimate time, the time that we spend thinking and planning, is less," says Cheryl.

Susan and Andrea have two infants. They find that the only time they have for their own relationship right now is during naptime. Cheryl and Jeanine, whose son is a little older, agree that when you have an infant it's very hard to do anything other than baby care. "When Adam was born," says Cheryl, "a friend of mine said that 'For the next two years he's going to take a lot of what you have.' I think just now we're beginning to feel like maybe we can think about actually scheduling regular time in. We're the kind of people who committed to Adam. We made a commitment to being with him and having him, so we were willing to give up two years to get that going."

Rosita talks about the changes in her relationship with Gabriella since they had the children. "There's so much stress, of just the everyday stuff. And it's not just that there's stress. We don't have time for each other as much as we used to. I love my kids dearly, but there are times I wish that I could just, on a Sunday, say to her, 'Hey, you want to go out to dinner and a movie?' and just go. We can't do that. That requires babysitting and planning. So we have given up a lot as far as our social life and our sex life go, because of the kids."

◆ Did You Know . . . ? ◆

For most couples, marital satisfaction goes down after the birth of a baby.

Cowan, C. P., & Cowan, P. (1999). *When partners become parents: The big life change for couples.* Mahwah, NJ: Lawrence Erlbaum Associates.

In our relationship, Suzanne was most keenly aware of these feelings when our children were infants still being breastfed. She sometimes felt like a "third wheel," with Beth and the baby having formed a strong attachment and Suzanne not sure where she fit in. Fortunately, these feelings faded for Suzanne as the babies got older and became interested in other things besides nursing. But you should not feel that your best strategy is to wait for things to change. There are things you can do now to alleviate some of this discomfort. If you feel left out of the parenting loop, talk to your partner and work to get yourself back in it. You could have an arrangement where, when you come home from work, your partner hands the baby to you and she disappears for a while, leaving the two of you to have special time together. You can be in charge of at least some of the feedings. This is so even if your partner is breastfeeding. She can pump some breast milk and you can bottle feed it to your infant. This is what we did. You can have special activities that just you and your child do together. You might want to sign up for a mommy-and-me class, or be the one to take him to soccer practice on Saturdays, or just take him to the park or the movies every weekend—just the two of you. Be sure to be involved in the activities that are not so much fun, too. Nobody is crazy about changing diapers, but doing your share of diaper changes will make you feel like a real parent in a hurry.

Are Two Mothers Better Than One?

There is something unique about our families, and we should not ignore that. The fact that both of the parents in our families are mothers really does make a difference. Women are expected to be the main parent, the primary caregiver, for their children. Although that statement is less true today than it was thirty years ago, it still holds. We are the ones who are expected to stay home with a sick child, to attend school conferences, to be involved in school programs. Fathers are not generally assumed to be as involved in day-to-day parenting activities (there's a reason why the phrase "soccer mom" has become so popular, while "soccer dad" is virtually unheard of). So what happens in families with two moms and no dads? You can get two very involved parents who actively participate in their child's life. You can also get two very overextended, stressed out parents who try to do everything. Two women trying to be "Super-Mom" can lead to unnecessary pressure and strain.

Mothers have a tendency to give everything they have to their children, and ask for nothing for themselves. Families with two mothers are at special risk for becoming overly focused on the children and their well-being. Lesbian mothers can feel guilty for wanting any time alone, or time with their partner. Try not to fall into this trap. Even though having children has changed everything in your life, you are not being selfish or a bad mother to want to have a break now and then. You need it, and having some time off will make you a better mother and a happier person.

Parenthood is the trump card of life; it supersedes any and all other relationships. And if you are not careful, it can replace your partnering relationship with a strictly parenting relationship. Having a baby brings about profound changes in the lives of new parents. Their relationship with each other is not the same as it was. Most commonly, couples talk about their loss of personal freedom and the decreased time they have alone with each other as the most stressful changes. Lesbian couples, in addition, mention the decrease in emotional intimacy and sharing as particularly stressful.[1] We tend to value our emotional connection with our partners, and we miss it when it changes.

All relationships need time and energy to flourish. Once you have children you will, by necessity, give them a great deal of time and energy. Time and energy are limited resources; the more you give in one area, the less you have to give in another area. Your relationship with your partner may have to take a backseat for a while. The danger is that your relationship with your partner may continue to fade into the background, until you find yourselves feeling like two strangers. Women, in particular, are at risk for always placing their children's needs above their own. While you do have to be selfless a lot of the time as a mother, you do not have to be selfless all of the time.

It is important to maintain a strong couple relationship, separate from your relationship as co-parents, for several reasons. This will make you a better parent. The more support you get from your partner, the better able you will be to parent. It is good for your children to see a loving relationship between their parents. You also need a close, loving adult relationship for your own sake! All of us need to feel loved and supported. It is important for your own sense of well-being and fulfillment to be in a satisfying relationship. And remember, your children won't be children forever. At some point they will leave the nest, and it will be just the two of you again. It would be nice, when that happens, if you and your partner still have a close attachment with one another.

Keeping that special couple bond going requires both of you working together. You must give your own relationship time to flourish and grow. This means that you must have time away from the children, and during this time you must do things unrelated to the children. So you can't, on your one night out in months, go to the children's store in the mall to pick up some new outfits for your little ones. The two of you can go to the mall on your one night out, but you should do something just for the two of you. Go to the movies or the lingerie store or browse at the bookstore. Go out to dinner at your favorite restaurant, but do not spend the evening talking about the kids. In fact, we try to make it a rule on our dates that the children are off-limits as conversation topics. It does seem kind of artificial at first, but soon you will find that there are other things the two of you can talk about.

Just as it is important for families to have traditions, it is important for couples to have their own private traditions. If there were certain things the two of you did before you had children, try to maintain at least some of them now. If you never had a childless period together, try to create some adult-only traditions. For example, have a candlelight dinner to celebrate each of your birthdays (hire a sitter or do it once the children are asleep). Decide, every September, that the two of you will take a day off together to celebrate the beginning of the school year. Drop the children off at their grandparents' and go camping for a week-

---

♦ Did You Know . . . ? ♦

In a group of lesbian mothers of infants, eighty-one percent found raising a child to be much better and much harder than they had anticipated. Most (sixty-four percent) reported some feelings of jealousy and competitiveness toward their partners about bonding with the baby.

Gartrell, N., Banks, A., Hamilton, J., Reed, N., Bishop, H., & Rodas, C. (1999). The National Lesbian Family Study: 2. Interviews with mothers of toddlers. *American Journal of Orthopsychiatry, 69*(3), 362–69.

end. Whatever works for the two of you, make a point of having some special routines.

Rosita acknowledges that "We end up going to bed late at night because, you know, getting ready for bed, and by the time the story's done, and everything, it's nine o'clock. And then we have to go downstairs and get lunches ready for the next day, and we have to do laundry and everything else once they're not around, because we don't want to take away from their time. So when our heads hit the pillow, we hit the pillow." She and Gabriella have begun hiring teenage girls in the neighborhood as occasional babysitters.

Division of Labor: To Work or to Stay Home

All couples with children have to come to some arrangement about who will earn a living, whether one or both partners, and who will provide childcare. How do lesbian families deal with these issues? At least one study has shown that in lesbian families where the children were born to the couple (as opposed to stepfamilies), the biological mother tends to be more involved in child care, and the nonbiological mother tends to spend more time working outside the home, at least in the children's early years.[2] This has been our experience. When our older daughter was born, Beth continued to work part time while Suzanne continued full time. Beth became a full-time stay-at-home mom just before she became pregnant with our second child. This arrangement works well for our family.

There is no way to know, at the present time, just how many lesbian couples make this type of arrangement as opposed to other types. Lesbian couples are probably more flexible than heterosexual couples, in that it is still a presumption in heterosexual families that if anyone stays home it will be the mother. In our families, if anyone stays home it will be the mother, but which mother? The answer may depend not on a priori assumptions but on preferences, financial concerns, and logistics.

Lauren needed to return to work full time once her maternity leave was finished. "I actually own my practice with one other physician, so I took six weeks off and then I had to be back full time. I have a fairly demanding schedule, so Julie has been staying at home with Nathaniel. She takes care of him full time during the day, and then I pretty much take over at night." For Deirdre and Meredith, the flexibility of Meredith's work schedule helped determine their childcare division. "Because Meredith had a lot of consulting contacts and part-time work opportunities and I really didn't," explains Deirdre, "we knew that she would be the one who would work part time and I would work full time."

Sometimes the work situation changes over the years, as children get older and parents' interests and careers change. In Paula and Nancy's case, when their children were young, Paula worked only part time, spending the rest of the time at home. This continued until one day Nancy decided "that she had had it, that the practice of law is not what it's cracked up to be and she was quitting. She was staying home and being the house mommy and it was time for me to get a job. I did, and so then she became the house mommy."

Whatever the arrangement in your family, both stay-at-home mothers and employed mothers have unique pressures and concerns.

Stay-at-Home Mothers

There are days when Beth looks around and says to herself, "What is going on here? Here it is, the twenty-first century, I am an educated woman, and I am spending my life making sure my family has clean clothes and watching *Teletubbies*? And I am a lesbian, for God's sake! How did this happen?" In general, stay-at-home mothers get lip service about what a wonderful choice they have made, but they don't get much respect. Stay-at-home lesbian mothers do not even get the lip service. They are in a sort of no-woman's land. And this can be a problem for the full-time mom who is lesbian. Although there are a lot of us out there, it is not likely that there is another lesbian stay-at-home mom in your neighborhood. The stay-at-home lesbian mom is at risk for feelings of isolation and loneliness. She may find herself feeling alienated from her lesbian friends who do not have children. Her childless friends are still leading adult-centered lives. They socialize at night, which is difficult for parents of young children to do; they can do things on the spur of the moment, which is impossible for parents of young children to do; and they do adult things that do not involve children.

Stay-at-home moms may face more challenges regarding their family, in that they are more likely to be having casual conversations with strangers (at the park, the store, mommy-and-me classes). Employed moms usually are working with the same people they always have been and so do not face this as often. Jeanine still feels a bit uncomfortable when faced with the prospect of responding to innocent remarks from strangers about her family. "The most difficult thing is if I have Adam at the park. He's a rather tall child for two; he looks like he's about three,

three and a half, maybe four. People say, 'Well, is his dad tall?' It's still a struggle for me to say, 'I have a partner; he doesn't have a dad.' And I really have to work on saying that, because eventually Adam's going to say it—'I don't have a dad, I have two moms.'"

This type of thing happens less often to Cheryl, who works full time and has fewer run-ins with people at the park. "For me, I have more ongoing relationships with people at work or at school, and it doesn't take me a long time to say, 'I've got a female partner.' But I also have ongoing relationships with people." This is a different situation than revealing aspects of your life to someone you are unlikely to see again.

As we know, coming out is an ongoing process. Even if everyone you know knows that you are a lesbian, there are bound to be new people coming into your life who don't know. We sometimes think that Ellen DeGeneres is the luckiest lesbian in the world—she had her picture on the cover of *Time* magazine with the caption "Yup, I'm Gay." Now everyone knows and she need not ever come out again. For those of us who have not appeared on the cover of *Time*, however, things are a little more complicated. We find ourselves having to explain over and over again to people that we are lesbian. As mothers, the number of people who will know you are lesbian has greatly expanded from what it once was. It may take some getting used to—coming out to the woman at the park may make you uncomfortable.

It is important to reach out to other lesbian moms. Consult the resources at the back of this book for ways to contact national and local groups. A lot of the groups have regular meetings and events, and it can be good for both you and your child to attend. If it is not possible for you to attend such a group, you may have to settle for long-distance contact. If you do not have a computer, check out your local library. Many of them now have computers that people can use to access the Internet. Take advantage of these opportunities; it is important to remember that you are not alone.

Another thing you can do is to not be afraid to befriend other parents in your neighborhood. The older your children get, the more opportunities you will have to get to know other parents. From Gymboree to Little League to dance lessons to PTA, the other faces you see will start becoming familiar. You have more in common with other parents of similar-aged children than you have differences. Strike up a conversation about the coach or the tuition or how your child has suddenly started refusing to eat anything that isn't orange. You are all parents and you can relate to each other on that level, if nothing else. Focus on the similarities ("we're parents") and not the differences ("they're all straight and I'm not"). You need to make connections with other adults who are going through what you are going through.

Employed Mothers

Any mother who works outside the home has her own set of concerns. Sometimes going to work is a necessity rather than a choice, and it can be heartbreaking for a mom to have to go to work when she would rather be home with her children. Other times work is almost a guilty pleasure, with a mom secretly delighted that she gets to be out in the adult world while someone else cares for her child. Most employed mothers fall somewhere in between, being generally happy with their situation while feeling occasional twinges of regret for what they are missing and wishing they had more hours in the day.

The lesbian mom who is employed can face unique pressures. If she is a stepmother or a nonbiological mom, she may not have the same acknowledgment of her parenthood at work that other mothers have. Of course this is doubly true of the woman who is not out at work. Being out is a personal decision, and sometimes fear of losing your job makes being out at work impossible. But being evasive about your personal life becomes much more difficult once your personal life includes a child. In addition, like any employed mother, the lesbian mother may feel a real pull toward being at home with her child. Women, much more than men, are expected to be the primary caregivers. Even if your child has two mothers, you are still one of them, and you may find yourself feeling much more torn about working full time than you had expected.

Being the main, or only, breadwinner in the family can put pressure on the employed mother. You feel the weight of being the one responsible, not just for yourself, but for an entire family. You can start to feel trapped by your job, realizing that your family is relying on not only your paycheck but also your benefits. Even a job that you have always liked can start to feel like a burden from which you cannot escape. It is easy to begin to feel resentment toward your partner, who gets to stay at home all day and play with the baby. Even though you know that staying at home with the baby is not a vacation, you may still feel this way.

The employed mother can sometimes feel like a visitor in her own home. She comes home from a long day at work, looking forward to being with her baby, and the baby only wants to sit in the stay-at-home mommy's lap. It seems like the two of them have their own universe and they do not need anyone else. The employed mother can easily begin to feel like a second-class parent. It can be a shock for a lesbian mother to find herself playing the stereotypical role of "daddy."

Of course in many cases today there is not one employed mother but two. In many lesbian-headed families both moms are full-time employees, working forty hours or more outside the home. This situation is in some ways unremarkable; most heterosexual-headed families with young children have two employed parents. Every popular magazine and television talk show is filled with advice for "working" parents, and much of it is as applicable to "working" lesbian parents as anyone else.

Division of Labor inside the Home

Apart from the decision about who, if anyone, stays home to care for the children, there remains the issue of dividing the tasks in the home. Psychologists have compared heterosexual relationships with gay and lesbian relationships. One difference that emerged was that gay and lesbian relationships are generally more egalitarian than heterosexual relationships. Heterosexuals were much more likely to follow a traditional male/female division of work, for example.[3] Other psychologists have looked at what happens to heterosexual couples when they have their first child. They have found that for most couples the division of labor becomes even more pronounced at that time.[4] This means that it is quite common for parents of new babies to fall back on conventional roles.

In lesbian couples with children, both partners contribute equally to the household tasks and to decision making. However, biological mothers tend to be more involved with the childcare responsibilities. The difference between lesbian partners in terms of childcare, however, was less than the difference between husbands and wives in childcare. What this means is that for many of our families (and we are talking about families with young children), biological mothers tend to do more of the childcare. And nonbiological mothers do more of the childcare than do biological fathers in heterosexual families.[5]

Many lesbian parents try hard to balance their childcare responsibilities, even if one partner has much less time with the child than the other. For Margaret and Sarah, the amount of time they spend with Alexa is not comparable. Sarah works full time at a very demanding job, while Margaret works part time and is home with Alexa the rest of the time. Still, their arrangement is that Sarah takes Alexa to day care the one day a week that she goes; she is the one who bathes her; and they always do the food shopping together. So, as Margaret says, "It wasn't as if Sarah was spending that much time, but she was doing very essential things. So I think it made a nice balance. It wasn't a time balance at all; that's very skewed." In Julie and Lauren's family, Julie is home with Nathaniel, so when Lauren gets home from work she takes over. Rosita feels that she and Gabriella aren't "really dividing the responsibilities, we're sharing them. However, since I do work more hours than Gabriella does, she does spend more time with them." As lesbians, we tend to value egalitarian relationships and strive to have them, even when children enter the relationship. In this area we have a distinct advantage over heterosexual women, who are generally unsatisfied with the amount of help they get from their husbands.[6]

Single Moms: Doing It All

Some lesbians have chosen to become mothers by themselves, without a partner. Others find themselves single parents as a result of death or the end of a relationship. All single mothers face tremendous responsibilities in raising their children without another parent. The responsibilities are so vast and never ending, in fact, that the single mother may find that she has no time or energy left for herself. Between going to work, arranging for childcare, cooking, cleaning, chauffeuring your child to all her various activities, checking homework, reading stories, and so on, you probably feel that there is not enough time in the day as it is. Is it even possible to think about getting some time for yourself?

Diane remembers "dating," in the early years of Alyson's life, as more often than not a family event. "For the first few years I was out, I was in graduate school too, and there's not a lot of time for relationships. Any relationships that I would pursue would be with Alyson in tow. Every-

---

♦ Did You Know . . . ? ♦

Most single lesbian mothers see advantages and disadvantages in being single parents. They enjoy not having to negotiate with another person about parenting decisions, but they miss having a partner to help and share in raising their child.

Gartrell, N., Banks, A., Hamilton, J., Reed, N., Bishop, H., & Rodas, C. (1999). The National Lesbian Family Study: 2. Interviews with mothers of toddlers. *American Journal of Orthopsychiatry, 69*(3), 362–69.

---

body knew that I had a child. I would do very few events without her, not too many parties or going out or anything like that."

Gina also spent time as a single mother, and found that being a parent did lead to difficulties in relationships with other women. "It [being a parent] affected every relationship I've ever been in. One relationship I had before Kathy, where I was very, very involved with this woman, ended because of my having a child. She started out, obviously, knowing, and moved in with me, and then couldn't take it and took off."

Single lesbian mothers are in a different situation from coupled lesbian mothers. Unless they go out of their way to broadcast their lesbianism, single mothers will generally be assumed to be heterosexual by other people. This can be an advantage, in that your child may not be stigmatized as the child of a lesbian right away. There will not be any awkward introductions at the parent-teacher conferences or on the playground. It can also be a disadvantage, in that you are assumed to be someone you are not. You will have to go out of your way to let other people know who you are, in a way that women with partners will not have to do. Single parents also have no breaks, no one to bounce ideas off, no one to help with the day-to-day routine of children. On the other hand, single mothers have an intense relationship with their children. They do not have to contend with another parent who may want to do things differently. Single mothers need support as much as anyone else. While they will not have a partner to provide that, they can rely on friends and family to play the role of sounding board. It is very important for single mothers to have that support and to have time away from their child as well.

Pressure to Be Perfect

Before we have children, we fantasize about our child and about the kind of relationship we will have with our child. Most of us identify things we want to reproduce from our own childhood. We may want to continue particular family traditions or stress the same values. We are also aware of things we want to make sure we do not repeat. We want to avoid the mistakes our parents made and do better than they did in certain areas. Once our child is actually here, we may find our ideals difficult to live up to. We realize that, despite our best intentions and greatest efforts, we are not going to be perfect parents either.

Yvonne has found this to be true of herself. "I think we're all trying to fix things that happened in our family when we were young. And it's like 'Well, I'm not going to do that.' You're trying not to be like your parents in all those ways that you didn't want them to be. So that's sort of that perfect thing. But I think by the time your kid gets to be six years old, you've had a lot of time to realize that the truth is, you're going to make mistakes. You're not always going to do it perfectly. There are going to be things you wish you didn't do and things you wish you did do. I think that it's a universal thing of motherhood to always think that somehow you're not quite doing it right, that you would do it better if you did that and if you did that."

Sarah is quite conscious of her desire not to be like her mother. As she explains, "My mom was just so horrible, so I feel like I have that in my blood, I have that in my genes. How do I make sure that I'm not that? I feel like I've got the monkey on my back to not be who my mother was. So far, none of that has ever come out, but I always wonder if it's working somewhere. I want to be not a perfect parent, because I'm not perfect, but I do get disappointed in myself. Like when I'm sitting there and reading work stuff and I can't pay attention to Alexa. How can I tell her I don't have time for her? How can I tell her that I have things to do? But once in a while I don't have a choice, or my head's just not there—it's swamped with work and other things that are going on. And that's where I get very disappointed in myself. I don't want to be like that."

Deirdre can look back now to the time when Kelsey was a baby as the time that she struggled with her desire to be perfect. "I think definitely in the beginning we were trying to be the perfect family, period, and that was very hard on all of us, because I was working full time at the time. I had to go back about three months after Kelsey was born. I did not want to go back; I wanted to be with her. But finances were such that I had to go back. So every single second that I was with her I wanted to be perfect. And it made me crazy. There would be no time to relax for Meredith and myself. Our relationship focus was very much on Kelsey and how to be perfect parents and so on. And that was hard. We've learned since then, with Tyler; we're more relaxed." When Meredith was pregnant with Tyler, Deirdre was diagnosed with breast cancer. "That was quite a challenge. We definitely focused on what was most important." Deirdre has recovered, and she and her family are moving on from "a long year."

As mothers, we all have to come to terms with our own limitations as parents, even as we try to overcome them. As lesbian mothers, we can face another kind of pressure to be perfect. We often feel that we are under particularly close scrutiny. We feel that people may be looking at our family situation as less than desirable, perhaps even as detrimental to our children. As a result of this perception, some of us feel extra pressure to be "perfect parents." We are not talking here about wanting to be the best possible parents that we could be. All parents feel that way. We are talking about wanting to be even better than everyone else, so that no one will be able to point to our family or our child and say, "See, lesbians don't make good parents." We are talking about the desire to prove to the world that we are good parents and that our child is doing as well as, if not better than, the average child being raised by straight parents.

How does this pressure exert itself? It can present itself as a vague underlying feeling that you owe your child more than the typical parent owes a child. You may feel you need to be especially nurturing, loving, and available to your child, to make up for the difficulties he will face as he gets older because he has a lesbian mother. You may find yourself being somewhat defensive when talking about your family. You may feel a keen sense of competitiveness with other parents or children. It may be very important to you that everyone notices how well-adjusted and successful your child is—the child of the lesbian mother. Or you may feel that you want to be a role model for other lesbians.

Becky admits to feeling this pressure "every day." "This is the first year that Samantha has been in school. She's in kindergarten. I think that it became more noticeable when she became a part of the world by going to school. The pressure certainly feels self-imposed. I don't want to say that the school system is doing it or the teachers are doing it or anything like that. But there seems to be a pressure to do the job really well, because people are watching. They have their mindsets about what lesbian and gay families represent—that they represent less than ideal family situations, and things along that line. So it feels like there's pressure that she has to go to school every day looking a certain way, and that she has to perform well. I want to make sure that whatever observations her teachers make, that they're not looking at the two of us, her parents, as being unfit."

Yvonne noticed these feelings in herself, although she experienced them more strongly when her son was younger. "You feel like you should be the perfect example of a family because other people think it's a little weird that you're wanting to do this anyway."

It is completely understandable to have these feelings. Many of us have had experience with being told that we should not have children.

We've heard it said that it is unfair to bring a child into a lesbian household. (As we noted earlier, we've even heard this from some lesbians!) Why wouldn't we feel that we have something to prove? While it is natural to have these feelings, it is important that we get past them, both for ourselves and for our children. As Karen notes, this pressure is entirely self-imposed. While the responses of other people can contribute to it, the pressure to be perfect is something we create.

We believe that the women most likely to suffer from this pressure are those who still have unresolved negative feelings about their own lesbianism. Those feelings—feelings of guilt, embarrassment, and shame—can hang on for a long time, even after you think you have completely accepted and embraced yourself and your sexuality. One of the surprising aspects of being a parent is that you find out that some of the issues you thought you had settled long ago are front and center again. In this case your striving to raise a perfect child in a perfect family may be your way of compensating for the fact that you are a lesbian. It masks your secret fear that you are not as good as everyone else.

So what should you do? First, don't beat yourself up more for still having these feelings. Society works very hard to put them there, and you can't blame yourself for having been affected by that. Self-acceptance for lesbians is often a long journey. Be proud of how far you have come already. Second, acknowledge the fact that you still have a way to go. Talking with another lesbian—your partner, a friend, or a professional—often helps clarify these issues.

The truth is that probably very few people are looking at us with a skeptical "let's see how good a job a lesbian mother does" attitude. Most people are too busy with their own lives to be judging us. There are a few people out there who think having a lesbian mother is inevitably harmful for a child. And the people who have that attitude will never change their opinion, even if all of our children turn out to be Nobel Prize winners. You can spend the rest of your life trying to prove something to these people about your abilities as a parent and your worth as a human being to no avail whatsoever, except at a high cost to yourself. So accept that you are not going to change some people's beliefs about lesbian motherhood no matter what you do.

Think about how much pressure you are putting on yourself and your child. We know that too much emphasis on performance and achievement is damaging to children. It puts them at risk for feeling inadequate, anxious, and incompetent—exactly the opposite of what we want to accomplish. Children who have parents who push them to achieve tend to be tense, goal-oriented, and unable to take pleasure even when they do succeed. We do not want to set our children up for a lifetime of feeling like they don't measure up to some standard. We do not want to spend our lives feeling that way either.

If you are the first ones in your circle of lesbian friends to take the plunge into parenthood, you may feel a certain pressure to portray your experience in an overly positive light. Maybe you would like to convince your childless friends to take the plunge into parenthood with you. Maybe you want to assure your skeptical friends that their doubts were unfounded. Maybe you just like the status that being a mother brings you. Or you feel you owe it to the community to have a picture-perfect family life so that you can be the role model. All of these factors could lead you to try to present a rosy image of parenthood, either by glossing over the difficult aspects of parenting and focusing only on the good parts or by trying to force your family to live up to some idealized image. In this case the problem is not so much a deep-seated feeling of inadequacy as it is a heartfelt desire to give the community what you think it wants. You may say to yourself, "What the lesbian community needs is a happy, loving family with successful, flourishing children, and that's what I am going to give them. Even if it kills me."

The sentiment is nice, but it is misplaced. Yes, we all want you to be happy, and to have happy children, but we don't expect you to be happy all the time. And we certainly don't want you to drive yourself crazy trying to be something you are not.

No family is perfect, no child is perfect, no mother is perfect. But love and commitment to each other makes a family as perfect as it can be.

The Legal Maze: Our Families and the Law

When children enter our families, through either birth or adoption, in almost all cases only one partner is that child's legal parent. In some cases both mothers are able to adopt the child together, but this is the exception. Generally speaking, one parent is the legal parent and the other is, legally, a stranger. It is important for us to consider the legalities involved when a child enters our families. Unfortunately, to say the least, our families do not enjoy the same automatic protection that heterosexual families do. It is a sad reality that, at the happiest time of your life (bringing your child home), you are forced to consider what will happen if you split up or one of you dies. We don't like to think of these possibilities, certainly, and yet we must. As responsible parents, we need to do all that we can to protect our families. There are a number of ways we can do this.

Legal Options

Second-Parent Adoption

Second-parent adoption is becoming possible in more states. This is the best option for lesbian-headed families. In second-parent adoptions, the second (that is, nonbiological) parent is granted full parental status, without the other parent giving up any of her rights. Often, as in our case, the state issues a new birth certificate with both mothers' names listed. This document must be recognized in all fifty states. It guarantees that both parents have equal standing with regard to the child. In the event of one parent's death, the surviving parent automatically assumes full legal custody of the child. In the event that the couple splits up, it guarantees that both parents' rights and responsibilities for the child will continue.

The biggest drawback of the second-parent adoption is its expense. You should plan on spending several thousand dollars, when all is said and done, before the process is complete. It can also be somewhat time-consuming, often taking months or even a year from start to finish. Depending on the state in which you live, you may have to go through a number of procedures you wouldn't have anticipated. Undergoing a physical exam by your physician, being fingerprinted, agreeing to a background criminal check, and having a social worker conduct a home

---

♦ Did You Know . . . ? ♦

As of this writing, the following states, through either statute or appellate court ruling, allow second-parent adoptions: Illinois, Massachusetts, New Jersey, New York, Vermont, and Washington, DC. The following states have had second-parent adoptions approved by lower court rulings: Alabama, Alaska, California, Colorado, Connecticut, Indiana, Iowa, Maryland, Michigan, Minnesota, Nevada, New Mexico, Ohio, Oregon, Pennsylvania, Rhode Island, Texas, and Washington.

Price, J. R. (2000, July/August). A state-by-state adoption guide. *Alternative Family Magazine, 3*(4), 23–26.

---

study may all be required of both of you. Whether you find these requirements humiliating or just absurd, they will result in a binding legal recognition of your status as a family. Second-parent adoption provides an important safeguard for your family, one we hope you will never have to use. We also feel that those people who go through a second-parent adoption are sending an important message to the courts and the legal system—that we feel our families are important and deserving of legal recognition.

Legal Custody, Guardianship, Wills

In some states that do not allow second-parent adoption, another legal remedy, legal custody, is available. In this case, the second parent can file for full legal and physical custody of the child. This does not require the child's mother to give up any of her rights. This protection is not as strong as an actual adoption. It is easier to terminate custody than to terminate parental rights. However, it does offer some legal protection.

Generally, depending on the particular state, there are fewer requirements for custody than for second-parent adoption. Often no home studies or court appearances are involved. All that is required is filing papers. It usually costs less than a full adoption. If this is the best you can do where you live, then it's the best you can do. In most cases, this level of legal protection will be all you will ever need.

What is available varies from state to state. Because we are not lawyers, and as the law is changing so quickly in this area anyway, we are not going to offer you specific advice on what you can accomplish in your state and in your particular situation. We would recommend, in general, consulting a lawyer about the possibilities of guardianship. At the very least you can name your partner in a will as your child's legal guardian in the event of your death. Courts generally, although not always, abide by the deceased parent's wishes.

Letters of Intent

There are some places where neither second-parent adoption nor second-parent custody is available to lesbian parents. If you live in such a place, you must do what you can yourself to protect your family. We suggest consulting an attorney, then drawing up papers specifying your plan to raise your children together and to both be considered equal parents. Each of you should have copies of this, as should your attorney. You should be aware that this is not a legally binding document. However, it will be evidence of your intentions regarding your children. In the worst case scenario, if you end up in court battling for custody or visitation, you will have this to show the judge what the situation in your family was. Given that this is not binding, an individual judge may give it a great deal of weight or no weight, as he or she chooses. But again, if this is the best you can do, then it is what you should do. For single mothers, wills are essential in expressing your wishes about who should care for your child in the event of your death or incapacitation.

Now We're a Family

Becoming a family is a monumental, life-changing event. Every aspect of your life, from your personal finances to your relationship with your partner to how you spend your free time, is different from before. Your responsibilities are greater than a new heterosexual parent's, because you must take steps to ensure whatever legal protections you can for your family. The early years of family life, in particular, can be very stressful. Give yourself time to adjust to your life as a member of a new family.

What You Can Do to Adapt to Your New Roles

1. Recognize that a new baby or child will completely alter your familiar existence, at least for a while. A newborn requires constant care. An older child, newly joining your family, will change the routine and dynamics of everyone in the household. Accept that this initial period is one of adjustment for everyone.

2. Try not to let one parent become the "expert" and the other be the "parent of last resort." Both of you are new at this. Help each other, but make sure you get to be as equal in the parenting tasks as you can be.

3. Set aside time to spend together, just the two of you. It need only be twenty minutes once a week if that is all you can afford right now. But during this time you must promise not to talk about the children or about running the household.

4. Keep some of the important rituals the two of you shared before you had children. You won't be able to maintain all your old habits, and you won't even want to. But pick the ones that are most

important to you and keep those alive. If you always go out to dinner on your anniversary, continue to do so. If one of your favorite things is watching old movies together, be sure to do it once in a while.

5. Go on dates. Get a babysitter once in a while. Your children will be fine in someone else's care for a while, and you need to have an adult afternoon or evening.

6. Maintain your physical connection with each other. Give your partner a backrub before bed, or have her give you a massage. Don't let your children be the only ones who receive your physical affection.

Notes

1. Stiglitz, E. (1990). Caught between two worlds: The impact of a child on a lesbian couple's relationship. *Women and Therapy, 10*(1/2), 99–116.
2. Patterson, C. J. (1995). Families of the lesbian baby boom: Parents' division of labor and children's adjustment. *Developmental Psychology, 31*(1), 115–123.
3. Peplau, L. (1981). What homosexuals want in relationships. *Psychology Today 15*(3), 28–38.
4. Cowan, C. P., & Cowan, P. (1999). *When partners become parents: The big life change for couples.* Mahwah, NJ: Lawrence Erlbaum Associates.
5. Patterson, C., op. cit.
6. Cowan, C. P., & Cowan, P., op. cit.

◆ CHAPTER 4 ◆

How to Help Our Children Better Understand Our Family

All children gradually come to know their family. As children get older they gain a better understanding of what it means to be a sister or brother, son or daughter, cousin, niece or nephew, or grandchild. They come to know all the members of their extended family and how they are all related to each other. This can be a very confusing process, even given the simplest of family relations. Our older daughter still thinks it very odd that her mothers are also sisters and daughters. But as lesbian mothers we have an additional challenge in helping our children come to understand our families. That challenge is helping our children come to understand that our family, although different from most, is a family just the same.

Our responsibility as parents is to promote a positive and supportive image of our families. Our families have value and legitimacy regardless of what public opinion may say. Parents do have an influence over their children's viewpoints and behaviors. Parents build within their children a sense of morals, beliefs, pride in themselves, and confidence in who they are and where they come from. Given this, it is our responsibility to broaden their thinking, beyond what is presented to them by the general public, to also include their reality and experiences. Our children will eventually come to understand that their family is viewed as something unusual by other people. They will not be perceived as being "just like everybody else," even if, in fact, their family is in many ways just like everybody else's. We want our children to understand that "different" does not mean "worse." We want them to have the mindset that will enable them, when faced with prejudice from others, to know that the problem lies with other people's ignorance and not with them. We want our children to feel proud of themselves and their family.

When our older daughter, at the age of four, asked us if two women could get married, our answer was immediate and definitive: "Yes, Bailey, two women can get married. Getting married means that the two people love each other and want to spend the rest of their lives together." When she followed up and said that her friend had said that two women couldn't get married, we chose to focus on why her friend would think such a thing, not on the narrow-mindedness or discriminatory thinking of others. After all, he was only four at the time too, and it is always more productive to focus on the positive instead of the negative. We suggested that he said that because he didn't know any women that were living together. It could be that the only married grownups that he knew were like his mom and dad. If he knew all the different types of families like our daughter does, he probably wouldn't have said that. For that moment that is all our daughter needed to hear. She proceeded to ask what we were going to have for dinner.

Some might say that we should have discussed things more completely with her at that time. We disagree. You should discuss issues with your children only to the extent that they can understand them and to the extent that they want to understand them at the time. Pushing the issue and trying to inculcate political correctness into a four-year-old will not work. Imagine if our answer had been something like this: "Well, yes, your friend is right. Two women can't get married because gay people are discriminated against. Do you know what being discriminated against means? It means that you can't do things that other people can do because they don't like you. Mommy and I would like to be married, but it's against the law. Someday, if we're lucky, we may be able to get married like other people." Can you imagine the impact this might have on a four-year-old? Can you imagine the questions that would follow? "People don't like you? Why? Does everybody dis . . . disc . . . whatever that word is, does everybody not like gay people? Are the police going to arrest you? When people do things against the law they get arrested, right? Are the police going to make you not live together anymore?" There will be plenty of time to introduce and discuss the broader societal issues that face families like ours. At this point, as a preschooler, Bailey was not cognitively prepared or emotionally ready to deal with these complexities.

As developmental psychologists, we know that children of different ages have very different capabilities in terms of understanding the world. They also have different emotional and social needs. As we help our children understand their family, we need to take into account these capabilities and needs. As a preschooler, your child's thinking is still very concrete and self-centered. Your preschooler's primary emotional need is to feel safe and protected by her parents. Presenting the idea that people out in the world don't like you and that unknown individuals have the ability to keep you from doing things is no way to accomplish that. Grade-school-age children are beginning to understand that different people see things in different ways. Their tendency, though, is to think that people who see things differently than they do are wrong. While they still need to feel safe and protected by their parents, children in grade school have an overwhelming need to feel accepted and liked by their peers. During adolescence, children acquire the ability to think in more abstract ways. They can understand that different viewpoints can reflect different experiences and perspectives. Their emotional bonds with peers become stronger, and they begin to look to them as much as to parents for emotional support. Sensitivity to your child's needs and abilities will be key in helping them come to feel proud and comfortable in their lives and in their families. The golden rule of communication with your child on any topic is to keep it simple and age-appropriate.

Children born to a lesbian or a lesbian couple or adopted at birth have no other immediate experience to compare it to. For them, their family is all that they know and is quite normal. It's the rest of the world and its broader context where our family arrangements are in the minority. When your child moves out into the broader world and starts to gain experience, he will begin the discovery that his family is not like all

---

♦ Advice from a Lesbian Mother ♦

"Be totally honest with who you are, because the children see right through it, and I think it detracts from who they are as human beings if you're not."

—Diane

---

others and vice versa. Bailey is always quite comfortable in correcting anyone who addresses us incorrectly (Mommy or Mama). She will quickly say, "That's my mama, not my mommy. My mommy is at home." Or sometimes she'll say, "That's my mommy, not my mom. I have a mommy and a mama." Her comfort and matter-of-factness are not always equaled by ours. It's not that we live in the closet, not by a long shot, but we wouldn't necessarily tell the checkout clerk at the supermarket, the dry cleaner, or the gas station attendant we've seen once in our lives the nature of our relationship as an introduction. In a way these experiences are certainly amusing. In another way they remind us that no matter how comfortable we are and continue to be with our own homosexuality, there are situations that our children are far more relaxed in because it's what they know. It is already their reality and one that we, as parents, are still creating for ourselves, having defined ourselves as lesbian later in life. This chapter focuses on helping your child understand the uniqueness of your family that will become apparent to her once she is exposed to the outside world.

Regardless of how and when children come to know that they are raised by a parent or parents who are gay, there are a number of ways to help your children come to understand and be comfortable with their family. Of course this assumes that you, as a parent, are comfortable with being a parent who is gay. There are also effective ways to handle the special circumstances of stepfamilies and adoption, which you will find in Chapters 13 and 14.

Here are our specific suggestions for what lesbian mothers need to do to help their children understand their family. The first few suggestions concern things mothers can do themselves, mentally and emotionally. The rest of the suggestions are things that mothers can actively do to increase their children's awareness and understanding.

Be Aware of Your Child's Point of Reference

We were reminded of the importance of this the other day, when Suzanne was watching a tape of an *Ellen* episode while she was on her exercise bike (yes, we have all the *Ellen* episodes on video). Bailey was in the room with her. At one point in the show, Ellen happily announced that she had a date with Lori. Bailey, then age five, said "A date? I don't know about that."

Suzanne, huffing and puffing along, asked, "What do you mean?"

"Two girls can't go on a date," explained Bailey casually.

Suzanne, after nearly falling off her exercise bike, composed herself enough to ask, "What about Mommy and me?"

"You two don't date," answered Bailey.

Well, she had us. After fifteen years and two children, we don't date. But that wasn't the point.

Suzanne explained to Bailey that, yes, two girls can date. She mentioned several of our lesbian couple friends who Bailey knows. "You know Alice and Barbara date, and they're two girls, right?"

"They don't date. They live together."

Outsmarted again. But Suzanne persisted, explaining that two girls can date, two boys can date, or a girl and a boy can date. It all depends on what the two people want to do. Bailey finally reluctantly agreed that, yes, two girls could go on a date. Suzanne was careful to use the words "gay" and "lesbian" in her explanation. Bailey has certainly heard those words before, but obviously she is still putting the meaning of them together.

This incident really surprised both of us, but it probably shouldn't have. Even though Bailey has been living with lesbian parents since the day she was born, the mainstream culture has a powerful effect on the way she views the world. This underscores the importance of exposing our children to nonheterosexual images and characters. Our example, and even Ellen's, is not enough. The message that the world is heterosexual, and only heterosexual, still seeps in, and we have to be ready to counter it. It also illustrates how easy it is for us to overestimate the connections and associations that our children are able to make. Bailey knows that both her parents are women, that we love each other, and that we are "married in our hearts," but she was unable to infer from all this that women can date each other. The lesson is not to assume that our children will automatically put things together.

Yvonne, who is a single mom, was reminded of how children's points of reference are not always what we think they are. She and her son recently attended a holiday party given by some friends of hers. "A lesbian couple that we knew, who have two children who are adopted, have a big party every year. This time it gave me the whole idea about what frame of reference means. At one point during the party the couple's oldest girl turns to me and says, 'Where's his other mommy?' And I said, 'Oh, honey, he doesn't have another mommy. I'm the only one in our family. We only have us.' And she goes, 'Oh.' I thought it was very interesting. The party wasn't specifically a gay and lesbian party. It was a party that included people from all over their lives. But her frame of reference was that people have two mommies."

If your child was born into a lesbian family, and you live in a very strong gay and lesbian community, with many families like your own, you may find that your child will come to see having two moms or two dads as the norm. This certainly will change as your child gets older and becomes familiar with more traditional families. You don't need to worry that your child will carry a skewed picture of families around with her for the rest of her life. What you can do is emphasize, again, that there are all different kinds of families—even some that have a mom and a dad!

Keep in Mind How Lucky Your Child Is to Have the Family She Has

Many of the mothers we spoke to expressed the belief that their children are lucky to be in a lesbian family. Lauren is amazed at people who see the fact that her son has lesbian parents as problematic. "I've actually had people say to me, 'Oh, he's starting off with such a burden.' I think that he's going to have two parents who really love him and really wanted him, and we worked hard. I mean we went through fertility treatment and all kinds of things, and he truly is the center of our lives. I think he is going to be far better off than a lot of kids with single parents or divorced parents who are fighting."

Deirdre cites the belief common to many lesbian mothers, that two moms are better than one. "There's only one thing that counts and that's love. Attached to that would be respecting your children and helping them develop a strong sense of themselves and helping them develop in a creative way, that they feel that they are themselves. And I think they get a double bonus there, because we both are caring for them and are devoted to them and have chosen to do this. There are no accidents here. We just basically love being with them; that's the most fun in our life, and I don't know if all parents can say that."

Keep in mind the benefits your child will have as a result of having you as a mother. She will get to have as a role model someone strong enough to go against what society tells her is right and instead do what she feels is right. She may have the benefit of having two mothers to love her and nurture her. She will know that she was a wanted and cherished child. Your child is a lucky one.

Talk to Your Child about Your Family and Your Lesbianism

All children love hearing about their birth and their entrance into their family. When you tell your child the story of how she came to be your child, talk about how you and your partner were so happy to become parents. (Of course, this is if you had your child while in a lesbian relationship. If this was not the case for you, you can still talk about how your family came to be.) Our daughters love to hear about how Mommy and Mama went to the special doctor's office where the doctor would help get a baby started growing, and how excited we were when it worked, and how much fun we had getting their room ready, and on and on until we talk about the day we brought each of them home from the hospital.

As your child gets older, questions will arise that pertain directly or indirectly to your lesbianism. Are you and Mommy married? Why aren't you and Mommy married? Why don't I have a daddy? How come you didn't fall in love with a man? When these questions do come up, answer them honestly and specifically. Again, let your child take the lead in letting you know how much information she wants. Margaret remembers when Alexa asked her if she had a daddy. "I was very surprised, so my answer was just very direct. 'No, you don't have a daddy.' She said, 'I don't have a daddy?' I said, 'You have two mommies,' and then her immediate next question was something very object-oriented—'Can you pass me that? Can I have this?' She just went right on from that. I think her question was answered." Alexa will certainly ask more questions in the future,

---

♦ Advice from a Lesbian Mother ♦

"I think the one thing that we've picked out is not making a big deal that you're a lesbian, not really focusing on it that much. Kids don't know that they're different until someone tells them that, their peers or their parents. It can be a good thing or a bad thing—they can either take that in a pride sort of way or they can feel different. We really don't have an answer for that at this point. Everybody sort of has her own take on it."

—Susan, on the attitudes expressed
in the lesbian mothers' support group
to which she and Andrea belong

---

though for the time being she got the information she wanted. "But her cousin's comment was the best," adds Sarah, "because she said, 'You know, Alexa doesn't have a daddy, she has two mommies. She's the luckiest!' We'd agree."

Children have a way of letting you know when you haven't answered their questions thoroughly or clearly enough. They will ask you again or tell you that they didn't understand. Children also have a way of letting you know you're giving them too much information or that they've already gotten the answer they want. They change the subject or tell you they don't want to talk about it anymore. An important point to remember here is that whenever you are answering your child's questions, you must be honest. Don't tell her something that isn't true; she will figure it out or find out eventually.

Because children understand concepts in different ways at different times throughout their childhood, parents must remember that they will be discussing the same issues multiple times as the child grows. One conversation about donor insemination or adoption will not be enough. Your child will eventually have follow-up questions. Your responsibility is to be open and available for discussion. Your child will sense your comfort or discomfort, and nothing sends a child packing faster than the impression that you don't want to talk about something. Let your child guide the level of complexity she is after. When she runs out of questions, let it go until next time. There will be another time.

Sometimes children ask questions because they want information. Sometimes they ask questions because they want reassurance or comfort or they want to understand something other than the specific thing they are asking about. We need to be mindful not only of our child's intellectual capabilities but also of her emotional needs. A child who asks, "Why aren't you and Mama married?" may just want a factual answer to a mild curiosity. On the other hand, the child may be wanting assurance that both her parents love each other and are planning to stay together. Or she may be beginning to realize that her family does not look like other people's and she wants to know if that is okay. Or she may be feeling embarrassed that her family is different. In these examples, a simple straightforward answer about having a commitment ceremony or being married in your hearts, or even about the evolving religious concept of marriage, will not give your child what she needs. She needs the opportunity to express her feelings, to have them validated, and to be reassured.

Preschool-Age Children

How you talk to your child depends, of course, on your child's age and level of development. You need to be aware of your child's intellectual abilities as well as her emotional maturity. In general a child's thinking begins in a very simple, one-dimensional way. As far as toddlers and young preschoolers are concerned, their life experiences are like everyone else's experiences. Children younger than school age simply don't consider other people's perspectives long enough to realize that others don't have exactly what they have. Their emotional and social development is similarly self-centered. Although they do become increasingly interested in playing with peers as they get older, and doing so in a truly cooperative and reciprocal fashion, their main emotional focus is still their parents. Preschoolers' most pressing need is to know that they are loved and that they can count on their parents to help them and comfort them.

A couple of years ago we were preparing to donate a large amount of infant clothing to charity. Bailey became upset about giving things away that had once been hers and her sister's. We tried to explain that there were many people in the world who don't have the things that we have. The idea that there are children in the world without food, clothing, toys, or a home was incomprehensible to her. She thought we were telling her a story and preferred to keep the clothes for her baby dolls. We did eventually drop the clothes off to charity, without our daughter, we might add, to avoid uncharitable comments.

What's going on in this situation? Is our daughter selfish? Does she lack compassion? Not at all. Her problem was her age. At the time, she was four years old and had no direct exposure to families or people who are in need. Although she has tremendous imagination for creating imaginary friends and fantasy play (she's a princess or ballerina one day

---

♦ Did You Know . . . ? ♦

Preschool children whose parents talk to them about feelings are better able to judge others' emotions at later ages. Make-believe play also contributes to their understanding of other people's feelings.

Denham, S. A., Zoller, D., & Couchoud, E. (1994). Socialization of preschoolers' emotion understanding. *Developmental Psychology, 30,* 928–936; Youngblade, L. M., & Dunn, J. (1995). Individual differences in young children's pretend play with mother and siblings: Links to relationships and understanding of other people's feeling and beliefs. *Developmental Psychology, 66,* 1472–1492.

---

and an astronaut other days), this play is very concrete. She's seen princesses, ballerinas, and astronauts on television and read about them in books. It is easy for her to pretend to be something that she knows about. Her ability to think in the abstract is not developed yet. In other words, when it comes to understanding that in the real world people have very different experiences, she, as with all preschoolers, is going to have a difficult time. If you ask them, however, to pretend that they're butterflies or elephants, that's no problem because they know what those things are.

What's interesting, then, about children younger than school age is that many issues are not issues, at least for now. Notions of discrimination, prejudice, hate, and homophobia will not register in their minds beyond maybe recognizing them as words they've overheard you use from time to time. Concepts such as adoption, insemination, pregnancy, and so on need to be discussed in very concrete and simple terms. Our nephew, who is now a young adult, cringes at the thought that when he was three he believed that children were born through the belly button. Yes, it's true. Don't you know? You simply unzip it or stretch it out to allow the baby to be born. Oh, if only this were true. He actually, for a time, believed that some day he too would grow up and have a baby. And he did mean he would *have* the baby. You see, completely fantasy.

The advantage of talking to your preschooler about her lesbian-headed family is that her ability to understand what you're saying is going to be quite limited. Keep it simple and concrete. Her emotional understanding is also fairly simple. She wants to know that you love her and you will always be there when she needs you. So if she asks about marriage, tell her that you are married in your hearts (or talk about your commitment ceremony, if you had one), and emphasize that you love each other and will love her forever. That is really all she wants to know.

School-Age Children

School-age children present a different situation. They are beginning to understand that there are differences between people and that not everyone lives in the same circumstances that they do. Their thinking is still fairly concrete, and they tend to see things in black and white. They are old enough now to recognize that two people may have opposing ideas; however, they are likely to think that one of them must be wrong. They are only starting to comprehend the notion that people may see things differently and that people can disagree.

◆ **Did You Know . . . ?** ◆

How well school-age children are liked by their peers is related to a number of important later outcomes. Children who are actively disliked by their peers tend to have low self-esteem, poor school performance, and future behavior problems.

Bagwell, C. L., Newcomb, A. F., & Bukowski, W. M. (1998). Preadolescent friendship and peer rejection as predictors of adult adjustment. *Child Development, 69,* 140–153; Parker, J. G., & Asher, S. R. (1993). Friendship and friendship quality in middle childhood: Links with peer group acceptance and feelings of loneliness and social dissatisfaction. *Developmental Psychology, 29,* 611–621.

School-age children are beginning to form a more sophisticated identity. While preschoolers will describe themselves in terms of physical characteristics and favorite activities, school-age children are beginning to describe themselves in terms of personality traits and abilities. They are increasingly interested in forming friendships with other children and are more capable of doing so. They can communicate with others better, are more able to consider others' feelings, and are more able to empathize with others. Belonging to a peer group, and feeling accepted by others, is very important now.

Children at this age can easily understand issues like insemination and pregnancy. You can use commonsense discussion about conception and films showing the process of fetal growth. Books and videos are helpful here, because although children can now understand the concepts they still have difficulty visualizing them. They are still very dependent upon concrete images to help them learn and understand. Children can understand adoption and foster parenting now. They can comprehend why circumstances may have made it impossible for a birth parent to care for a child.

They are more likely than preschoolers to have questions about why things happened the way they did. While they can understand the mechanics of donor insemination perfectly well, they may wonder why a man would choose to be a donor. They may worry, for the first time, that their friends may think they're weird because of their different family. School-age children are just starting to put together their own self-concept, so they may have a difficult time figuring out what having a lesbian mother means about them. We will give suggestions in a later section on answering the tough questions, but keep in mind that, for children of this age, their primary concern is how they will be perceived by their peers.

Adolescents

Once a child reaches adolescence she is much like an adult in her cognitive abilities. She can now rise above purely concrete thinking and begin to consider abstract concepts. For example, teenagers can consider experiences that they have not had or may never have. They can put themselves into others' positions and consider how others would feel and think. But in another way, adolescents' thinking becomes more egocentric than it was during the elementary school years. Adolescents tend to think of themselves as the center of everyone's attention. They become very self-conscious and sensitive to real or imagined criticism from others. At the same time, they tend to have an inflated opinion of themselves. They see themselves as unique, special, and having viewpoints and feelings that no one else has ever had or could possibly understand.

During adolescence, relations with peers become even more important, with most adolescents becoming involved in cliques. Cliques include small numbers of adolescents who are generally the same gender and age and have similar interests. The process of sexual maturation is completed in adolescence. Adolescents begin to think of themselves as sexual beings and are interested in forming intimate relationships with others.

♦ Did You Know . . . ? ♦

Most children have high self-esteem during their early childhood. Self-esteem tends to drop during the first few years of elementary school. This is probably because once they are in school children begin to compare their own abilities, appearance, and other characteristics to those of their peers. Self-esteem rises again in the later elementary school years and, contrary to popular belief, most adolescents continue to have high self-esteem.

Marsh, H. W., Craven, R., & Debus, R. (1998). Structure, stability, and development of young children's self-concepts: A multicohort–multioccasion study. *Child Development, 69,* 1030–1053. Powers, S. I., Hauser, S. T., & Kilner, L. A. (1989). Adolescent mental health. *American Psychologist, 44,* 200–208.

Your adolescent's ability to understand her family makeup is not hampered now by a limited intellectual capacity. She can also comprehend that prejudice and ignorance exist and can affect her. Her questions will no longer center around how her family came to be; she will be more concerned with what effect it will have on her. Remember, at this age having a bad hair day can make your daughter feel self-conscious, embarrassed, and like a focus of scrutiny. Imagine how having a lesbian mother might make her feel! This is not to say that all adolescents are going to feel embarrassed about their lesbian families. But if it is going to happen, this is the time you will find it.

Keep in mind during this period that your child's concerns are related to her self-image and her peers' reactions. You can reassure her that her true friends will not abandon her. You can remind her that people come from different backgrounds, and that sometimes something perceived as different will cause some initial discomfort. You can even use your adolescent's egocentrism to your advantage, by pointing out that having a lesbian mother really does make her part of a special and unique group. Her ability to understand her family and the ramifications of having a lesbian mother are essentially the same as an adult's. One of the ultimate benefits is that our sons and daughters are probably more aware of diversity and the need for tolerance than the average person their age.

Listen to Your Child When She Talks about Your Family and Your Lesbianism

As important as talking to your child about what having a lesbian mother means is, it is just as important to listen to your child when she talks about it. Not only what she says, but how she says it, will let you know how she is dealing with the effects of having a lesbian mom. Your child must feel free to talk to you about how she feels. If she is feeling uncomfortable or embarrassed at some point, it has to be okay for her to tell you that. Do not respond with anger or hurt feelings, even if that is how you feel. Instead, offer empathy. Try putting a label on her feelings for her, rather than telling her not to feel that way. For example, if she says, "I was the only one in my class who didn't go to the father–daughter dance last week," you can respond with, "I'll bet that makes you feel sad." Responses like "I can't believe they still have father–

daughter dances nowadays" or "You probably didn't miss much" are not going to make her feel like you are receptive to hearing about difficulties she may be having as the daughter of a lesbian. Encourage her to talk about her feelings by showing that you are open to whatever they are. Ask her if it's hard sometimes not having a father. Let her know that you understand that sometimes it is hard. You can then proceed with suggestions about how you might handle next year's father–daughter dance. Maybe she could go with an uncle? Maybe your family could do something special that evening? In this way, you have dealt with the immediate situation while letting her know that you will listen to her.

Keep in mind, when your child asks a question, that there are always two possibilities as to why she is asking. One obvious possibility is that she wants information. The other is that she is looking for emotional reassurance. A good rule of thumb is to assume that your child wants both, information and emotional reassurance, and to provide both. Going back to the example of having your child ask, "Why didn't you and Mommy ever get married?" give her an explanation that she can comprehend. If she is over the age of seven or so, you can tell her that the laws right now say that only a man and a woman can get married. The law might be changing soon, but that is the way it is right now. That answer gives her the information that she asked for. So your job is half done. Always assume that she is asking the question out of some emotional need as well. Whether she is wondering about your commitment to your partner, or sensing that her family is different, or just catching on to how homophobia operates, she needs more than just information. Ask her what made her wonder about that. Ask her if it bothers her that you and Mommy aren't married. Try to get her to say more about what prompted the question, so you can provide the appropriate reassurance. If she is not forthcoming, you can tell her how you feel about the situation. "I wish Mommy and I could get married. It makes me a little bit sad that we can't. But I think that someday the law will change. And since Mommy and I love each other so much, we will definitely be the first in line!" Try to tie your remarks to what you think her concern is, if she hasn't stated it.

Listening to how your child talks about your family, both to you and to others, provides an important clue as to how well your child is dealing with having a lesbian mother. See how comfortable your child is when a new person meets your family. Listen to how she talks to her friends about your family. You probably played the "pronoun game" at some point in your coming-out process; see if your child is doing that (for example, "We went to the amusement park last week. My mom and all of us went on the roller coaster" as opposed to "My moms and I went on the roller coaster"). See if she becomes tense when she is out with you and your partner in public. These are all red flags that your child is feeling something—whether discomfort, embarrassment, shame, or something else. You won't know until you ask.

Our older daughter shows no sign of embarrassment or sadness when she answers people who ask where her daddy is. She simply says: "I don't have a dad, but I have two moms, a little sister, and a cat. I also have a nana, a pop-pop, and . . ." If the person allows her to continue, she will attempt to list every single relative she can think of. We are very pleased with her comfort and ease, but we don't kid ourselves. She is only six. What she can talk about quite matter-of-factly now may start to cause her embarrassment later on. We know that we have only begun the process of helping our daughters understand their family.

If Possible, Make Sure Your Child Knows Other Children with Gay Dads or Lesbian Moms

In all likelihood, your child is going to be a member of a minority as she grows up. Most of her friends, if not all of them, will have heterosexual parents. This may be difficult at different points for your child, and it will help her to know that she is not the only person in the world who has gay parents. She can find support from other kids who have felt the same way. It will also be good for her, even if she never has any difficulties, to realize that she is part of a community. The gay and lesbian community is very proud of its children. Since it is only fairly recently that many of us have been openly lesbian mothers, we are a very child-centered, affirming group of parents. As parents, we tend to place a strong emphasis on diversity, respect for all people, and pride in ourselves and our families. Try to make sure your child gets to benefit from being a part of this group.

Sometimes exposing your child to other lesbian families takes no effort on your part. Many of the mothers we spoke to have lesbian friends, even a whole circle of lesbian friends, who have children. Stacy's next-door neighbors are two women with an eight-year-old child. Irene and Kitty have "a really good friend who has a seven- or eight-year-old that Bradley really likes. She also has twins that are three or four that the kids really like. We don't see them very often, but they do know them, and we were with them a lot in the very beginning. That was part of the reason: so that the children could see other lesbians with kids." Deirdre and Meredith "have several sets of friends that have children too, and several other sets that are still in the process of trying to have children in different ways." So their children know "a lot of lesbian families."

You may have to make a special effort to get to know other families with gay or lesbian parents. Rosita and Gabriella belong to a local gay and lesbian parents' group. "There are over eighty families right now. We get together for barbecues and holiday parties. We get together at people's houses. We have a few of those mothers that we call and have play groups with; so, yes, Katya and Sofia know a lot of kids that have two-mother or two-father homes." Karen and her daughter Jessica are also involved in a local parenting group that "we've been participating in since she was about six or seven months old that's been ongoing." Their group is larger. "It probably now has 200 to 250 families. And they're two-mom families, single-mom families, two-dad families, single-dad families, families with more than two or three parents, and it's set up as a group for lesbian and gay families." Jessica is still fairly young. "I don't think that at five it matters a whole lot to her right now. I think this is something that's going to matter to her as she gets older."

When your child is as young as Jessica is, the benefits she will get from participating in a gay and lesbian family group are probably no different than the benefits of playing with any other children her own age. She will get a chance to socialize, have fun, and learn to get along with other children. As your child gets older, she will get different things from the group. She will be able to feel like part of a group of people who are proud of who they are. She will get to know other children who know what it's like to have lesbian moms. She will have the opportunity to talk about her experiences with people who really understand them, because they have had the same experiences.

Gay pride parades and festivals are becoming more child-friendly. Many pride events are including activities specifically geared toward children, with clowns, face painting, games, and activities. Some larger cities set up a children's center where families can play while other adult-oriented events are going on. Contact the local organizers of your nearest pride event for details. These events can be another opportunity for your child to realize they are part of a larger community.

Your children may not ever form close friendships with any of the children they meet at the group functions. "The reality, in terms of my ex's kids and other people's kids that I've known, is that they don't necessarily choose to be best friends with somebody with a similar family. You know, they choose their friends based on their friends and whatever else happens," notes Karen. The goal of having your child involved in one of these groups is not to have her find a best friend. The goal is to let her see that there are other families like hers out there and to feel proud of being part of a wonderful community.

Point Out the Diversity in Human Relationships to Your Child

Some lesbian mothers just do not know other lesbians with children and may not live close to any towns or cities with support groups or gay pride events. If this is your situation, there are still things you can do to show your child that there are many kinds of families. Your gay and lesbian friends who do not have children can play an important role in your child's understanding of different types of relationships. Margaret and Sarah do not know too many other lesbian parents. However, they make a point of talking about their lesbian friends as another kind of family. When they socialize with "a couple without children, I say they are two moms," says Margaret. "I want Alexa to see it as a lesbian relationship as well, so that if she doesn't have other peers in terms of having lesbian parents, at least she sees that there are lesbian couples. I want to identify the couples. I tell her, 'There aren't any kids, but these are two moms.'"

It is important to recognize and validate gay and lesbian relationships for your child. This will help reinforce the idea that there are all kinds of families—even ones without children. It also helps them to see that other gay and lesbian relationships are out there.

Expose Your Child to Books, Television Shows, and Videos That Feature Gay and Lesbian Parents as Characters

There are books written for children about families with lesbian mothers or gay fathers (see "Resources" at the end of this chapter). Cheryl and Jeanine are already exposing two-year-old Adam to this kind of thing. They have gotten him a book that "presents all different kinds of families—families with people with disabilities, families where grandparents are taking care of children, a gay male couple taking care of children, and a lesbian couple. On the last page, they have pictures of all of the various families they talked about. And it's always amazing. Adam doesn't have a lot of language yet, but if you say to him, 'Where's your family?' he points to the lesbian women. And one of them is me and one of them is Jeanine. It's amazing that here he is, basically a preverbal child, but he still sees his family in books and that's an important thing to him. He already knows who his family is. It's amazing."

Keep an eye out for television shows and movies that have gay or lesbian parents. These are becoming more common all the time. Make a point of doing this, even if you feel that your child does not need it. We are swimming against a very strong tide, and we need to remember that.

Talk to Your School-Age Child about Discrimination and Prejudice

Make a point of talking about things like racial discrimination, prejudice, and civil rights, once your child is of school age. There are lots of opportunities to do this—just pick up a newspaper or watch the evening news, and a relevant story is bound to appear. This need not be a lengthy lecture, and it probably shouldn't be. You don't want to turn your child off by seeming to be too moralistic. Point out the story, whether it's about police brutality or some episode of employment discrimination, and ask your child what she thinks about it. Try to help her look at the situation from both sides. That is, ask her how the person who was unfairly treated feels. Also ask her to think about why the person who acted badly did so. This will give you an opportunity to talk about how ignorance and irrational fears can lead some people to treat others unkindly.

Our children should be aware of these things because we want them to grow up to be the kind of people who don't discriminate. They are also probably going to be exposed to some form of discrimination themselves, as children of lesbians. We want them to understand why people might do that. If they do experience some harassment at some point, we don't want them to feel that it means there is something wrong with them. We want them already to understand that discrimination is a sign that something is wrong with the person doing the discriminating.

Expose Your Child to Lesbian Family Resources—Don't Force Them on Her

Some children are very interested in joining groups, reading books, and learning about other gay and lesbian families. Others are not. You should allow your child the choice of whether to be involved or not or how much involvement she would like to have with these things. Joanne's son Will, for example, is in high school and does not really care to be involved in any lesbian family groups right now. "Part of it," says Joanne, "is he's so busy. We've talked about it, and he's said, 'What am I going to do there?' He doesn't have time." In Will's case, part of his reluctance stems from his feeling, quite correctly, that most of the groups involve children younger than he is. Irene's children have a similar disinterest. "I have looked around a little bit on-line for stuff for kids, but they're just not real interested in that. They're more interested in Pokemon right now. Maybe when they get a little bit older, they might, but they just don't think it's that big a deal."

You should let your child know about things like on-line sites, groups, books, and so on, but let your child take the lead. Your child may truly be unconcerned about having a lesbian mother and feel that spending time talking or thinking about it would be a waste of time. If she is too busy being a kid—playing soccer, going out with her friends, listening to music—then the best thing you can do is to let her be a kid. She knows that these things are out there, and she can explore them if she wants to. There may come a time when she wants to think more about these issues. For some children, this could be when they reach adolescence and start thinking more about themselves and their family. For others, adolescence may be the time when they become much less interested in thinking about their unique family and much more interested in starting to lead independent lives. Your child's interest should determine how much involvement she has with these things.

If your child is not as interested as you would like, you can take comfort in knowing that maybe all she needs to know is that there are other kids out there with lesbian moms. Just knowing that groups for kids like her exist may make her feel less alone. Her lack of interest in pursuing the opportunities you have shown her probably means this is not a terribly important issue for her. As we said in Chapter 2, do not make the mistake of assuming that having a lesbian mother will be a big issue, much less a problem.

What If Your Child Is Having a Real Problem?

There are cases, of course, where a child's apparent lack of interest indicates that a problem does exist. Sometimes the child's disinterest is masking a sense of shame, fear, or confusion. How is a mother to tell when this is the case? Listen carefully to your child's responses when you talk to her about groups like COLAGE, or local children's groups, or gay pride events. If her objections to becoming involved seem to be centered on other activities she would prefer to do, then there probably is nothing to be worried about. If, on the other hand, she insists that she is not interested and can't give any reason, or if she becomes upset and refuses to talk about it, then there may be a problem. Let your child know that if she is bothered by anything related to your being a lesbian it is okay for her to tell you about it. Remind her that you know it's hard sometimes and you want to help her. If she still doesn't want to talk about it, let it go for the moment. Bring the topic up again later and see what kind of response you get after your child has had some time to think about what you have said.

If you are still concerned that your child is having some difficulty with your lesbianism and she won't talk to you about it, try to get someone else to bring it up with her. An adult, someone your child likes and trusts, maybe an aunt or uncle or close family friend, could try broaching the topic. Your child may be more willing to talk about her feelings with someone other than you. Her reluctance to talk to you may be because she is afraid of making you feel bad.

If all else fails, you may want to consider seeking professional help (see Chapter 5 for specific tips on choosing a therapist). A skilled clinician may be able to get your child to open up about what is going on.

Resources

www.colage.org
COLAGE (Children of Lesbians and Gays Everywhere)

This is a great on-line resource for children of gays and lesbians. Children can join and get a newsletter, they can find out about local groups for children of gays and lesbians, they can get a pen pal, and they can join various e-mail lists. The web page also has lots of information for kids. This is really a terrific resource.

www.familypride.org
Family Pride Coalition
P.O. Box 65327
Washington, DC 20035-5327
Telephone: 202-331-5015
Fax: 202-331-0080

The Family Pride Coalition is a national group that offers advocacy and support for gay, lesbian, bisexual, and transgendered parents and their families. You can find local parenting groups as well as information about legal decisions affecting our family, research done on our families, and so on. Joining the FPC entitles you to a quarterly newsletter that will keep you informed on what is happening in our community.

www.familieslikemine.com

The web site of Abigail Garner, an adult daughter of a gay man and a straight woman, contains columns she has written as well as resources, answers to frequently asked questions, and so on.

www.geocities.com/WestHollywood/heights/6502

The web site of Sol Kelley-Jones, a teenage activist daughter of two lesbian mothers. Sol has been very active in working for civil rights for gays and lesbians and their families. Her site contains lots of photographs, news releases, and presentations.

Heather Has Two Mommies, by Lesléa Newman (1989). Boston, MA:
Alyson Publications.

This well-known children's book (geared toward preschoolers and early elementary school children) tells the story of Heather, who has two mommies—Mama Jane and Mama Kate. It talks about the process of alternative insemination in a way that a young child can grasp. The moral of the story is that all families are different, and they're all good.

Zack's Story, by Keith Elliot Greenberg (1996). Minneapolis, MN:
Lerner Publications.

This book, written for older elementary school-age children, tells the story of Zack's family. Zack's mother and father were divorced when he was young, and his mother now lives with a woman, Margie. Zack talks about his family, what kinds of things he does with them, and how he feels about all this. There are many photographs of Zack and his family.

Who's in a Family?, by Robert Skutch (1998). Berkeley, CA: Tricycle Press.

A picture book showing all different types of families.

Love Makes a Family, edited by Peggy Gillespie (1999). Amherst, MA: University of Massachusetts Press.

Beautiful photographs of lesbian, gay, bisexual, and transgender parents and their families. Includes biracial couples and families whose members are of different races. Young children will enjoy the photographs, while older ones will like reading interviews with family members.

ABC A Family Alphabet Book, by Bobbie Combs, Desiree Keane, and Brian Rappa (2001). Ridley Park, PA: Two Lives Publishing.

This is a basic alphabet picture book for preschoolers, but this one features families with two moms or two dads. Two Lives specializes in books for children from gay- or lesbian-headed homes. Also check out *123 A Family Counting Book,* by Bobbie Combs and Danamarie Hosler (2001), also from Two Lives.

♦ CHAPTER 5 ♦

Dealing with Others: Family, Professionals, and People in Our Children's Lives

As lesbians, we are well aware that how open we are about ourselves with other people is a central issue in our lives. As lesbian parents, the circle of people who will come to know that we are lesbians increases exponentially. Not only are there more people who will learn about our lesbianism—our children's teachers, their friends, their friends' parents, their pediatrician, and on and on—these people are central to our children's lives. It was relatively easy for us as childless lesbians to shrug off insensitive remarks or outright rejection from others. It is quite a different thing to have such responses affect our children. The last thing we want to have happen is for anyone to give our children a hard time because we are lesbians.

A lesbian without children has some choice in deciding to whom she will come out. She can be out at work or not; she can come out to friends who she trusts; she can live as open or as closeted a life as she chooses. A lesbian mother, however, does not have the same kind of choice. Our children make that impossible. Our family life is now something for the world to see. We will be coming out to more people than we ever have before. Not only that—the stakes are higher. If we met with an insensitive or homophobic response when we were childless women, we could dismiss that person, challenge that person, or laugh it off. The possibility that our child might be met with an insensitive or homophobic reaction, however, is a very different thing. It makes many of us respond on a gut level. As Sarah put it, "Sooner or later homophobia is going to hit her. And then I'll go chase the kid with a baseball bat."

There are, of course, many "others" we will have to deal with. We talk about dealing with teachers and schools in Chapter 7; clergy in Chapter 8; ex-husbands and attorneys in Chapter 12. That still leaves quite a few important people. In this chapter, we shall give advice on how to handle the many professional people who come into your child's life, as well as the nonprofessionals (like scout masters, sports coaches, and so on) who are important to your child.

You may think you came out years ago. You may have lived openly all of your adult life as a lesbian. You may think you know all you need to know about coming out and being out. But as a lesbian mother, you are right back to square one. In addition to all the new people whom you now have to deal with, you will probably find your old relationships changing as well.

Official Recognition—for the First Time

Heterosexual couples have their relationships recognized in a number of ways. Most of them get engaged, which is a public declaration of their intention to be together and viewed as a couple. They get married, which gives their relationship religious and legal legitimacy. The wedding ceremony, typically involving all their family members and many friends, is a powerful symbolic ritual that forever changes the way society looks at the couple. Lesbian couples, on the other hand, do not have these rituals. Some of us do have commitment ceremonies, but we are all aware that these ceremonies do not carry any legal significance. Some of us are able to declare our partner as a "domestic partner" for insurance purposes or for limited benefits (for example, some cities do allow same-sex partnerships to be registered, so that partners will be able to take days off from work in the event of one partner's death). How romantic!

The truth is most of us have had no official recognition of our relationships. Once we have children, however, that does change. Many lesbian mothers have found, often to their surprise, that having a child can lead to getting their relationships sanctioned in some official ways. Sarah, for example, found the church ceremony for Alexa's baptism particularly moving. In the ceremony, she, Margaret, and Alexa walked down the church aisle together, stood at the front of the church, and had the priest pray for them as a family. It was, Sarah feels, the closest thing they will ever have to a church wedding.

We had a similar experience, although not in a church. Since we live in New York, Suzanne was able to arrange a second-parent adoption for our daughters. In both cases we had to appear in court for the judge to finalize the decree and declare us both our children's parents. Both times we entered the courtroom with our lawyer (same judge both times) and stood before the judge as he asked us standard questions, such as if we really were who we said we were and if all the information we had submitted was true. After all that was finished, he asked us if we promised to care for this child and love her forever. With tears in our eyes, we both said yes. Then he came down from the bench, shook our hands, and posed for pictures with our family.

Thinking about the very brief ceremony later, we wondered why it had been so emotional for us. After all, not a single thing about our family had changed as a result of it. We were together and would be, whether both Suzanne and I could be our daughters' legal parents or not. We had felt that, since we could go through the adoption process, we probably should, but it was not of vital importance to us to get a piece of paper affirming what we already knew. After giving it some thought, we realized that it was the first time that anyone in any position of authority had acknowledged our relationship in any way. We may not be a "couple" in any official sense, but we are definitely a family. And, while we may think that public affirmation does not matter, the truth is it does.

Unofficial Recognition— Sometimes for the First Time

Some psychologists have examined the process of becoming a lesbian family. One change that often takes place once a child enters a lesbian family is that the parents of the lesbian mother often become more accepting of their daughter. The presence of a child often makes formerly disapproving, even rejecting, family members change their attitudes.

Joanne has seen a big change in her parents' feelings about her being a lesbian mother. "Initially, my father wanted to kill me, and my mom cried for weeks, you know, all of that. But they've come around. They've changed a lot. My son is the only male child in the whole family that carries the family name. My parents have worked hard; I have to give them credit. They adore him, and he gets to go there and visit them on a really regular basis."

Although it may surprise you, having a child could bring estranged family members closer to you. There are many ways that the presence of a child can ease strained family relations. Suddenly you all have something new to focus on and talk about. Instead of rehashing old disagreements and opening old wounds, you can rely on your child to provide endless topics of new and more pleasant conversation. Your family has a reason now to keep in closer contact with you, to talk to you more often and to visit more often. You have reason now to ask them for advice, and to share "war stories" about their experiences. They may feel that they now have something in common with you.

Yes, it would have been nice to have the acceptance all along; you should have had it all along, and nothing can change the fact that you didn't have it for all this time. Try not to dwell on that. Your child has given you a great gift. You may have your family back.

When Support from Your Family Doesn't Come

Not all responses from our own families are positive. Even family members who seem to have accepted our lesbianism may have difficulty accepting the idea of us as parents. Sometimes having a child, or even planning to have a child, can cause new problems with family members. When Rosita told her family that Gabriella was pregnant, "They had their reservations. They asked me, 'How could you bring a child into a world that is so prejudiced against homosexuals?' I said, 'Well, you know, we bring children into a world that's prejudiced against everybody. I will teach my children not to hate anyone on the basis of anything, and if my children decide to be straight, I will not punish them for it.' They looked at me like that's a ridiculous thing to say, and I said, 'No, not if you look at it from my and Gabriella's point of view. I would never hold it against them if they were straight, and it should be the same with you guys. You shouldn't hold it against me that I'm gay, because it's not a choice.' I think that broke a lot of barriers."

There may be some initial shock, as many people just assume that lesbians do not have children and so have never considered the possibility that you would be a parent. Often the first reaction is similar to the one Rosita's parents had, asking about the effects of bringing a child into a lesbian home. People may even ask if you think it's fair to bring a child into that type of family, the assumption being that the child will be subjected to untold ridicule and teasing from other children. It is also true that having a child forces your family members to admit to themselves that you are a lesbian and that this is not just a phase. The mother of a friend of ours likes to pretend that her daughter and her partner are just friends and roommates, even though she knows that this is not the case. Once our friend and her partner have a child, her mother will not be able to maintain this pretense.

Sometimes family members do not change their position. Irene says, "The only person who's really had a problem with it [her relationship with Kitty] is my baby sister. She suddenly turned real religious a few years ago, and her church says it's all wrong. She won't let me bring her twins over here. We've talked about how we've been trying to have a baby, and she says if there is a baby that the twins will never know this child. She's been real ugly about it." In some cases time will change people's minds, or at least soften their positions, but not always.

In most cases, very harsh negative responses come only from those people who were fairly negative to begin with. The truth is that not everyone comes around with time. If you have lost family members because of your lesbianism, you need to grieve that loss. As with any loss, the best way to get through it is to acknowledge the pain and, in this case, the hurt, that comes from having that person no longer in your life. You may, in fact, have to cut off contact with someone who cannot refrain from making hurtful, negative remarks to you. Your children should not be around such a person, and your children come first. As Deirdre put it, "Even if it's a family member, they're not going to confuse my children. Because if they're not being accepting, they're the ones that aren't being caring and loving and being a real family member. So, to me it's real clear. You care about one another or you don't, and if you don't you're not a part of our lives. Life is way too short."

Being Out as a Family

The manner in which we deal with people is of paramount importance in how others will receive us. Margaret has been very pleased with "the feedback that I've gotten absolutely directly from people about being out and the extent to which we're open. I guess we are more open than most people, which I didn't know. And people have told me that what has made them feel comfortable is that we're so blasé about it, you know.

This is a completely normal thing, and that's just how it comes out. We feel very comfortable ourselves; people pick up on that." Our level of comfort with ourselves comes across very strongly. If we seem uncomfortable with who we are, this will be apparent to the people we are talking to, and they will probably be uncomfortable as well.

Rosita is a teacher, and "every teacher in my school—and I work with 110 teachers—knows that I'm gay, knows that I have two kids, and I have never had a problem. As a matter of fact, my children visit the school, and everybody's wonderful to them. They get Christmas presents from them. I think a lot of this has to do with the fact that I'm so open, and that I'm very friendly and very approachable. That's, I think, part of the key. I'm a very approachable person. And honestly, I don't have a chip on my shoulder. When somebody says to me, 'I think being homosexual is a sin,' my answer is, 'Well, okay, you're entitled to your opinion. You just have to let me live.' People get disarmed by that. I tell people, 'I'm not out to prove that I'm right or I'm wrong, or that you're right or you're wrong. I'm just out to live as decently as I can and be a good, honest person.' And it's worked out for us."

Our fear of a negative response from others is often unrealistic. Most of the mothers we talked to had experienced no problems with anyone regarding their lesbianism. Rosita explains: "I find that when you deal with people one on one, rather than with a mob, people tend to see you for a human being, and they're much more accepting. It's the mob mentality that changes things."

Tara feels it is important that she, rather than her children, tell other people that she is a lesbian. "They've never run into a situation where it isn't okay to talk about it, yet. I think for the most part they don't have to disclose it, because we're so open. Anybody that they would hang out with would know. Other families at school know. I would never put them in the situation where they would have to tell someone that they have two moms." Presenting yourselves openly as a family is the best way to being treated as a family.

Most people are not expecting that a child will have two mothers. Our family configuration may initially take them by surprise. That does not mean that they are not accepting. They may just need a moment to get over their initial surprise. The presumption of heterosexuality is strong. It is good for people to have their presumptions corrected, and it is good for us to give them the chance to do so.

Dealing with Professionals

When dealing with the professionals who help care for our children—their doctors, health care workers, au pairs, and so on—the best approach is an up-front discussion before the professional deals with your child.

Physicians

Doctors have an ethical obligation not to discriminate against patients who are gay or lesbian. The American Academy of Pediatrics has a similar ethical obligation. So a doctor cannot ethically choose not to treat your child because you are a lesbian. While that is good to know, we do want more than someone who is grudgingly treating our child. We want someone who is at the very least accepting of our family, if not openly supportive. So how do you find such a doctor?

A good place to start is to ask people you know for a referral. If you know other lesbian parents, you can ask them if they've found a pediatrician they like. Ask your heterosexual friends whether they think their pediatrician would be a good one for your family. Check out the web sites listed in our "Resources" section at the end of this chapter for locating gay-friendly physicians. You will want to interview prospective doctors to get a sense of which one you feel comfortable with. Especially during your child's first two years of life, you will be seeing the pediatrician a lot, for routine checkups and immunizations. You will probably have lots of questions about your child's development, and you need to feel at ease in asking them. This is in addition to all the questions any parent would have for a pediatrician (Is this doctor covered in my insurance plan? What are the office hours? What if I have a question after hours? Are there separate waiting rooms for sick and well patients?).

◆ Did You Know . . . ? ◆

"The creation of the physician–patient relationship is contractual in nature. Generally, both the physician and the patient are free to enter into or decline the relationship. . . . However, physicians who offer their services to the public may not decline to accept patients because of sex, color, creed, race, religion, disability, ethnic origin, national origin, sexual orientation, age, or any other basis that would constitute invidious discrimination."

From the *Physician–Patient Relationship: Respect for Law and Human Rights*, written by the Council on Ethical and Judicial Affairs of the American Medical Association, June 1994.

If you have a partner, we suggest that you both go on this initial appointment. Make it clear that you are both your child's parents. During the meeting, notice whether the physician looks at and addresses both of you, or if he or she stays focused on only one of you. If the latter happens, this is probably a sign that this particular physician is not entirely comfortable with your family. If the doctor starts throwing around code words like "alternative family" and "lifestyle," this probably isn't the best choice for your family. What you want is someone who acknowledges both of you as parents and treats you as such.

Lauren began the process of interviewing pediatricians prior to Nathaniel's birth. She was particularly concerned, given her unusual family makeup (Nathaniel's father, John, plays an active role in his life, as does Lauren's partner, Julie), that they find an accepting doctor. "Before Nathaniel was born we interviewed pediatricians and we all three went (although on occasion, Julie was at work and wasn't able to make a couple of appointments, so John and I went). When John and I went there was a feeling that we were a straight couple, so we would actually tell them otherwise, because we wanted to make sure that everything was going to be comfortable. We had one doctor who said, 'Well, I'm not treating your lifestyle, I'm treating your child.' So we knew that that was not the pediatrician for us. But the one that we chose was very comfortable and understood that any one of the three of us might be bringing Nathaniel in when need be. He actually had an illness when he was, gosh, about eight or nine months old, and was hospitalized. And the hospital staff said only parents could stay over night, and I said, 'Well, he has three parents and that better not be a problem.' And they said, 'Okay, okay, no problem,' so all three of us were able to sleep in the room with him."

Lesbian mothers sometimes make the assumption that they will feel more comfortable with a female doctor, rather than a male doctor. In our experience, this is not always the case. We got a recommendation for our pediatrician from straight friends of ours who have a daughter a year older than our older daughter. The practice has one male physician, three female physicians, and a number of female physician's assistants (PA). We interviewed one of the physician's assistants while Beth was still pregnant, and the practice sounded like it would be a good fit. The PA we spoke with didn't have a reaction one way or another to a family with two mothers. Once Bailey was born and we began taking her to her many appointments, we found that we liked the male doctor the best.

He was the only one to give a really positive response to our family situation. When we told him that we were both Bailey's moms, he looked up, smiled, and said, "Oh, that's great! You know, we have another patient here who has two moms." We then chatted a bit about our family. On subsequent visits when Suzanne couldn't come, he always asked Beth how her partner was. He is the doctor we see for the girls' checkups. If he is not available when they are sick, we will see one of the other doctors or PAs, but we stay with the practice because of him.

Mental Health Professionals

There may come a time when you feel that your child would benefit from some sort of professional counseling. This could be for any number of reasons. Your child may have difficulty paying attention and sitting still in class, and you or the teacher may suspect he has attention deficit disorder. He may be experiencing a drop in his grades and you don't know why. You may believe that your child is using drugs or is showing signs of an eating disorder. We certainly hope that you don't run into any of these problems. If you do, you want to have your child treated by someone who is competent, knowledgeable, and comfortable with your family.

Getting counseling for your child, or for your child and your family, is a bit trickier than getting medical care. In both cases, of course, you have the right to treatment from a respectful, caring professional. There is an important difference between medical treatment and psychological counseling. In the case of medical treatment, when it comes right down to it, the antibiotics prescribed by a homophobic physician will work just as well as those prescribed by a gay-friendly physician. You should not have to put up with disrespectful behavior, but the physician's attitude will not alter the effectiveness of the treatment. The case of psychological care is very different. Treatment by a homophobic counselor can do irreparable harm. Mental health treatment involves talking to the counselor about very personal, intimate aspects of one's life. If the counselor you and your child are speaking with is going into the therapy with a preconceived notion that homosexuality is not healthy, or that your lesbianism must be a contributing factor to your child's difficulties, then you may be setting yourself up for disaster. Not only will your child not get the help he needs; he may well end up with more problems than he started with.

Now that we have frightened you, let us try to reassure you. The overwhelming majority of mental health professionals are not homophobic. Their training, for the most part, encourages them to be open to people from all types of backgrounds and families. We will get into the particular types of education that different types of professionals have, but suffice it to say that counselors have been trained to be nondiscriminatory in their practice. Some do slip through with their own prejudices intact. But there are so many mental health professionals out there that you should be able to find one who will treat you and your child with acceptance and respect.

So how do you find such a therapist? Your first stop should be your pediatrician's office. We give this advice to any parent who suspects a child is in need of counseling. There are two reasons why going to a pediatrician is important. First, he or she can rule out any medical conditions that may be contributing to or causing your child's difficulties. Your pediatrician sees children all day long and may be better able to determine whether your child's behavior is outside of the range of normal. It may be best, depending upon your child's age and your particular concerns, to speak to the doctor outside your child's presence. This will give you a chance to talk freely about your concerns without fear of embarrassing your child or making him self-conscious.

The second reason for going to your pediatrician first is that he or she should be able to provide at least one, if not more than one, referral to a mental health specialist. Ideally, you will have established a trusting relationship with your child's doctor by this time. Ask directly if your doctor feels that the people he or she is recommending would be experienced and comfortable dealing with a child in a lesbian family.

You can get referrals from other sources as well. Local gay and lesbian parenting groups, even if you are not affiliated with them, are usually happy to refer you to providers their members have used. You can look in local alternative or gay newspapers for advertisements. There are even some mental health clinics in large cities that cater to the gay and lesbian population.

Once you have your referral, your next step is to interview this person. This meeting is different from an evaluation of your child. In the interview, as in the initial interview with prospective pediatricians, you will want to bring up any concerns you have directly. Ask the provider if he or she has any experience working with children in gay or lesbian families. If not, ask how comfortable he or she would be in treating such a child. If you feel that your child's problems are in any way related to your lesbianism or your relationship with your child, you probably should not have your child treated by someone who has no experience in dealing with gay or lesbian families. Even if the inexperienced therapist is open-minded, you do not want to spend your time educating him or her about the issues faced by children of lesbians.

There are a number of different types of therapists to whom you might take your child for treatment. The different types have different levels of education and training, and come from different perspectives.

Child and adolescent psychiatrists are medical doctors. After completing medical school, they had advanced training in pediatrics, psychiatry, and child psychiatry. They are the only providers who can prescribe medication. Their training has been on curing disease, not on understanding the social and psychological ramifications of being gay or lesbian. As a group, psychiatrists tend to be more conservative than the other groups of providers. You could very well find a child psychiatrist who is experienced in dealing with children of gay and lesbian parents, but this is not likely. You should be aware that this is not an explicit part of their training.

Child psychologists went to graduate school. They have at least a master's degree, and usually a PhD. Their training focused less on the disease model of mental health and more on the dynamics of interpersonal relationships. They also studied normal developmental processes. The type of treatment they would offer would be some sort of child or family therapy. They may suggest parenting classes. If a child psychologist feels that your child would benefit from medication, he or she will consult with an MD.

Social workers generally have a master's degree. Their training is the most liberal and progressive of the three types of providers we have discussed. Their education focuses on things like diversity and oppression. Social workers have almost certainly had training in dealing with members of minority groups, if not specifically gays and lesbians. Their training, however, is the least extensive of any of the groups we have mentioned.

So what would we do if one of our daughters developed a behavior problem we thought worthy of treatment? We would, as we said, first seek the advice of her pediatrician. What we did after that would depend on what type of problem our daughter had. If one of our daughters was having a problem that was social or emotional in nature—say, extreme shyness, an inability to get along with peers, or disobedience and defiance to authority—we would not consult a child psychiatrist. Instead, we would go to a psychologist or social worker. Ideally, we would take her to one who was experienced in working with children of gay and lesbian parents. If that were not possible (if we lived in a fairly remote area and our choices were more limited, for example), we would be sure that whoever we took her to see was open to our family. We would interview some prospective therapists until we found one that we felt that we and our daughter could work with productively.

There could conceivably be some circumstances in which we would bring our child to see a child psychiatrist. If she were showing some behaviors that seemed to have a physiological basis, we would not hesitate to bring her to a child psychiatrist. Currently, problems such as hyperactivity or attention deficit or obsessions and compulsions are disorders that appear to have such a physiological basis. A child psychiatrist, in our opinion, would be the most appropriate person to treat such disorders. We would only consider a child psychiatrist, though, if our pediatrician and we felt that she would benefit from medication. Incidentally, sometimes pediatricians will prescribe medication for psychological conditions (for example, treating childhood or adolescent depression with a prescription for Prozac). In our view, any diagnosis like depression warrants counseling in conjunction with any medication that may be prescribed. If your child is prescribed medication for any psychological disorder, insist that he receive counseling as well.

Other Professionals

Your child may have need of services from other professionals at some point in his life. Speech therapists, physical therapists, dentists, optometrists, and so on may be involved in treating your child. Generally speaking, these professional relationships will not be as long-lasting as the relationship with your child's pediatrician or as emotionally intense as the relationship with a mental health care professional. We recommend that you mention the fact that your child has two mothers when and if that information is relevant. When we first started taking the girls to the dentist, Beth said at the initial meeting, "The girls have two moms. The dental insurance is through their other mother, Suzanne. Here is the insurance form." The dentist showed no interest at all in this piece of information. What are his feelings on lesbians having children? We really have no idea. But we don't need to know that. What we do need to know is that he will treat our daughters as he would any other patient. And he does.

There are a few things you should keep in mind when dealing with professionals. The first is, when you come right down to it, these people work for you. They may not act like it (in the case of most doctors, for example), but they do. You and your child have the right to be treated respectfully. You do not have to hire someone who has any type of problem dealing with your family.

The second thing to keep in mind is that you never want to put your child in a situation where he is being treated by someone who actively disapproves of his family. It is our job to protect our children from that. Someone may be recommended to you as the best speech therapist in the area, for example. But if that person turns out to hold unyielding homophobic attitudes (for example, asking your partner not to attend conferences because as a nonparent she has no right to be there), then that person is not the best speech therapist for your child. Your first responsibility is to be the guardian and advocate for your child. You can, and should, express your concerns to the person who is treating your child. If that professional is unable to assure you that your child will be treated in a way that is respectful of his family, then you must find someone else.

You may at times find yourself forced to deal with professionals whom you do not know. If your child requires a visit to the emergency room, for example, he will generally be seen by whoever happens to be on call. In this case, you do have to take who you get at the time. Even in such a situation, however, do not feel that you have to allow yourself to be mistreated. Explain your family situation to whoever needs to know about it. If you believe that your family is being treated differently than a heterosexual family would be treated, insist on speaking to a superior. You can also contact your own physician.

Dealing with Other People
Who Are Important to Your Child

In addition to the professional people who are in your child's life (doctors, teachers, and so on), there are many other adults who also play a role. We are talking about scoutmasters, soccer coaches, dance teachers, camp counselors, and, as our children get older, their employers. These adults come in and out of our children's lives but can be very important to them while they are here.

In one way, of course, the issues are the same as they always are. We want our child to be treated like any other child and not made to feel unwelcome because he has a lesbian mother. What is different about these people, as compared to the people we have been speaking about, is that they are not trained professionals. Your child's scoutmaster or soccer coach is probably going to be another parent who is volunteering his or her time. Your child's ballet teacher has been trained to dance; your teen's boss at the fast food restaurant has been trained to flip burgers. There is no code of ethical standards that they have sworn to uphold. There is no Hippocratic oath they are breaking if they fail to treat our children kindly. They are not working for us in the same way as the professionals are. It's a little harder to be authoritative with someone who is volunteering than with someone you are employing.

Not everyone who passes through our lives needs to know, or has a right to know, about the intimate details of our lives. So first you must decide how much any particular person needs to know about your family. If your child takes gymnastics and this involves you taking him there once a week so he can tumble around for an hour, it is not imperative that you sit down with the gymnastics instructor to have a heart-to-heart talk about your family. Most of the mothers we spoke with handle extracurricular activities in a more casual manner. They do not make a point of announcing the nature of their relationship. They do not hide their relationship either. Both moms show up at games or swim meets or recitals. It's probably obvious to the other parents as well as to the coach or instructor that the child has two mothers.

Sometimes the people who are in charge of extracurricular activities can really help smooth the way for your child. Bailey was involved in Girl Scouts this year. When we signed her up, we filled out the application with both our names. Each of us, at different times, had picked Bailey up from the meetings, but we had never formally had "the talk" with the parents who were the leaders. Recently Beth was helping out at a meeting with Bailey's troop. One of the other little girls asked Beth, "Are you Bailey's mom?"

Beth said, "Yes, I am."

"But I thought that that other lady was Bailey's mom." She obviously remembered seeing Suzanne with Bailey at some point.

"Yes, Bailey has two moms."

Bailey chimed in, "I call one of them 'Mom' and the other one 'Mama.'"

Before either Beth or Bailey could say another thing, Bailey's troop leader jumped in. "Bailey has two moms. Isn't she lucky?"

The little girl smiled and said, "Yes."

Dealing with Neighbors and Other Adults

The way in which you deal with your neighbors and your child's friends' parents is necessarily different from the way in which you deal with professionals. Obviously, you do not have the option of hiring a new group of friends or neighbors if the ones you have don't measure up in some way. We don't get to choose our neighbors, and as our children get older we will be less involved in choosing their friends. Fortunately, most lesbian mothers find others to be pretty accepting.

"When we first moved into the house where we are now, we had a window that looks right up the stairs. We needed something to cover it. And the rainbow flag fit perfectly, so I put it over the window," laughs Irene. "A lot of people really didn't know what it was. It took a few weeks before everybody realized, 'Hey, they're lesbians over there,' but we haven't had a problem over here at all. The kids are always all over at our house."

Joanne makes certain that anyone coming to her house knows that Will is a member of a lesbian family. "I tell his friends' parents before they come over. I've only ever had one babysitter, and I talked to her parents before she ever babysat. If they have a problem with it, I don't want it to be his problem. But I've found that pretty much everyone is very supportive."

Again, openness is the best policy. A good approach, in coming out to new people, is to explain that your child has two moms. We find that if we bring this up as part of an introduction, people tend to be more at ease. So Suzanne might say, for example, "Bailey and Rowan have two moms. I'm a professor at the college and Beth is home full time with them." This way, people can respond to any part of the statement they want to—whether it's "Oh, what do you teach at the college?" or "How does Beth like being home full time?" or even "Two moms? How did that happen?" By the way, we have never gotten the last response. People are very unlikely to respond negatively to this kind of approach, in our experience.

Privacy: Do We Have to Tell Everyone Everything?

Sometimes people may respond to the information that our child has two mothers as an invitation to ask personal, prying questions. While this can be the result of genuine curiosity, and the person asking doesn't mean any offense, it can still be quite disconcerting. Do you really want to talk about the details of your insemination with someone you don't know? Should you have to answer a question on how long after you were married you knew you were a lesbian? People can feel that your openness about being a lesbian gives them license to be nosy about your private life. Do not make the mistake of feeling you have to answer every question that anyone asks.

Becky and Anne have taken the approach that they will not tell people which one of them gave birth to their daughter, Samantha. Their decision to keep this information private sends a strong message to others that some topics are just off-limits. Your response to a too-personal question needn't be a hostile one. "We don't answer that question" or something like "Out of respect for my son's privacy, I don't usually talk about that" will get your point across. Couples who do what Becky and Anne do usually say that they don't like to highlight which parent is the biological one, as that implies that the other mother is somehow less of a mother. Whatever the reasons, making a decision beforehand on what information you will share and what you will not is a good idea.

Negative Reactions from Others

Fortunately, outright rejection or negative responses from others are rare events. Rare, but not unheard of. Rosita had to deal with such a situation in a courtroom with a judge. The judge, ironically, was the one who granted her second-parent adoption. "When we were adopting the girls, we did a second-parent adoption in our state. And the judge, a very nice man, looked at me, and he said, 'You know, one of your responsibilities as an adoptive parent is to bring up your children as law-abiding citizens.' And he said, 'You know, the relationship that you are in is not a legal one.' And my answer was, 'Your honor, if I could speak candidly without, you know, being thrown out?' He's like, 'By all means.' And I said, 'My relationship, although it's not a legal one, is not an illegal one. And I'm waiting for you boys to make up your minds. If you want to draw up the marriage decree right now, I'll marry Gabriella here. I don't have a problem with that. I'm waiting for you guys.' So you know, I said, 'I understand that. I'm not ever going to encourage my children to break the law, but you know, I'm not in an illegal relationship, and you can make it legal for me. I can't. It's up to you, and the ball's in your court.' And he let it go at that."

Irene had a situation with a neighbor who tried to blame Irene and Kitty for problems that her own son was having. "Bradley is pretty open about it [having two moms]. We had a real problem with that for a little while; he was going around the neighborhood telling everybody that he had two moms, that his moms were lesbians. A parent came and confronted us about it. She had this horrible, bratty son who used to try to beat up Bradley. They had once had this big fight, where we ended up calling the police on this little boy. He'd been smashing Bradley into the wall and taking his bike and all this stuff. And this lady came over and said, 'Well, you need to talk to your son about lying, because he goes around and tells everybody his mother is a lesbian.' And I said, 'Well, I'm not going to talk to my son about anything, because he's telling the truth.' Kitty's jaw hit the ground, and this lady's jaw hit the ground, and she said, 'Well, that's why my son's having all these problems.' 'Well, I don't think so. He's not in the bedroom with us. Your son is just a brat!' Yeah, he already had a record with the police. The police knew exactly who he was. He was only nine years old. That's the only time we've been confronted about it." By being open about the fact that she was a lesbian, Irene took away her small-minded neighbor's ability to use the information against her. She also did not allow her neighbor to turn the conversation away from her son's misbehavior and into a conversation about something else. In both this instance and Rosita's experience with the judge, homophobes are left with nothing to say when we respond to them with dignity and pride in who we are.

Resources

www.ama-assn.org

The American Medical Association contains quite a bit of information that is of use to the general public, including a doctor finder (you can look up the training and areas of specialization of your physician), a reference library, and consumer health information. This is also a professional site, so it includes things that are relevant to AMA members but not the rest of us (such as upcoming meetings, elections, and so on).

www.aap.org

The American Academy of Pediatrics has a listing of parent resource guides, which are booklets written on general parenting topics as well as specific medical problems, such as dealing with asthma. The guides are available for purchase. The site also includes an address for a pediatric referral service—no on-line referrals as of yet.

www.glma.org

The Gay and Lesbian Medical Association was founded in 1981. It promotes tolerance and respect for gay and lesbian healthcare workers as well as improved care for gay and lesbian patients. The web site has an on-line referral for physicians who are affiliated with GLMA (they are either gay/lesbian themselves or are accepting of those who are). You can get referrals based on your area code, city, or state.

www.apa.org

The American Psychological Association is the official organization of psychologists. The web site offers its ethical guidelines and standards, some general information on psychological treatment, and a referral service. The site also includes research that may be of particular interest to lesbian mothers—check out this link to a summary of the studies that have been conducted on children of gays and lesbians: apa.org/pi/parent.html.

www.psych.org

The American Psychiatric Association web site offers information on common psychiatric disorders (afflicting both adults and children), as well as advice on how to choose a psychiatrist.

www.aacap.org

The American Academy of Child and Adolescent Psychiatry is the web site for those psychiatrists who specialize in treating children and adolescents. The site contains features like Facts for Families, which describes various childhood disorders or situations that are often stressful for children (for example, parental divorce). It also includes a glossary of symptoms affecting adolescents. There is a bit of advice on choosing a psychiatrist.

www.aglp.org

The Association of Gay and Lesbian Psychiatrists is a professional organization. Like most professional sites, it has information about such things as membership and upcoming events, which are of no interest to the rest of us. What the site does have is some (fairly technical) references from journals on gay and lesbian issues. It also provides some referrals to gay-friendly psychiatrists.

www.gayhealth.com

This site offers the latest news, information, and advice on matters related to health care for the GLBT community. One of the features allows you to search for a healthcare provider in your area who has asked to be listed as gay-friendly. Pediatricians and mental health professionals are listed.

◆ CHAPTER 6 ◆

Helping Our Children Deal with Others

The biggest concern that most lesbian mothers have is Will my child be teased? We all know that children do tease each other, sometimes quite cruelly. With good reason, we worry about how our children will be treated and how they will handle it if they do, in fact, get teased. We want to be able to advise our child on the best way to handle questions about his family. We may also wonder if, someday, even our own child may ask us to hide our lesbianism from other people, so he won't feel embarrassed or self-conscious. How should we respond to two opposing feelings—wanting to protect our child and wanting to live openly as who we are? These are issues all of us need to be prepared to face.

Preparing Our Children for Questions

At the very least, your child will have to answer questions about his family. Help prepare him to talk about his family in a way that will help him avoid problems. We like the advice one mother we know gave to her son about talking to his friends. She told him to tell his friends that he has two moms, and if the friends have any questions about that they can ask his moms themselves. So far there have been no takers, and the son has not had any problems. That approach not only forestalls endless questions from other kids, it also lets her son know that she will be there to help and support him. He knows he is not alone. You can give your child the same advice in talking to adults. If he has two moms, he can say so. If they want to know more about it, they can ask you. Just as you do not have to answer every question posed to you, your child also has the right not to answer every question he is asked. He has a right to his privacy. Tell your children, flat out, that they do not have to talk about anything that makes them feel uncomfortable. Different children draw the line at different points. Paula and Nancy's son Thomas recently did a school project where he made a family tree, complete with the man who was his sperm donor. Not all children wish to be as open as Thomas. Starting at the beginning of the elementary school years, you should talk to your child about the issue of privacy. Let him know that sometimes people ask rude questions, even if they don't mean to be rude. Tell him that he can say, "I don't want to talk to you about that. It's private," anytime he wants to.

Come Play at Our House

Many lesbian mothers report that their house is the one where the neighborhood children prefer to play. This came up so often in our discussions with lesbian moms that we started to wonder why that is. We thought probably part of it is that women are usually more child-centered than men, so a house with two women is bound to be a popular gathering place. We suspect that a larger part of it is that, as lesbian mothers, we are naturally concerned that our children have friends who accept them. We worry that they might be ostracized because of our lesbianism. For that reason, many of us go out of our way to make the neighborhood children feel welcome, to ensure that our children will have friends.

For Tess, the popularity of her house as a place for the local children to play helped her daughter overcome a problem with teasing. "A couple of the boys teased her a couple of times about it. 'You have a lesbian mom, your mom's a dyke,' and she said, 'Yeah, and so?' But after that, the boys ended up coming over to our house. Our house is usually the house that the entire neighborhood is in, or playing out in front with the basketball hoop or whatever. So, after that, the boys were like, 'Hey, you know what? Your mom and Barbara are cool!'"

Margaret and Sarah have also found their home to be the one where all the neighborhood children come to play. They feel this will be a real advantage for Alexa as she gets older. "I think it's great that she's seen mommy-and-daddy couples endorsing us. All the neighborhood children—they love to come here. They are going to be very important people in her life. They already are. She'll be on the bus with them; she'll be in school with them. That the neighborhood would be like this was a benefit that we could never have anticipated. My hope would be that if a more peripheral person makes a negative comment, then she can interpret the information for herself. She'll also know 'Well, how weird can it be if Jane and Katie and Sam all think my moms are so cool and they hang out at my house all day?' I hope that that will buffer the situation for her. I think sometimes when people have difficult times within themselves, it is helpful to look outside yourself for a gauge. She'll have those gauges outside, because she has so many people here that are so close to her in that way. It's fine with them."

Your house does not need to be the most popular place for the neighborhood children to play for your child to have friends. Promoting friendship between our child and children who have heterosexual parents is another thing lesbian mothers can do to help smooth the way. "We're also trying to get Adam involved in relationships with kids with straight parents," explains Cheryl. "We're trying to open ourselves up with those parents about who we are. That way, for the kids that Adam's playing with in the neighborhood, his having two moms is just a natural thing."

When Teasing Does Happen

Teasing is a part of childhood for most children. Your child may be teased because he wears glasses; because he is taller or shorter or thinner or heavier than other kids; or because he doesn't wear the "cool" kind of sneakers. We know that most children, at some time, will be teased by someone about something. We would like it not to happen at all, but if it does happen we want our child to be able to shrug it off, to not feel hurt or demoralized, and to experience it as nothing more than a momentary problem. We hope that our child has good friends who treat him kindly and that teasing is a rare occurrence. We all know how to talk to our child if he is teased for wearing glasses, for example. We reassure him that there is nothing wrong with wearing glasses, that he looks good in them, that this other child is being mean, and that his real friends know that our child is just fine. We may give him pointers on how to deal with this particular child, either by ignoring him or coming back with a stinging retort. If the teasing is particularly troublesome to our child, most of us would not hesitate to intervene, speaking with the teacher or the child's parents if necessary to bring it to a halt. This is part of our job as parents.

If the teasing is about our child having a lesbian mom, however, that is something else. In addition to all the feelings we would have about our child experiencing any teasing—anger at the teasing child, protectiveness and sympathy for our child—we can add another layer. We can feel guilty about making our child vulnerable to this kind of response; we can feel irate about a society that inculcates homophobia in its children; we can feel hurt that someone is attacking us through our child. In short, this kind of teasing pushes our buttons. We need to be ready to handle this situation, if it comes up, in a way that is appropriate, helpful to our child, and not an overreaction.

Most lesbian mothers feel that teasing or other difficulties our children face because of the fact that we love women requires two types of responses. The first is to deal with the child or other person who is bothering our child. The second is to talk to our child about the problem.

Although her children have not yet experienced any teasing from other children about having two moms, Rosita already has a plan for how to deal with that, should it come up. "I'm the kind of person that doesn't take it lying down, you know. I'd probably get into the car and go over to the kid's house and say, 'Listen, your kid said this to my kid today, and I'd like you to address this with your child, because it's not right.' I'm not in your face, but I do address things directly. I don't hide."

At one point Will got into a fight with a new friend who taunted him about having a lesbian mother. Joanne took the incident as an opportunity to emphasize her belief in openness. "I talked to Will about it, a lot. I explained to him that in my experience being out was the safest place to be, because then people couldn't hold it against you. How can they hold it against you if they already know?" She also encouraged Will to use his other friends as support. "I tell him, if your friends know you're struggling with something, they can be really helpful, and they want to be helpful. But if they're left out, they might be angry. So he thought about all of that a lot. One day he just decided to come out to them, and they've all been pretty much a cheerleading group." Since then Will has not had any problems.

When your child is not capable of handling a situation on his own, either because he is too young, he is very upset, or he asks for your help, then you should directly intervene. Generally speaking, a child still in elementary school will need two kinds of help in dealing with teasing and hurtful remarks. He will need to be reassured that nothing is wrong with him and that he has lots of friends who know that. He will also need you to tell him how to deal with the situation or to deal with it for him.

For example, say your child invites another child over to your house to play, but the other child's parents do not allow it because your child has lesbian parents. How should you handle this? It's most important to acknowledge your child's feelings—that he is hurt, confused, and probably angry, maybe even a little angry at you. After all, if you weren't a lesbian then he wouldn't be having this problem. Let him know you understand this, and that he has every right to feel upset. Explain to him that sometimes people do things out of prejudice. His friend's parents are not mean; they just don't understand or want to know people who are different from them. It's too bad—for them, their child, and for your child. "I plan to tell Jessica that some people don't like things that are different," says Karen. "They don't like people who have different colored skin. Some people don't like the people that we choose to love and care about, and it's unfortunate that there are some people who feel that way." You can suggest that he invite another friend over, or that you all do something fun as a family. Give him some advice on dealing with his friend. He could say, for instance, "I'm sorry your parents feel that way. I would like to be friends with everyone." Remind him that most people are not like his friend's parents.

Occasional teasing is a different problem than outright rejection. A child who is rejected by his peers is one who is actively disliked and avoided by most, and sometimes all, of his age-mates. Rejected children exhibit aggressive, hostile, and immature behavior, which in turn leads to further negative responses from other children. Active rejection by peers in childhood is predictive of later difficulties in adolescence and adulthood. On the other hand, a child who is generally well liked by others, and has some close friends, may encounter teasing from other children at some point. This occasional teasing, while painful when it happens, is not going to lead to significant future problems. Remember to look at the whole picture of your child's social relationships, not just at the infrequent teasing.

As your child gets older he may wish to handle teasing or hurtful comments on his own. If he only wants to get your advice rather than ask you to do anything, then respect his wishes. We aren't always going to be there to protect our children. They do need to learn to stand up for themselves. By the time your child is old enough to want to deal with difficult situations on his own, you would hope that you have raised him to be confident enough to know that nothing is wrong with him.

Lesbian Mothers Who Are Still in the Closet

We all know that there are lesbians who live virtually all their lives in the closet. There are lesbian mothers who do the same thing. Some of you who are reading this book fall into this category. There are many reasons, both societal and psychological, for making the choice not to live openly as lesbians. The one couple we interviewed who was closeted while their children were growing up was Marie and Shirley. They had inarguably good grounds for not being open. When they got together in the 1970s in a rural town in the West, they knew that there was no chance of their relationship being tolerated, much less accepted. As divorced women, they believed with good reason that they could lose custody of their children. So concerned were they about the repercussions of their relationship being revealed that they did not even tell their children that they were a couple. "We had separate bedrooms all those years. We never really came out and told them. We didn't show our affection. We argued in front of them, but we didn't touch or kiss or anything in front of the kids. But back then, twenty-four years ago, we would have been run out of town," explains Marie.

It wasn't until long after the children were grown that they came out to them. Marie recalls, "It was the same time Ellen came out on TV. Our daughter-in-law invited us over for some cake and ice cream, and afterward she said, 'There's something I want to ask you.' And we said, 'Well,—what?' And she kind of hesitated. We said, 'What do you want to know? Are we lesbians?' She said 'No! Well, yes.' So I did tell her. And she decided we needed to have a big party, you know, to let everybody know. Because she said all the kids know." So they had the party with all their children and their spouses, and now everyone officially knows. Of course they suspected before this, but they never brought it up. Marie feels that "in one way, it was a good thing to hide it." They protected themselves and their children from a hostile world. "In another way, we should have told them. The kids do feel that they've been left out of a large part of our relationship." Shirley adds, "They felt like it was a part of their life that was missing. They weren't able to share in our life."

Times have changed in the last twenty to thirty years. But there are still some pockets where being out as a lesbian mother could be damaging to you or your child. The women who are most at risk are those women living in isolated rural areas, and who have discovered their lesbianism after having children. Living in an area with no support groups, no gay community of any kind, and no tolerance among the local populace can make it very difficult to live openly. If this is your situation, and you feel that living openly would expose you or your child to danger or ostracism, you do have options. Today, if you have access to a computer, you have access to a strong and supportive gay community. You can take advantage of the larger society's growing acceptance of gays and lesbians, even if your immediate surroundings are not so accepting. (See "Resources" in Chapter 4 for publications, on-line groups, and so on.) Once your children are old enough to understand concepts of discrimination and prejudice (around the middle of the elementary school years), you can explain to them that although there is nothing wrong with your family, some people who don't know any better think that there is. You might say something like, "We need to be careful about talking about our family to people who might not understand. If someone asks you about us, you can say that your parents are divorced. You and your mom live with your mom's friend now. No one needs to know more than that."

Of course the obvious solution, if you live in an area where your lesbianism cannot safely be disclosed, is to move somewhere else. You and your child will be better off living among tolerant, accepting people. We realize that for some people this is not a possibility, for whatever reason. We urge you to try to make arrangements to relocate to a more friendly area. You don't necessarily have to move to a big city. The suburbs of big cities, or smaller towns that are near colleges, are usually more progressive than where you are now. The difficulties in relocating and finding a new job will be well worth it. In the meantime, think of our suggestions on living the closeted life as temporary measures you are taking until you can live somewhere openly.

Closeting Yourself for Your Child

Some of the mothers we spoke with, and these were mothers with adolescent children, had made the decision to not be as open as they would like to be about their sexuality. In these families, the children themselves had asked their mothers to "tone it down." In Gina's case, her daughter Carla's request for more discretion came when the family recently relocated to a new area. "I used to be very, very open," sighs Gina. "We moved here. [Before then] I was out; I didn't care. I was very, very open there. I moved here, and I became closeted. The women I work for—I'm very, very close with them. They have absolutely no idea that I'm a lesbian—whatsoever. They think Kathy's my cousin. For my daughter's sake, I'm not out anymore. Because she asked me not to, you know, because she's at this age now. I have to respect her wishes right now—and my job."

Gina is in a fairly unique situation. She is living in a new, smaller town, and fearful of jeopardizing her employment if she comes out as a lesbian. She also functions as a single parent. Her partner, Kathy, has never had a parental relationship with Carla. So there are no occasions when Kathy acts as another parent. Also, Carla is a senior in high school and beginning to lead her own independent life. Interestingly, Carla has made the decision to tell her boyfriend and her best friend that Gina is a lesbian. What seems to be happening with Carla is not that she does not want anyone to know that her mother is a lesbian. She just wants to be able to choose whom to tell and when to tell them. In fact, says Gina, "Carla just recently told this other girl, because this other girl told her that her mother's a lesbian. So Carla said, 'Oh, so is mine!'" In this case, Carla is not so much asking her mother to go back into the closet as she is asking her to let Carla decide when she wants to reveal personal information. Joanne has noticed that recently Will has wanted her to be less visible as a lesbian too. "My son has a lot of issues going on around it, has had for about two years now, and has asked me to 'tone it down.' So I'm not as politically involved as I was. I still give money, but I'm not really involved in the political process, and that's been my source of activism. I agreed to do that, because I felt it would happen anyway, and I'll probably stay that way until he's through this."

Lesbian mothers comment, not infrequently, that their adolescent children ask them to remove bumper stickers or other visible signs of gay identification. There may be two things happening here. Your child may be feeling like he is the center of attention and everyone is looking at him. In other words, he is overestimating the impact that your rainbow sticker will have on other people. The other thing that may be happening is that your child, like Carla, is beginning to want to lead an inde-

---

♦ Advice from a Lesbian Mother ♦

Gina's daughter is a senior in high school. Gina, her partner, and her daughter recently moved to the suburbs from a big city. "Just be open and respect your children's views on who you are. Don't force yourself on them. Don't make it that you have to be out of the closet, because that's who you are, and it doesn't matter what your children feel. If you throw yourself and your sexuality at them and their friends, it's going to be hard. So let them be who they are, and just let them go on and decide whether or not they want to be proud of who you are as a lesbian. But have respect for them as children and then as adults."

—Gina

---

pendent life. He would prefer to be the one to decide whom he wants to know about his family.

So what should you do? Pick your battles. Talk to your child about what, specifically, he wants you to do and why he wants you to do it. If he wants the bumper sticker off the car because he thinks that people stare at it on the street and it makes him feel uncomfortable, then fine, take it off. Many of us don't make a point of wearing rainbow jewelry or T-shirts emblazoned "Dykes Forever" everywhere we go, and for a similar reason. If he is feeling the need to be the one in control of his personal life in this area, then that is certainly okay too.

As mothers, we want to do whatever is best for our child. We certainly do not want to make our child feel uncomfortable or self-conscious. As lesbians, we recoil from being asked to deny who we are under any circumstances, even in small ways. And as lesbian mothers, we wonder how we could have ended up with a child who would ask us to hide who we are. What we have to remember is that one of the hallmarks of adolescence is thinking that everyone is looking at you, and that not fitting in with the group is a fate worse than death. So we didn't "end up" with a child who wants us in the closet; we have a child who is going through a phase of wanting desperately to fit in. This may make it easier for you to handle it when your adolescent asks you to take the rainbow bumper sticker off your car. The same bumper sticker, we might add, that has adorned the family car since he was a toddler. Do not take this as a rejection of everything you have tried to instill in him, or as a denunciation of you as a parent. It is neither. What it is is a perfectly normal adolescent desire to look like everybody else. He will outgrow this, as surely as he outgrew temper tantrums and believing in the tooth fairy. Until he outgrows it, you can talk with him about what he wants you to do and why he wants you to do it.

If he is asking for more major concessions, such as never appearing in public with your partner or lying to someone about being a lesbian, then you need to talk to him about what is bothering him. While indulging his wishes to be like everyone else is fine up to a point, it is not good, for you or him, to agree to become completely closeted. What he needs to learn, and what he will learn with maturity, is that there are more important things in life than fitting in with the crowd. Not only do adolescents attach entirely too much importance to that, but they also grossly overestimate how much attention other people are paying to them. Your adolescent needs to find out that other people are not as interested in his life as he thinks they are. He is also probably overestimating the negative impact on his peers of the news that he has a lesbian mother. This is not to say that there may not be some negative fallout; there certainly could be. But most kids find that their real friends stand by them.

You can talk to him about his concerns, reassure him that there are lots of kids out there with lesbian moms AND friends who know that, and come up with some compromises to make him feel better. You can remove any public displays that bother him, and promise not to be affectionate with your partner in front of other people. You do not have to, and should not, lie about your relationship to anyone. You do not have to broadcast it either. We recommend that you make one thing nonnegotiable: You will not lie about your relationship with your partner when asked.

On a few occasions, when he's had games or events that parents can attend, Will has asked his mother to come alone. "Like a couple of times he's said to me, 'Will you come to this with me and will Denise stay home?' He's like that. And so we talked about it, and we decide if that's the best way to deal with it. Usually she stays home," says Joanne. Will is in early adolescence, when the yearning to fit in and the sense that everyone is looking at him are at their peak. Denise has only been Joanne's partner for a short time, so he is still getting used to having her in his life. In this situation, Joanne feels that going along with his wishes is the thing to do.

Our job as parents changes as our children develop. When they are very young, we do everything we can to make the world a safe place for them. As lesbian mothers, that means we must ensure that the people they come into contact with know about our family. As our children get older, we help them to handle questions and teasing in a way that helps them feel good about themselves and their family. As they mature into adolescence and young adulthood, we negotiate with them about revealing personal information to other people. The theme that remains constant is our concern for our child and our respect for ourselves.

♦ CHAPTER 7 ♦

Dealing with Schools

Next to their family, children's most important and enduring influence is their schooling. The quality of their educational experience affects them for the rest of their lives, in many different ways. As lesbian mothers, we have more than the usual concerns about what type of school our child attends and what curriculum she will be learning. We want to have our child in a school that, ideally, values all types of families, tolerates no trace of homophobia in its faculty or students, and makes our child feel comfortable. From choosing a school for our child, to deciding whether and how to come out to the teachers and administrators, to dealing with a homophobic teacher, we have a lot to do to insure our child the best possible learning environment.

The First Step: Choosing a School

Some of us, because of where we live or financial constraints, do not have a choice in where we send our children to school. They will attend the local public schools, and there will be no debate about it. The fact that your child attends the local public school certainly does not leave you without choices or a say in matters. You have more influence than you may realize when it comes to your child's educational experience. For those mothers who do have a choice, the prospect of looking for the right school for our child is exciting as well as daunting.

Lesbian mothers who are lucky enough to live in an area with a number of accepting schools should take advantage of their circumstances. Of course you will be interested in hearing about all the things that any parent would want to know—the curriculum, the student-teacher ratio, accreditation, tuition, and so on. But you also want to find out how your child, as a member of a lesbian family, will be accepted. The best approach is to visit the school as a prospective parent, gathering all the information you can about the school. Then talk to the director or principal individually about your child's family and any particular concerns you may have. Tara's children go to a progressive private school. "Right from the beginning, in the opening interview for the school, we came out to the school and told them. And when they've done family studies we're very out, and the teachers are very supportive of including our family structure and style in everyday conversation."

Ideally, you would like to find a school that has an active philosophy of inclusiveness as well as a diverse student body that includes children of gay or lesbian parents. Even if you are not in the enviable position of having to choose among inclusive schools, you can investigate the local public school's philosophy. Asking questions of your public school principal can let him or her know what your concerns are and what you will be looking for.

Questions to Ask Prospective Schools

♦ Does the curriculum include diversity and inclusiveness as part of its program? A diverse elementary school curriculum would have lessons on different cultures and civil rights. Secondary schools would include issues of cultural and ethnic identity and diversity in today's society.

♦ Does the school library contain books about nontraditional families? If it does not, you can make suggestions for appropriate additions to the library.

♦ How diverse are the students and their families? You may think you know the answer if your child will be attending the local public school, but you might be surprised. Some student bodies are less diverse than the local neighborhood because many of the white students go to private schools. Some student bodies are more diverse than the local neighborhood because children from a nearby neighborhood also attend.

♦ Does the school have any explicit teaching about gay and lesbian issues? Some schools do have special lessons, or even special days, set up to talk to children about different types of families and acceptance of people who are different.

♦ What is the sex education curriculum, and does it discuss only heterosexuality?

Preschool

Not all children attend preschool, but it is becoming increasingly likely that kindergarten will not be the first formal schooling experience for most children. The latest statistics show that most three-year-olds in the United States do attend some sort of preschool. We are very strong advocates of the value of preschool, for reasons having nothing to do with the fact that we're lesbian mothers and everything to do with the fact that we're developmental psychologists. Preschool gives children all sorts of skills that will help them in elementary school—they learn how to be part of a group, how to take turns, how to get along with other children, how to listen to instructions. They are also ready for some basic academic learning—numbers, letters, colors, and so on. Children at this age do not need to be in school all day, and they should not be in a rigorous academic program that puts a lot of pressure on them. But a preschool program, even on a part-time basis, is a wonderful way to introduce school to your child.

Preschool, as it turns out, is also a wonderful way for lesbian mothers to get introduced to the schooling process. For many of us this is our first step in bringing our child into the world, where someone else will be regularly caring for our child. It is the first time we are becoming part of a school community. It is also likely to be the easiest, most uncomplicated school for you as a lesbian mother, in terms of coming out. Your child is too young to have any feelings of reluctance or hesitation about being "outed." His classmates are too young to tease him about his fam-

---

♦ **Did You Know . . . ?** ♦

The more preschool experience they have had, the higher kindergarten students score on school readiness tests. More preschool experience is also associated with a more positive attitude toward kindergarten.

Birch, S. H., & Ladd, G. W. (1997). The teacher–child relationship and children's early school adjustment. *Journal of School Psychology, 35*, 61–79.

---

ily situation. The curriculum is not much more than ABCs, so you needn't worry so much about inclusiveness, per se. Preschools are generally small, so you will most likely be dealing with only the teacher and the director. And generally, educators who work in preschools will do all that they can to make your child feel welcome.

Karen's daughter, Jessica, was the first child of a lesbian mother and a gay man at her preschool. "From thirteen months to two years and nine months, she was in an infant–toddler center that didn't have any other children of gay and lesbian parents, although there's another child there now. It's a small center, with twenty-five kids. There were no identified lesbian and gay staff, but we were very out there nonetheless. It was just something they weren't quite used to, but they did fine with it." You would not expect a child as young as Karen's to experience any problems related to her parents being a lesbian woman and a gay man. A preverbal child would have no capacity to understand if there were any problems. What was valuable for Karen was that she got to practice being out with educators in a school. Having already been out with Jessica's preschool will make it easier for her to be out at Jessica's elementary school.

When our older daughter started preschool, we spoke to the director about our family, and she was quite accepting. We then spoke to the young woman who would be Bailey's first teacher (although staffing changes happened and she turned out not to be her teacher after all). We introduced ourselves and Bailey and said that we wanted her to know who is in Bailey's family—specifically, that she has two mothers. The young woman, who was just out of college, looked somewhat confused for a moment. Then realization of what we were saying slowly dawned on her. She turned to us, gave us an overly bright smile and said, "Oh, that's okay." We very much wanted to respond, "Yes honey, we know it's okay. We weren't actually asking for your approval, believe it or not. We just want to make sure you are going to be nice to our little girl!" But, of course, we didn't. We smiled brightly back, told her how nice it was to meet her, and got out of there.

We left the school that day feeling concerned and unsure about what to do. On the one hand, the school was beautiful, it was close to home, had a very good student–teacher ratio, and we liked the director. On the other hand, this would be our baby's first school experience, and the teacher didn't seem to have a clue as to how to handle our family. Once we thought more about it, we decided to give the school a try and see how things worked out. As it happened, they worked out beautifully. We met the woman who would end up being Bailey's first teacher, and she was great. She told us she had seen our application form, so she knew about Bailey having two moms. She asked us what she called each of us, so that she wouldn't make any mistakes. Bailey loved school, loved her teacher, and had a wonderful experience. On Mother's Day she made two cards. On Father's Day she made a card that said, "Have a happy day." When the class project was drawing pictures of their mothers, Bailey had two up on the wall: "Bailey's Mommy" and "Bailey's Mama." Incidentally, the first teacher we had met was someone we got to know as well, and she was a very kind and accepting person. We were just the first lesbian family she had ever dealt with, and so she was initially thrown off balance.

That is an important point to remember. Not all of us live in areas where there are lots of other children with lesbian or gay parents. For some of us, our family may be the first such family that teachers and principals encounter. They may be unsure about how to respond to us at first. This does not necessarily mean that this is not the right place for our child. It would be great if we could all enroll our children in schools that have many other lesbian and gay parents and that have a curriculum that explicitly teaches about the diversity of families. But if that is not the case, our child can still get a valuable education in an accepting environment.

When you are looking for a preschool for your child, you need to let the director know that your child has two moms before you enroll him. Let the teacher know as well, and be sure to let her know what your child calls each of you. If you are a single mother, you will of course want the director and teacher to know that as well. If your child seems to be the only one with lesbian parents, you could let her know that you will be happy to answer any questions that may come up. As the time approaches, make suggestions on how you want Mother's Day and Father's Day handled. (For Father's Day, we suggest that our daughters make either a Father's Day card for their grandfather, or a Happy Day card for us.) You can make recommendations for books that the preschool could add to its collection.

Elementary School

Elementary schools can go from kindergarten through fifth grade, sixth grade, or eighth grade. Parents who are looking for a suitable school for their children can visit prospective schools with very clear goals in mind.

Karen is currently in the process of looking for a school where her daughter, Jessica, will attend first grade next year. Where they live, "there's just been no money put into public schools, and so we've been applying to all the private schools for her this coming fall. We've been very open as well. I want to find a school that not only talks about lesbian and gay families, but also really celebrates that area of diversity, a place that is really supportive of Jessica and her lesbian and gay family. I don't want her to be in a school where she's the only child of a lesbian and gay family, even in her class. I want her to be in a place that's not so unusual. She's in a school now where it's not unusual that kids have two moms, or two dads, or a combination thereof, and I want her to see those as viable families, rather than as something that's strange."

How Open Should You Be with the Elementary School?

The answer is simple. You should make a point of letting your child's principal and teacher know that your child has two mothers. Your kindergartener or first-grader should not be in the position of having to explain his family to an adult. The teacher also needs to know that your child has two mothers so that she can be sensitive to this in class. Instead of automatically referring to the children's parents as "your mother and father," she could make a point of referring to them as "your parents." She can be ready when your child talks about having two moms. If you are a single mother, your child's teacher needs to be sensitive to this as well. In that case, there is probably no reason to make your sexuality known to the teacher, but you can still emphasize how important it is to you that your child be in an accepting, diverse environment.

We had a pleasant surprise when we were getting ready to enroll our daughter into elementary school. Bailey attends kindergarten at our local public school. We had filled out all the required paperwork several months before school began. The forms, of course, asked for information about "mother" and "father," so we crossed those out and wrote "mother 1" and "mother 2." Our plan was to talk to the principal and the teacher when the beginning of the school year was closer. What happened, instead, was that the principal called us at home. He had gotten a copy of the paperwork, where we had written that Bailey had two moms. He was almost apologetic when he called, saying he didn't want to intrude, but he wanted to know if there was anything he could do to help make Bailey feel more comfortable in school. He even asked us for suggestions on books he could order for the library. Needless to say, we were surprised and very touched. We certainly felt very confident about sending Bailey to school there. At a "Get Acquainted" meeting prior to the start of the school year, we both met and talked to Bailey's future teacher. We introduced ourselves as Bailey's parents and said that we wanted her to know about Bailey's family. She responded quite positively. We ended up chatting about the college where Suzanne teaches and the teacher had taken some courses.

Alyson, Stacy's daughter, has been attending the same private school since the first grade. "She goes to a unique school. It's a Waldorf School, and all the children stay together in the grades one through eight, so all the kids and the teacher know each other very well. The children just naturally know about each other's family situations and respond to each other and support each other in different ways." This illustrates an important point. For the most part, it is news that your child has two mothers only when your child is a new student at a school. If your child attends the same elementary school all the way through, the other children will know about your family. The principal knows, and the teachers will probably be aware as well. You will still want to meet with each new teacher at the beginning of the school year to introduce yourselves as your child's parents.

Junior High or Middle School: The Transition

In the sixth or seventh grade, depending upon your local school district, your child will be leaving elementary school behind and moving up to an intermediate school. Middle schools are a midway point between the very different environments of elementary school and high school. In elementary school, children stay with the same class all day. They have one teacher for the bulk of their classes. In middle school, they begin moving from class to class, meeting different groups of children. They will have different teachers for different classes. They will be taking much more responsibility for themselves.

As our children are becoming more mature, we must start to pull back a bit. It is no longer necessary to have a talk with each teacher, to let him or her know about your family, at the beginning of every school year. We do not recommend, as we did for elementary school children, that you meet with the principal when your child enters the school. Our

♦ **Did You Know . . . ?** ♦

The transition from primary school to secondary school (from elementary school to middle or junior high school) is associated with a decline in grades. As compared to their experience in elementary school, secondary school students get less personal attention and fewer opportunities to influence classroom decisions.

Eccles, J. S., Lord, S., & Buchanan, C. M. (1996). School transitions in early adolescence: What are we doing to our young people? In J. A. Graber, J. Brooks-Gunn, & A. C. Peterson (Eds.), *Transitions through adolescence* (pp. 251–284). Mahwah, NJ: Lawrence Erlbaum Associates.

children are now old enough to understand that their family makeup is different from most other children's. They are not going to be confused if a teacher refers to "your mom and dad" in the way a younger child might.

When your child starts middle or junior high school, we recommend that you put both your names on the registration forms. Then go to the open house or "meet the teachers" functions together and introduce yourselves as your child's parents. These open-house events are not like conferences you had with your child's elementary school teacher. They are not opportunities to get together and have a chat about your child's progress, abilities, and so on. The teacher will be talking to the parents as a group, to explain what the class will be doing that year. Of course individual teachers run these events in their own styles. Some will conduct formal presentations, while others will offer an informal walk-through of the classroom. In any case, you will not be having a heart-to-heart talk with the teacher. A simple "We're Bailey's parents—it's nice to meet you" is about all you can expect.

Irene's children have not been in a lesbian family for very long, and in that time they have had no problem at school. "One of their teachers is a really good friend of mine, and her son is a friend of Bradley's. She's known that I'm a lesbian since I left my husband. And it's a real little town. One of the teachers at Bradley's middle school is also a lesbian, and when we went to his open house, he said, 'Oh, you have to go meet this teacher; you'll really like her.' I said, 'Really, why?' He said, 'Because she likes rainbows too,' so we went and met her, so of course she knows. We just don't hide it. We go to enroll the kids in school, I put Kitty down as able to pick the kids up too, and she goes to school functions with us."

High School

High school is yet another step on our children's road to independence.
Now, not only are they moving from class to class, they are choosing
some of their own courses. They will most likely be tracked into a college preparatory track or a nonacademic track. They will need to worry
about graduation requirements, college entrance exams, advanced place-
ment courses, and more. They will be attending a school with many
more activity choices, and in most cases many more students, than they
have had before.

While in some ways the high school experience has not changed
since most of us were there, in other ways it is a different place. Young
people are identifying themselves as gay or lesbian earlier than they did
when we were growing up. Many high schools have gay and lesbian
clubs. The topic of homosexuality is discussed much more openly than it
was even ten or fifteen years ago. So on one hand, there is much more
openness about homosexuality. On the other hand, adolescents are still
adolescents, and are prone to strong feelings of wanting to fit in with the
crowd. (See Chapter 10, "Sexuality and Our Children," for a more detailed discussion of adolescent psychological development.) Homophobic attitudes are common among high school students, and some of our
children may prefer to be discreet with their classmates rather than risk
being teased.

Lisa has seen this effect on her older son. "My son, my sixteen-year-
old, has become a tiny bit more closeted. For example, I work now in a
gay youth project with someone, and we're going to do it at some of the
area schools. He's fine about us coming and doing it for the staff, but he

would prefer that we don't do it for the kids. He said that they're really homophobic."

Homophobic Classmates: Your Response

We should not assume that our children will have any serious problems at school related to our lesbianism. Problems can occur, however, and it may be necessary for us to deal with a particular teacher or principal. Paula and Nancy's middle son, Thomas, did experience some teasing for a while in junior high school. "Finally in his third year they got a new principal in the school," says Paula. "And the new principal saw these kids teasing him in the hall about the second week of school, and called them into his office and read them the riot act, and called their parents, and it never happened again. It took a while to get the right principal and then it went away." An open-minded principal can and should put a stop to teasing. However, you should not feel that your only option is to wait for an enlightened administrator to show up.

If your child is being teased or bullied by another child, and this is not an isolated incident, it is appropriate for you to discuss the problem with the school. If your child is in elementary school, you would speak to the teacher first. If your child is in secondary school, you should first approach the principal. You want to keep the conversation focused on your child. It will not be productive to attack the children who are doing the teasing, or to criticize the insensitive teacher. Emphasize that your concern is your child's education, and you feel it is being compromised by what is happening. Come in to the meeting ready to offer possible solutions to the problem. If the problem is teasing, suggest that the teacher or principal speak to the child, or else set up a meeting with the other parents. Make sure you leave the meeting with a clear understanding of what will be done, and follow it up with a phone call a few days later to make sure that the plan was followed.

Homophobic Teachers: How to Deal with Small Minds

Your child may have to deal with a homophobic teacher at some point. It is unlikely that a teacher with such attitudes would go out of his or her way to make them known to your child, but it could happen. In this case, directly dealing with the teacher is the necessary first step. Again, resist the impulse to attack the teacher, and stay focused on your child. Your goal is not to turn a homophobe into someone who supports and values gay people and their families. Your goal is to get the teacher to behave in a professional manner. Talk about how your child was upset about some comments in class, and you are concerned because you want her to be able to focus on the lessons and not be distracted by other things. If you do not feel this meeting was successful, or if problems persist, your next step is to meet with the principal. If all else fails, insist that your child be removed from the offending teacher's class.

Legal Protection: The Law Is on Our Side

There are more legal protections now than there ever have been for students who are gay or lesbian. In a widely publicized case, a young man named Jamie Nabozny was awarded nine hundred thousand dollars by a federal jury that found that school officials were liable for not protecting him from abuse and harassment by fellow students. Jamie's experiences in school were extreme; he was taunted for years for being gay, severely beaten, and humiliated. Although he repeatedly told school officials what was happening, identified his attackers, and had his parents intervene, the school administration took no significant action. The court decision in

1996 set a precedent that public schools must treat abuse of gay and lesbian students as seriously as they would any other type of abuse.

This decision, as well as the high damage award, has made school administrators around the country much more aware of the issue of anti-gay harassment. While this ruling applies to students who are identified as lesbian or gay, it has strong implications for our children as well. If our children are subjected to anti-gay harassment at school—even if they themselves are not gay—school officials must take it seriously. There has not yet (thankfully) been a case of a child of a lesbian mother or gay father who has used this precedent to sue school officials for ignoring harassment. Certainly none of us would want to get to that point. But the obligation of public schools to protect all students is clear. Administrators would be foolish to ignore any type of harassment.

Following this ruling, the U.S. Department of Education, the Office of Civil Rights, and the Bias Crimes Task Force Subcommittee of the National Association of Attorneys General jointly issued a guideline to school administrators on harassment. *Protecting Students from Harassment and Hate Crimes: A Guide for Schools* tells school officials how to develop an antiharassment policy; how to respond effectively to reports of harassment; and how to create a safe and supportive climate in which all children can learn. The guide is quite specific in its suggestions. For example, it advocates making the antiharassment policy explicit, appointing one person in the school to oversee it and offering counseling to any student who has suffered from harassment. It also makes clear that schools should take these steps to avoid legal liability.

We like to think of these things as insurance policies. We hope we never need them, but it is good to know they are there. No document, statute, or program can eliminate all harassment. But knowing that the law is on our side should give us, and our children, confidence that any problems that arise will be dealt with appropriately.

Our Children's Education

Throughout their school years, our children will be exposed to two sets of curricula. The formal curriculum is the one that is taught explicitly. This includes the textbooks and daily lessons on history, geography, math, and so on. Then there is the informal curriculum. This includes what the children teach each other—about what games they play on the playground, what music they like, and how they want to dress. It also includes the implicit lessons from the teachers—such as whether girls are taken as seriously as boys, whether reading is a task or an exciting opportunity, how important it is to do your best, and so on. These lessons are imparted just as surely as are the ones on history.

As mothers, we are in a position to supplement the education our children are receiving at school with the one we give them at home. If despite your efforts the curriculum on diversity is still lacking at your child's school, then teach your child what you want him to learn at home. Get him books on the civil rights movement and about children in different countries. Help your child think critically about what other kids say, rather than just accepting it as fact. A child's school has an undeniable influence on him, but even that pales in comparison to the influence that we, as mothers, have.

What You Can Do to Enhance the School Experience for Your Child and Yourselves

1. Be a visible presence at your child's school. Become involved in the PTA, volunteer to be a classroom mother, help chaperone a field trip. Teachers and other children will be more comfortable with you if you are a familiar face.

2. Get to know other parents in the school. You will feel more connected to the school if you are acquainted with at least some of the other parents. You can also encourage your child to socialize with children whose parents you like.

3. Be sure that the discussions you have with your child's teacher or principal are not only related to gay and lesbian issues. Talk about the reading program, or the new gym, or after-school programs. You want to be seen as a concerned and involved parent, not just as the lesbian parent.

4. Make sure that the school's main office has it, in writing, that both you and your partner have permission to pick up your child from school.

5. Be on the lookout for Mom-and-Dad-isms. If notes from school are addressed to "Mom and Dad," if the school has "father–daughter" or "father–son" events, or if school projects have a nuclear family theme, speak to the teacher. You can say that you would prefer that they use "parents" rather than "mom and dad,"

as some children, like yours, do not have a dad. Ask if they could have "family night" events, rather than those calling specifically for fathers. Consider asking a male relative or friend to accompany your child to a father–daughter or father–son event if your child wants to go.

Resources

www.glsen.org
GLSEN National Office
121 West 27th Street, Suite 804
New York NY 10001
Telephone: 212-727-0135
Fax: 212-727-0254

The Gay, Lesbian and Straight Education Network (GLSEN) is an organization working to end anti-gay bias in schools from kindergarten through twelfth grade. They provide educational resources, including teacher training materials and curriculum resources. The organization has local chapters, which train teachers, serve as a resource for teachers, parents, and students, and advocate for GLBT youths in school. The web site also offers a great list of children's books, complete with reviews and suggested age ranges.

www.gsanetwork.org
160 14th Street
San Francisco, CA 94103
Telephone: 415-552-4229
Fax: 415-552-4729

The Gay–Straight Alliance Network is a California-based association that works to "empower youth activists to fight homophobia" by forming gay–straight alliances in schools. The site offers instruction on how to start a group as well as resources, news archives, and encouragement.

Gay Parents/Straight Schools: Building Communication and Trust, by Virginia Casper and Steven B. Schultz (1999). New York, NY: Teachers College Press.

The only book we're aware of that specifically deals with the educational needs of children from gay and lesbian-headed families. It offers information and advice.

♦ CHAPTER 8 ♦

Religion and Spirituality

It's a familiar story. You were raised in a faith. You regularly attended church or synagogue. Your faith may have been an important part of your life, or it may not have been. But somewhere along the line, you began to realize that you were not heterosexual. And you also realized that you could not reconcile this reality with the religious beliefs you had been taught. Individuals respond to this dilemma in different ways. Some abandon their religion, if not their personal faith. Others look for a more accepting faith. Still others remain steadfast in their religious convictions and either overlook the homophobic aspects of the religion or argue with those teachings. In all of these different responses, a kind of crisis of faith has occurred.

Now add children to the mix, and the issue becomes even more complex. Many parents feel it is important to raise their children with a grounding in religious beliefs. Often once people become parents they feel an increased need for religion in their lives, or at least in their children's lives. Lesbians who have not given formal religion much thought in their adult lives often begin to reexamine their faith and consider how they want to raise their children in terms of organized religion.

Children and Religion

As with any topic, children of different ages will get different things from being a part of a religious community. Early in a child's life, through the preschool years, being a member of a religious community gives children

117

a sense of belonging and acceptance. They can also begin to get a sense of the concept of God, and start to be exposed to very basic moral principles (like loving your neighbor). As children enter the elementary school years, they will start to have questions about the big mysteries of life. What happens when we die? Does heaven exist? How did life begin? Religious teachings are one way to answer these questions. It is important for children to hear the answers, not only to satisfy their curiosity, but to lay a foundation of faith that will serve them all through their lives. All of us will face difficult times in our lives. We will lose loved ones. We will face trying times of our own. Many people find that their religious faith is what gets them through these difficult times.

Most religions have some type of "coming-of-age" ceremony. Whether it is confirmation, bar/bat mitzvah, or adult baptism, these events symbolize a child's entry into adulthood. Such rituals are very meaningful to young adolescents. Today's society does not have many such rituals proclaiming the end of childhood. Churches and synagogues have many youth groups that provide social gatherings as well as more formal religious teachings. Adolescents can discuss with their peers how they want to lead their more complicated lives in accordance with their beliefs. There are many advantages that children can gain by being raised in a church or synagogue.

Gays and Lesbians and Religion

Lately the topic of homosexuality and religion has been in the news a great deal. One issue that has been generating so much attention is whether churches should perform same-sex commitment ceremonies (or gay marriage, or unions, as they are variously called). To a lesser extent, the question of whether noncelibate gay men and lesbians should be ordained as ministers has also generated controversy. There is a great debate among religious communities on these issues. While we were working on this book, the leadership of the Presbyterian Church (USA) voted to ban ministers from performing same-sex unions. The vote was close and very contentious. As of this writing, it has yet to be ratified by the church's regional jurisdictions. Other denominations have also faced internal dissent on this matter. One minister from the United Methodist Church was defrocked for performing a same-sex union; another was suspended for the same thing.

When these things happen, they tend to get a lot of news coverage. Through these kinds of actions, many gays and lesbians feel that churches are sending a strong message of "you are not welcome here" to members of our community. However, we see this kind of public disagreement as a positive sign. The issues of gay marriage and gay ministers are controversial now, in a way they were not even a few years ago, because so many more people now are in favor of gay marriage and gay ministers. These issues weren't controversial before because hardly anyone supported them. There are many people, gay and straight, in religious communities who feel that the time has come for full inclusion of gays and lesbians. Churches are undergoing a kind of revolution. There will continue to be setbacks. But the revolution has begun. We feel optimistic that churches will only grow more inclusive and welcoming in the years ahead.

Traditional Religion: Is There a Place for Us?

Rosita refers to herself as "a reluctant Catholic." Her partner, Gabriella, is the one who takes their daughters to church and to religion class, "because I refuse to go. I have no problems with God; as a matter of fact, God and I get along very well together. It's when priests and nuns decide to interfere that I have a problem. Gabriella is not more Catholic than I am, but she's much more forgiving than I am. How could I be a member of anything that professes to accept and love everyone, but then puts a huge question mark and a boot on my butt? Organized religion and I broke a long time ago. But as far as my faith in God goes, it's very strong, because my children wouldn't be here, and my life wouldn't be going as wonderfully as it is unless there was a God guiding it. I'm very strong religiously. I just do not like organized religion. I don't trust it. I don't like what it does to people."

When Rosita and Gabriella went to the church to have their daughters baptized, the priest refused to put both their names on the baptismal certificate, even though both women are the girls' legal parents. Gabriella's name is the only one on their baptism papers. "I didn't care," says Rosita. "I just said, 'Look, as long as the kids get baptized, I don't care. I know what my family is, and I know what my faith is. I just want to make sure that they're baptized.' So I didn't make an issue of it."

Margaret and Sarah also had their daughter baptized in the Catholic Church, and their experience was quite different. "Alexa had been baptized Russian Orthodox in Russia, and I had been there for that," explains Margaret. "But she had no baptismal certificate." They went to speak to their priest to discuss having Alexa christened. "The priest very rapidly said that he felt from his standpoint that we should delay it until her name change was completed [that is, until Sarah's second-parent adoption was granted]." Later, they realized "what he was doing, and he was brilliant in that he immediately knew what the political impact would be if it happened before" the second-parent adoption came through. In other words, this priest wanted to be sure that both Margaret and Sarah would be recognized as Alexa's legal parents, so that he could put both their names on her church record. Since Alexa had already been baptized, he told them that the ceremony would be "focused on you as a couple, as parents, sort of a blessing for you as a couple. And it was unbelievable. I mean people were amazed."

Sarah feels that, in a way, "it's frustrating, because they [the Catholic Church] do things like this, but of course they don't advertise it. The stuff they do advertise, or certain factions in the church do advertise, gives them a bad name in the gay and lesbian community. But meanwhile this kind of stuff is happening. And I'm sure it's happening, you know, in other Catholic churches with other Catholic priests, but the general assumption is, 'Well how can you be Catholic and how can you stay with the church, and how can you raise your kid with this church that condemns it?' When you look at what really goes on, it doesn't."

It often happens that what determines how gays and lesbians and their families are treated in different churches or temples is how welcoming the individual church or temple is. Individual priests or rabbis can be more or less welcoming, depending upon their own views and beliefs. It would be a mistake, for example, to decide that the Catholic

Church would not welcome a lesbian and her family because of the attitude of one priest or diocese. Many couples have had the experience that Margaret and Sarah had, which was a very positive and affirming one. Lesbians who want to raise their children within a traditional religious faith should feel that that option is open to them. It may take some time to find a place of worship where you feel comfortable, but don't automatically rule out traditional religions.

Shopping Around for a Church

Once we become parents, the issue of religion comes into play, in one way or another, for most of us. Should we have the baby christened? Shall we take our child to church on a regular basis? Do we want our child to attend religion classes, or even a religious school? If we decide that our child will be involved in a church or temple, how can we be sure that our child will not be exposed to anti-gay rhetoric?

As important as raising our child with some kind of faith is for many of us, it is just as important that we not put our child in a situation where he will be hearing negative things about his family. So many lesbians shop around for an accepting church.

Susan and Andrea's son is still very young, but when he is older, Andrea says, "we'll probably try to find an Episcopal church that's open." It can take a while to find one that is acceptable. Irene has "never really attended church regularly. We've talked occasionally about wanting to, and we did go with my sister to her church when she was baptized. I really didn't like it. I talked to the minister there, and he preached that homosexuality is wrong, so I just couldn't take my kids there. I really haven't found a church or anything that I could go to." Joanne considers herself "church phobic. But I take Will to different churches. We see a lot of different churches. I only to go churches that are open and affirming."

How do you shop around? This is a situation where having access to the Internet is, pardon the pun, a godsend. There are so many wonderful resources on the web for lesbians looking for welcoming places of worship, or wishing to explore religious philosophies. We have listed many excellent sites in our "Resources" section. While this list is not exhaustive (and it couldn't be; a complete listing of sites dedicated to homosexuals and religions would fill this book!), it will help you get started in your quest for a church or synagogue that would welcome your family.

The next step, after locating a church or synagogue that you would consider, is to attend a service. This will help you get a feeling for the congregation, the minister, priest, or rabbi, and the general tenor of that particular place of worship. If you like what you see so far, the next step is to make an appointment with the minister, priest, or rabbi. Say that you and your family are thinking of becoming members of a church, and want to talk about what that church has to offer. You will want to ask about what kinds of programs the church offers to children, if you are interested in that, as well as the services and programs for adults. You can then ask about whether the congregation has gay and lesbian members, and what the feeling is on homosexuality. Feel free to express your concern that your children not be told that their parents are sinful. During this meeting, of course, you will want to maintain a respectful, friendly attitude—you do not want to act like you are shopping around for the best deal on a used car. But you do want to make the point that you want to be sure your family will be as welcome as any other.

Some issues you might want to ask about at this meeting include:

- ◆ How does this church handle baptism? If you are a two-parent family, can both mothers' names be on the baptismal certificate? Even if you're not both legal parents, can both names be on the certificate?

- ◆ If there is Sunday School or other religious instruction, how is the issue of homosexuality dealt with?

- Are gay and lesbian unions performed here? Will you be recognized as a couple?

- As my child gets older, will he be able to participate fully in youth groups and other activities?

If you get a positive response, you and your family should try that particular church or synagogue out for a while. If you do not get the type of response you were looking for—if your questions were met with silence, equivocation, strong discomfort, or outright rejection, then move on and try to find a more welcoming house of worship. You may find that a different church within the same denomination is a better fit for your family. Whatever the case, do not feel that raising your children within a traditional religion is not an option for you.

Gay-Friendly Places of Worship

Probably the most well-known gay-friendly church in existence is the Metropolitan Community Church. The Metropolitan Community Church (MCC) was founded in California in 1968. The founding members were a small group of gay and lesbian Christians who wanted to establish a place of worship where gay men and lesbians could feel welcome. The church specifically ministers to gay, lesbian, bisexual, and transgendered people. Just over thirty years after its founding, the Metropolitan Community Church now has over three hundred churches all over the world. It is the single largest nonprofit organization in the United States that serves the gay and lesbian community. If you are not aware of the MCC and its place in the community, you should be.

Several of the parents we interviewed are members of the MCC. Cheryl and Jeanine go with Adam to their local MCC. "We try to," says Jeanine. "However, the church which we attend doesn't have adequate nursery care. Usually what happens is one of us has to walk Adam through the whole service and then the other person gets to go to the service, so we don't get to do it together. We typically decide not to go. But we've been talking lately about how we could maybe work it back in." Cheryl adds, "You know, so much of this is Adam's age. It doesn't have to do with lesbian and gay issues. I mean, he's two, and he's just not a good churchgoer.

"It's really important to us that he understands, and has a sense of God, and has a sense of Sunday school, and learns the values and the morals that he could learn from a church community, and also has the rituals of the coming-of-age in a church community. Those are the kinds of things that we really want for him, and that we had, and were very important in our growing up."

While Cheryl and Jeanine do plan to resume going to the MCC as a family, they do not feel that it is their only option. "There are many, many churches in the area that are open. That's not to say that we could walk into any church, certainly not, but we feel that there are many options of church for us."

The MCC is not the only gay-friendly place of worship around. Lisa and Robin and their sons "go to the Gay and Lesbian Synagogue and go to a Jewish Humanist Synagogue." Tara and her daughters are "members of the Unitarian Society. There's a very high population of lesbians who go there. We're called the welcoming congregation because we do in fact do trainings and promote lesbian and gay awareness as part of our congregational mission." Deirdre and Meredith belong to a Congregational Church. They have found it to be "an open and affirming church, and we're very involved with that."

Lesbian families who are interested in being part of a religious community have many options from which to choose. If you do not feel comfortable in a more traditional, mainstream religious setting, then exploring denominations that minister specifically to gays and lesbians is a good choice for you. You may feel that you want to make a fresh start with religion, after a negative experience with the faith in which you were raised. You may want to attend services where you can feel not only welcomed, but celebrated. You may want to have your children grow up seeing other gay and lesbian families leading spiritual lives. There are congregations out there where you can find what you want.

When Religion Is Used against Us: Dealing with Homophobic Religious Messages

If it were up to us, our children would never be exposed to anti-gay viewpoints from religious authorities, and so we would never have to face this issue. Certainly we would never knowingly bring our children to a church or synagogue that equates homosexuality with sin. However, it is not always up to us. Sometimes our children hear such messages on television or in the newspapers. Sometimes, despite our best efforts, they are exposed to them in a church or synagogue.

When this happens, we must help our children understand these messages and put them into perspective. If your child has seen a fundamentalist preacher on television or heard a radio evangelist, your task is relatively simple and straightforward. Tell your child that the person he saw or heard is using religion in a way it should not be used—to promote hate and intolerance. Explain that you believe God loves everyone, including gays and lesbians, and most religious leaders believe that as well. Point out that sometimes people get on television or radio in the first place because they say outrageous things. Remind your child that he should always be a smart consumer when it comes to so-called experts, and never to swallow what they say without thinking about it first.

The task becomes a little more complicated when your child is exposed to anti-gay sentiment from a religious leader whom he knows and respects. This is most likely to happen if your child attends services that you yourself do not—if your ex-husband takes the children to a conservative church, for example. Tess's oldest son is in that position, and he has been taught that homosexuality is a sin. Evan has come to terms with this aspect of his religious training on his own. "When he lived with his father, he was raised Mormon, and he knows that in the religion it's not accepted and it's not approved of," says Tess. "But he feels that God loves everybody and, taking the quote of 'What would Jesus do,' says, 'God still loves you, Mom, don't worry about it.'"

This is how you would like your own child to feel. He shouldn't have to disavow all religious principles because of some homophobic attitudes. You want to be careful not to condemn the whole religion, or religion in general. Doing this may make your child feel he has to choose between his mother and his religion. Do not make him feel that way. This is not fair to him. Instead, tell your child that even sincerely committed, faithful individuals have different opinions on the issue of religion and homosexuality. Many religious leaders believe that gay men and lesbians were made that way by God and that God loves them. Many gays and lesbians have deeply held spiritual beliefs and are very involved in their churches or synagogues. Whether you yourself are active in some organized religion or not, let your child know that homosexuality and religion can coexist. If you are in a situation where your child is regularly attending a church that condemns homosexuality (again, using the example of the ex-husband taking your child to such a church), consider taking your child to a more affirming church. This will let him see that not all religions are intolerant on the issue of homosexuality.

Personal Spirituality

It is not necessary to be involved with a formal religion to have a strong sense of spirituality. Many people find that they are able to maintain strong spiritual beliefs without benefit of organized religion. For some lesbian mothers, their own sense of what is morally right shapes all aspects of their lives as parents. Yvonne, as a single white mother of a Hispanic son, values respect and kindness for others and has taught her son to value those things as well. "He's a very sensitive child, and he already has a lot of empathy and kindness toward people whom other people reject. There's a little girl in his class who's autistic, and she's pretty severely impaired, and she's included in their classes. The paraprofessional who works with her has said to me on a couple of occasions, 'You know, Enrique's just really, really good with her. He's very gentle, and kind, and he always watches out for her.' And he'll say to me things like, 'I went to talk to so-and-so and they were sad because someone hurt their feelings.' He's very sensitive in that kind of way, and I think that having a lesbian mom, being one of those people who's different for some reason, has given him empathy for people who are different and he has more kindness around him."

Deirdre values tolerance and kindness as central to her personal philosophy. "That's who we surround ourselves with, and our spiritual lives are about that as well. My daughter does very well in nursery school and her teacher has more than once said what a wonderfully balanced and nice child she is, and what a good friend she is. And she's really amazed in a way because there's so many other kids that are nice, but they're into stuff. You know, how much stuff they have, how many Pokemon cards they have and all that kind of stuff, and my daughter's not like that. She knows what's most important, and she attaches herself to the same type of kids. There are many in the school like that, who know that friendships and people and relationships are the most important things."

Each of us has a personal philosophy about what it means to be a good person and how we ought to live our lives. Our experiences as members of a minority group impact each of us in our thinking about social justice. We should raise our children emphasizing our beliefs and values and allow our experiences as lesbians to influence those beliefs and values. Our children will be the richer for it.

One important closing thought on this topic should be remembered: Organized religion does not have a monopoly on morality or even spirituality. Some lesbian mothers prefer not to be involved in any formal religious practice, while at the same time working hard to instill a sense of spirituality in their children. We talk about the golden rule with our daughters, emphasizing how important it is to treat others kindly. One can be both moral and spiritual, and raise moral and spiritual children, without being a part of organized religion.

What You Can Do to Shape the Religious or Spiritual Life That You Want

1. When looking for a place of worship, be on the lookout for descriptors like "welcoming," "affirming," and "open." These usually indicate a gay-friendly congregation.

2. If you live near a college, find out if there is a campus ministry. Often ministries on campuses are more progressive than local ministries.

3. Remember that individual churches and synagogues are often much more open to gay and lesbian members than what the official position of that denomination would suggest. Many lesbian mothers are members of mainstream religions.

4. Consider taking your child to services from different denominations. Even if you are not shopping around for a congregation, you are exposing your child to different faiths and different religious communities.

5. As your children get older, point out the political agenda of many conservative religious leaders. For example, when someone appears on television campaigning for the latest Republican candidate, talk about how conservatives pick and choose their Biblical scriptures to match their political goals.

6. If you are not comfortable with organized religion, instill your own sense of spirituality and morality in your children. You could read books about Mahatma Gandhi and Martin Luther King. You and your children can volunteer at a homeless shelter, practice yoga together, or meditate together. Explain your personal philosophy of life. Talk to your children about why you believe in God, or why

you don't. Discuss moral decisions that you make on a regular basis (why you won't buy your fourteen-year-old a child's movie ticket; why you make it a point to visit your grandmother regularly, even though she is usually cranky and not a lot of fun; why, when the waitress gave you too much change, you returned the extra money to her rather than keep it).

Resources

Religious Resources Specifically for Gays and Lesbians

www.ChristianLesbians.com

This is a great starting point for anyone looking for a gay-friendly Christian church, as well as any woman who is trying to reconcile her lesbianism with her Christianity. The site lists gay-friendly churches by denominations (for example, United Church of Christ, Methodist, and so on). It also has message boards, e-mail lists, chat rooms, and good resources.

www.gaychristian.net

Another good place to start for lesbian Christians. This site also includes a listing of gay-affirming churches. It also has recommended books, articles on theology, support groups, and youth sites, as well as many links to other sites.

www.integrityusa.org

Integrity, USA, is a nonprofit organization of lesbian, gay, bisexual, and transgendered Episcopalians. There are currently about 60 chapters in this country. The web site provides a listing of local welcoming congregations, as well as a quarterly newsletter and other information about the organization.

www.ufmcc.com

Universal Fellowship of Metropolitan Community Churches. This tells about the church's founding, history, and beliefs as a ministry for gay, lesbian, bisexual, and transgendered people. It also has links to other sites, including a listing of all churches by geographic area.

www.mlp.org

The More Light Presbyterians organization was founded in 1974 and seeks "full participation of gay, lesbian, bisexual, and transgender people of faith." At the site you can find a local church that belongs to the organization, as well as links and other resources.

www.tamfs.org

That All May Freely Serve was founded in 1993 in Rochester, New York, in response to efforts to prevent a lesbian pastor from being granted a ministry in a Presbyterian church. The organization has expanded to become national in scope, advocating for "an inclusive church that honors diversity and welcomes lesbian, gay, bisexual and transgender persons as full members. Full membership includes eligibility for ordination to the offices of elder, deacon, and pastor." The site contains articles, sermons, lectures, books, and updates on church policy.

www.rcp.org

Reconciling Congregation Program is an organization that is part of a movement within the United Methodist Church to welcome all to its faith, regardless of sexual orientation. The site lists welcoming ministries and those belonging to the Reconciling Congregation Program.

http://members.aol.com/wabaptists/index.html

The Association of Welcoming and Affirming Baptists is a collection of churches, organizations, and individuals who are welcoming to all regardless of sexual orientation, and who are working toward full inclusion of all in the Baptist Church. The site lists churches (30 so far) that subscribe to its philosophy. It has resources and other links as well.

www.rainbowbaptists.org

The Rainbow Baptists, as the name suggests, provide support, information, and advocacy for lesbian, gay, bisexual, and transgendered Baptists. The site has very good links to other Christian organizations and sites, as well as links that are of general interest to lesbians and gays.

www.dignityusa.org

Dignity is a national organization of gay, lesbian, bisexual, and transgendered Catholics. The group has local chapters as well. The site lists its local chapters, as well as where and when mass is celebrated. It also has a newsletter and links to other sites.

www.glbtjews.org

The World Congress of Gay, Lesbian, and Bisexual Jewish Organizations is truly international in scope. You can follow the links to find a listing of U.S. synagogues (or those in other countries, if you are interested) that either welcome or specifically cater to gays, lesbians, bisexuals, and transgendered people.

www.usc.edu/isd/archives/oneigla/tb

Twice Blessed, the Jewish Gay, Lesbian, Bisexual, and Transgender Archives Online, has many features. In addition to a directory of congregations, it has chat rooms, boards, newsletters, news, links to videos and shopping, and more.

www.al-fatiha.net

The Al-Fatiha Foundation is an international organization dedicated to Muslims who are lesbian, gay, bisexual, transgender, and intersex and to their friends and families. It offers news, information, events, discussion groups, and mailing lists.

Stranger at the Gate: To Be Gay and Christian in America, by Mel White (1994). New York, NY: Plume.

Openly Gay, Openly Christian: How the Bible Really Is Gay Friendly, by the Rev. Samuel Kader (1999). San Francisco, CA: Leyland Publications.

General Religious Resources

www.uua.org
Unitarian Universalist Association
25 Beacon Street
Boston, MA 02108
Telephone: 617-742-2100

Unitarian churches are typically very gay-friendly. Many perform "services of union of gay and lesbian couples." Look for a church that proclaims itself "a welcoming congregation."

www.pcusa.org

The official site of the Presbyterian Church (USA). The Presbyterian Church has specifically addressed the importance of inclusion of gays and lesbians in the church. The site contains news about church policies and doctrines, directory of churches, and links to other sites.

◆ PART III ◆

Child Development and Lesbian Mothers

◆ CHAPTER 9 ◆

Gender Development, Boys Will Be Boys, Girls Will Be Girls, and Men in Our Children's Lives

We'll never forget the morning when our older daughter, who at the time was almost four, came down the stairs and announced that she could not wear her sneakers anymore because they had the color blue in them. We asked her why that was a problem and she quickly pointed out to us that blue was a boy color. She then added that she couldn't wear her jeans or sweat pants anymore because that's what boys wear and she is not a boy. She proceeded to give us a list of what she would be willing to wear: dresses and skirts, socks or tights, and shoes or sandals. Nothing else. Why? Because she's a girl.

Now Bailey rarely if ever sees her mothers wearing anything other than jeans or sweat pants, and she knows that we are both girls. However, this did not deter her. She gave us her wardrobe decree and was fairly persistent in sticking to it.

We began noticing something striking about the other children in her preschool class around this time as well. During playtime, the boys and the girls played separately. The boys usually played with trucks in one corner, while the girls played with the kitchen set or the baby dolls in another corner. Never did a boy venture into the girls' area, or vice versa.

The teacher's efforts to get the boys and girls to play together met with failure. Now at home Bailey is equally happy playing with trucks or dolls. Once, when we asked her if she ever played with trucks at school she gave us a horrified look and an emphatic "No! Boys play with trucks at school!"

So what was going on? Was our sweet daughter becoming a girly-girl right before our very eyes? Had all our careful avoidance of gender stereotypes been for naught? (This was a child who, as a baby, often slept with a doll on one side of her and a football on the other.) Or worse, was this hyper-femininity some sort of reaction to having two moms who are not particularly "feminine" in the traditional sense of the word? Was she trying to inject some version of femininity into her life that she felt was missing? Perhaps if she saw one or both of her parents behaving or dressing in a more traditional feminine manner she would not feel as pressed to take on that role herself?

Once we took a deep breath and thought about it, we realized that the answer to all our questions was no. What Bailey was doing is perfectly normal for someone her age. Preschool children are learning about themselves and how they fit into the world, and one of the things they are learning about is what it means to be a boy or a girl. They are like apprentices, studying the profession they are about to join. They like to surround themselves with others just like them, so they can watch and learn from each other. They exaggerate the qualities they see as defining their group, so girls will often eschew "boy colors" and male activities. Similarly, boys will often disdain "girl things" like dolls. Their rigidity about these kinds of things will gradually fade as they get older. They will start to feel more sure of themselves as boys or girls and even become more comfortable engaging in a wider range of behaviors, usually by middle childhood.

This experience we had with Bailey is an example of the kind of concern that affects lesbian mothers. We can't help considering what effect our lesbianism will have on our children's sex-role and gender development. After all, our children are not being raised in a household with an adult male. Some of our children do have a father who plays an active role in their lives. But many of them do not. And even those who do have a father in their lives do not have a father in their home all the time. What kind of effect will the absence of a father have on our children? Does the absence of a father affect boys and girls differently? Can two women really teach a boy how to be a boy—and what does "being a boy" mean anyway? These questions do occur to us, and they certainly occur to outsiders looking at our families. In this chapter we will explore these issues and their impact on our children.

Gender: What Do the Experts Say?

Let's begin at the beginning. As we all know, males and females differ from one another genetically, physiologically, and hormonally. They also differ from one another because they have been treated differently and have had different expectations placed on them from the time they were born. Many books have been written on this topic, and we have no intention of writing another one. Suffice it to say that the differences between the sexes are multifaceted, multicausal, probably overemphasized, but still very real. Children do not grasp the enormity or the subtlety of the differences. Although young children can identify boys and girls or men and women, they often do not know what underlies the distinction—they may focus on outer signs like clothing or hairstyles. In fact, very young children often do not even understand that there is a physical difference between boys and girls. It is not until about the age of four years that children truly understand that boys and girls are different because they have different sets of genitals. In other words they come to understand that there are two genders in the world that differ anatomically, and they identify themselves as either male or female. Psychologists call this "gender identity," the recognition that there are two different genders and that you belong to one of them.

A little later children come to understand that their biological features or anatomy are constant, unchanging entities. Surprisingly, it is not until about the age of six that children truly understand that their own gender is a permanent and unchanging part of them. Young children engage in magical and fantasy-based thinking. All things seem possible to preschoolers because they don't have a complete understanding of reality yet. So it is not unusual for a little boy to think that he may be able to give birth when he's grown up because he doesn't understand that his anatomical structures are stable. He clearly doesn't understand reproduction yet either, but that's a different issue. It is not uncommon for a little girl to think she can grow up and have kittens or puppies either, for the same reasons. We've even come across little girls who think that some day they will grow a penis. Again these ideas stem from the child's lack of understanding about biology and anatomy. Developmentally, by the age of six or seven, children will have come to understand that their bodies are stable entities and that that includes their reproductive anatomy. A little boy will now know that when he grows up he will be a man and he will not have babies. A little girl knows that she will be a woman and while she will grow breasts, she will not grow a penis. Psychologists refer to this concept as "gender constancy."

It is important to keep this developmental sequence in mind, because lesbian mothers, feeling anxious about gender issues in their children, can sometimes see a problem where none exists. It is easy to imagine a lesbian mom whose three-year-old son announces he's going to be a mommy when he grows up thinking, "Oh no! What have I done? He thinks everyone is female, or he doesn't know he's a boy, or . . ."—fill in the blank. She could easily turn herself into knots over this issue, when in fact it's not an issue at all. Her son thinks he'll be a mommy someday because he is three and doesn't know what he is talking about. A little boy being raised by heterosexuals could just as readily have the same belief. The difference is that the heterosexual mother is probably going to be less concerned about gender development in her child and so would probably think it's cute and let it go.

Once children understand that their gender is a permanent part of them, they begin seriously to focus on gender and what it means. They learn what types of behaviors are expected of boys and girls, how boys and girls are supposed to dress, and what toys and activities boys and girls prefer. These "gender roles" are learned very early in life. Of course parents, peers, and the media all play a part in teaching these rules about gender to children. But children themselves are active participants in learning about and incorporating gender roles into their own beliefs and behaviors. In a very real way, they are apprentices, trying to learn how to be boys or girls, and they want to get it right.

There are two periods of time where children are particularly inflexible about conventional gender roles. This is called "gender rigidity," the strict adherence to gender roles. One of these periods is in the preschool years. Bailey and her friends, in their sex-segregated playgroups, were busy solidifying their understanding of gender roles. Now that they understand they are girls, they busy themselves figuring out what girls are "supposed" to do. This is the time you see the gender rigidity and strictly sex-segregated social groups that we discussed earlier. Children this age will show strong preferences for gender-specific toys (dolls and dress-up clothes for girls, trucks and cars for boys). They will be aghast at the suggestion that they play with the toys belonging to the opposite gender. Girls will avoid playing with boys, and vice versa.

The other period of time when children show gender rigidity is around puberty—eleven or twelve for girls, a couple of years later for boys. Children at this age also prefer strictly sex-segregated social groups. Young girls commonly experiment with cosmetics, clothes, and hairstyles. Young boys commonly become inordinately interested in sports, cars, and loud music. Along with their sexual maturation usually comes an interest in members of the opposite sex, but their closest friends will still be same-sex friends. Of course these are generalizations, and every child does not show the exact same pattern. But it is safe to say that during the preschool years and early adolescence, your child will be more stereotypically feminine or masculine than she or he will be at any other time.

So it's good to know that your thirteen-year-old son will not be spending his entire life listening to rap music and memorizing football statistics. And your eleven-year-old daughter will probably develop interests beyond nail polish and teenybopper movie stars. Knowing that this is a temporary phase should make this period a little easier to handle. You can even take comfort in knowing that your child is going through the appropriate stages of social development at just the time he or she should be going through them. The old saying, "He's just going through a phase," is true in this case.

The Barbie Girl and Macho Boy Syndromes

There is, however, something else to consider. Some girls and young women really do remain on the high end of the femininity spectrum throughout their lives. These are the girls who start out playing with Barbie dolls and dress-up clothes. In high school they are never seen without makeup and wouldn't dream of participating in sports. As young women they focus most of their emotional energy on men and pursue careers that are stereotypically feminine. We all know this type of person. We have seen her all our lives. And most of the time, that person is not us. Most lesbians did not grow up like this (of course, as with all generalities, there are some exceptions). Most of us were at least somewhat interested in sports as we were growing up (seriously, would there be any summer softball leagues if it weren't for lesbians?) and not very interested in frilly girl things like makeup and the latest fashions.

Some of us had, and may continue to have, somewhat negative feelings about girls who did like those kinds of things. We may have looked down on girls who seemed to be so invested in what appeared to us to be superficial matters. Some of us may have resented those girls, because they seemed to be acting the way we were supposed to act. How many of us as we were growing up were criticized for the way we dressed or cut our hair? Most lesbians did not fit into the mold that was expected of us, and we heard about it one way or another. Young lesbians frequently encounter social ostracism or teasing from the more feminine girls. Often these were painful experiences.

Now, many years later, your own daughter could turn out to be one of those girly-girls. If you are sitting there smugly, the parent of a baby girl, secure in the knowledge that this will not happen to you, think again. We will talk about sex-role stereotypes in more detail later, but trust us, it could happen even to you. We know some lesbians who, when pregnant, secretly hope for a boy just so they won't have to deal with the "Barbie doll" syndrome. (In fact, one of us, we won't tell you which one, felt that way before our daughter was born.) If you have a daughter, she may well be more feminine than you are, maybe even more than you are comfortable with her being.

Of course you may not have a daughter. You may have a son. And you could face an entirely different set of circumstances. Your sweet little boy, the one who used to delight in helping you bake cookies and do housework, could turn into a very macho adolescent. The type of adolescent who listens to rap, watches wrestling, enjoys watching MTV videos that feature scantily clad women, and generally personifies every male stereotype that exists. Now this all may be perfectly fine with you (and it probably should be). But for some mothers, particularly lesbian mothers, these kinds of behaviors can be annoying, or even alarming. As was the case with the mother of the ultra-feminine daughter, the lesbian mother of the macho young man may feel that his machismo is a reaction to her lesbianism. She may view his behavior as a repudiation of her lesbianism. She may see his embrace of all things masculine as a rejection of the woman-only household in which he grew up. She may feel that he is trying to "make up" for something that was missing in his life. He didn't have a father to teach him how to be a man so now he is getting his lessons from the *Die Hard* movies and MTV.

There is also the personal response of the mother. Some lesbians feel uncomfortable around very macho males. They may feel reminded of past incidents of harassment. They may find unpleasant memories of earlier experiences with men resurfacing. Some may fear that their son is turning into the sort of man who, well, made them so happy to be lesbians in the first place. More benignly, they just may feel they suddenly have nothing in common with their son—as if an alien came to board in their home.

Lesbian mothers in these circumstances—be they parents of ultra-feminine girls or of super-macho boys—need to keep in mind several things. As we said earlier, nothing is permanent, and their children may just be going through a particularly rigid phase. Things could well lighten up in another year or so. Even if this is not the case, it is not time to panic. Children are individuals, and they come into the world with their own characteristics. Your children are developing their own personalities. Your child may not turn out to be exactly who you thought he or she would be in this area. You could look at this as a sign that your child feels free to become his or her own person (and how many of us felt that growing up?). A child who feels comfortable expressing himself or herself honestly is a positive reflection on his or her parents.

It may be necessary for you to reflect on your own past experiences, especially if you feel they have an impact on your responses to your child's current behavior. For example, if you find yourself driven to distraction over your daughter's nail polish and fixation with fashion, ask yourself why this bothers you so much. Maybe her style reminds you of girls you knew when you were young who had a similar style and who made your life miserable because you weren't like them. If this is the case, acknowledge this to yourself. Recognize that your daughter is your daughter, not one of the girls who made you so unhappy so many years ago. It might even be helpful to talk to your daughter about this, so that she understands why you have a hard time with some of her interests. If, on the other hand, after thoughtful reflection you conclude that what bothers you about the nail polish and the fashion fetish is that these things are becoming more important to your daughter than school is, by all means let her know this. Help her reorient her priorities.

This brings us to the final point. You are the parent, and you do have the right to limit your child's behavior. You can, and should, place restrictions on behavior you think is harmful. You do not have to allow your child to listen to music that promotes violence against women, for example. You do not have to allow your daughter to dress in micro-mini skirts and a pushup bra. You can insist that school remain a top priority, no matter what. Accepting your children's right to be themselves in the area of masculine or feminine behavior does not mean they need absolute freedom in this area. Do not let your own uneasiness, or even your child's accusations of your being unfamiliar with how things work ("Come on, Mom, this is how straight girls dress!"), cause you to allow any behavior that you feel is wrong. Explain your position and stick to your guns.

Does It Have to Be Either/Or?: Helping Our Children Find the Best of Both Worlds

Traditional sex-role stereotypes are certainly breaking down in our society. Today we have the whole nation watching women's soccer games; we have women as elected officials and more women doctors, lawyers, and business people than ever before. Similarly, men today are much more involved in their children's lives, more active participants in household chores, and less likely to expect their wives to stay home than in the past. Much, probably too much, has been written about these relatively recent changes in our culture. Some people even feel that gender roles are a thing of the past. When we teach college courses on child development and get to the section on stereotypes, the students almost universally proclaim that such things only used to exist, and they don't anymore.

Let's try an experiment. Imagine that your son is in kindergarten and wants to wear his sister's skirt to school. Would you let him? Of course you wouldn't. You know he would be subject to teasing, and maybe worse, from his schoolmates if he did so. Gender roles are still very much a part of our culture, as this example demonstrates. Although they probably are less rigid now than they were even when we were growing up, gender roles are not a thing of the past.

Androgyny is a blending of gender roles. In other words, an androgynous person is one who exhibits both typically masculine and typically feminine characteristics. For example, a man who is a professional football player and who hunts as a hobby (a manly man) can also bring Kleenex to the movies (he always cries) and enjoy cooking and house cleaning to relax. This would be an androgynous man. He is not con-

---

♦ Did You Know . . . ? ♦

Throughout middle childhood and adolescence, girls are more androgynous in their behavior and activity preferences than boys are.

Serbin, L. A., Powlishta, K. K., & Gulko, J. (1993). The development of sex typing in middle childhood. *Monographs of the Society for Research in Child Development, 58*(2, Serial No. 232); Galambos, N. L., Almeida, D. M., & Peterson, A. C. (1990). Masculinity, femininity, and sex role attitudes in early adolescence: Exploring gender intensification. *Child Development, 61,* 1904–1914.

---

fused about being male or female, and he shows, with equal comfort, behaviors that would be defined as masculine and feminine in our culture.

Studies of children and adults have shown that the more androgynous a person is, the greater is that person's self-esteem. Very feminine people often have low self-esteem. Highly androgynous people also show greater maturity in how they make moral decisions and more flexibility in their behavior. In short, feeling free to exhibit both masculine and feminine behaviors is a psychologically healthy way to be.

Many parents today make efforts to promote androgyny in their children. As lesbians, we are probably more motivated than most parents to encourage androgyny. Deirdre and Meredith have deliberately tried to promote androgyny in their son and daughter. "Our son, Tyler, is very expressive. Of course he's a baby still," says Deirdre. "We're just going to encourage that. He loves his trucks; he loves his dolls. Kelsey loves her cars and she likes her castles and princesses and stuff. We don't put any limits." Joanne feels her son, Will, "communicates better than any other male person I know. Part of that is because he has a lesbian mom. I've tried to teach him how to talk about his feelings, about what's really going on with him. He's also very sensitive. He's very, very aware of how other people might feel. He doesn't base all of his behavior on that, but he always takes it into consideration." Diane feels that Alyson has benefited from having "had very strong women around her." Alyson is "a very strong child and doesn't have a problem with coming up to the plate, as far as who she is and what she wants to do, and how she wants to do it."

Lisa feels that lesbian mothers of daughters often try to overcompensate with them on the issue of traditional femininity. "I've noticed in the lesbian community, especially with girls, the tendency to dress them really femmy." We have not noticed this tendency ourselves, but we

---

♦ **Did You Know . . . ?** ♦

Boys generally hold more stereotypical views of females than girls do. White children tend to hold more stereotypical views of females than African American children do.

Levy, G. D., Taylor, M. G., & Gelman, S. A. (1995). Traditional and evaluative aspects of flexibility in gender roles, social conventions, moral rules, and physical laws. *Child Development, 66*, 515–531; Bardwell, J. R., Cochran, S. W., & Walker, S. (1986). Relationship of parental education, race, and gender to sex role stereotyping in five-year-old kindergartners. *Sex Roles, 15*, 275–281.

could certainly see how that could happen. A lesbian mother, perhaps feeling sensitive about masculine–feminine issues, and perhaps feeling that others might be looking at her with a critical eye, may feel compelled to offset her own butchiness by making her daughter look like a princess. This is certainly understandable. What we would suggest to a mother in that position is to reconsider all the social and psychological benefits of androgyny, reflect upon why she is feeling the need to turn her daughter into a "super-girl," and relax. You don't need to prove you're a good mother by producing a princess.

They're Still Out There: Sexist Messages

So are our children going to grow up to be true free spirits, totally unaffected and unpolluted by sexist ideas and beliefs? Well, not really. What kind of stereotypes are our children exposed to? When your child goes to school, he or she will be taught predominantly by females, which in itself introduces a gender stereotype. Your child will hear stories about princes and princesses, fairy tales about living happily ever after, and more about adventurous boys than about adventurous girls. He or she will be exposed to movies and television shows featuring doe-eyed, curvaceous female characters awaiting rescue from rugged, handsome male characters (see nearly any Disney movie ever made). An enormous marketing machine will be aimed at your child, hawking everything from the ubiquitous Barbie doll to toy automatic weapons.

These stereotypes and sexist messages will get to your child, no matter how diligent you are in trying to keep them away. Most educated parents, be they lesbian, gay, or straight, are aware of the power of stereotypes and do their best to try to minimize their effect. Your child is being raised in this culture, and you have to expect that some of its influences will creep in. Not even the most hyper-vigilant parent can keep all mention of sexism away from their family. But keeping all sexist messages away from your child does not need to be your goal. A more attainable, and still worthwhile, goal is to provide a filter through which the most harmful messages don't get through, and the more innocuous ones can be explained.

There are many means you have available to you. You can limit your child's exposure to sexist movies and television. Believe it or not, you are not required by law to see every animated movie that comes to your local multiplex. You can teach them about stereotypes by pointing them out. For example, you can wonder aloud why Ariel (the Little Mermaid, for those of you new to the parenting game) would even want to give up her voice so she could be with the handsome human. You can make efforts to make sure that you don't provide only stereotypically masculine or feminine toys. You can encourage your daughter to dress in sweat pants or jeans sometimes, in addition to dresses and skirts (maybe you will be more successful at this than we have been). You can invite your son to assist you in the kitchen. These actions will all make it more likely that your child will grow into a person who values and exhibits both masculine and feminine characteristics.

The Question Everyone Asks:
What about Male Role Models?

A concern that is often raised by people about children being raised by lesbians is that of male role models. The fear is that children raised only by women will not know anything about men and how they behave. This is particularly important, many people think, for young boys who are being raised by women. They will not have anyone to show them how to "be men." They may become too feminine or too soft. It is also an issue for young girls being raised by lesbian mothers. They, presumably, will be totally unfamiliar with men and not know how to relate to them. They may either become too eager for contact with men, or else be completely uninterested in having any kind of relationship with men at all. It is not only outsiders who express these thoughts. Lesbian mothers, too, worry about providing male role models for their children and what the effects of not having a father may be on them.

So let us address these concerns. First of all, unless you are living on a desert island populated exclusively by females, your children will have men in their lives. They will have male teachers, coaches, and parents of friends. They will also have your male friends and relatives. It is just not possible for any child to only have contact with people of one gender. The notion that children of lesbians do not have men in their lives is false. Even if you do not go out of your way to assure male involvement in their lives, your children will still have it.

Lesbians as Male Role Models?

A number of the lesbian mothers we interviewed felt that having a lesbian for a mother eliminated the need for male role models at all. Lisa, for example, is not at all concerned about the issue of finding male role models for her two sons. "They've had plenty of women who are more butch and have some of the same energy as men do. It's hard to be concerned about something that just doesn't seem to be a problem." Sarah laughs. "You mean I'm not enough of a male role model?"

Lauren and Julie's son has a father in his life. Lauren notes that Nathaniel's father "is a very, very positive male role model. I think one of the nice things about having a dad is that he does have that. Actually we tease around saying that Julie is the bigger male role model. She can do many more things around the house and fix things and all those stereotypical things. I think one of the nice things about being women is that we're pretty flexible. Even I can do a lot more things, I guess, than traditionally you would expect women to be able to do. It's funny, because Nathaniel's dad is the better cook than either Julie or I. We're constantly trying to learn how to cook from him. And he's very emotional, so I think Nathaniel is going to get all the different varieties from the three of us."

Lesbians, by definition, are at least somewhat androgynous. After all, sleeping with women is considered to be a masculine trait in our culture. We do that. Possibly lesbian mothers are the most androgynous of all. We do it all—have sex with women (when we have the energy), cook, clean, go to work, take care of children, pay the bills, take out the garbage, do household repairs—you name it, we do it. We have an advantage over heterosexual mothers who are trying to model androgyny for their children. They may have to work at it; we don't. We are the embodiment of the androgynous life. Our children will inevitably be exposed to our engaging in both masculine and feminine behaviors. They will not be exposed to a sexist division of labor in their homes because they cannot be.

Our sons and our daughters will grow up seeing women performing all roles in life—both the "masculine" and the "feminine." They will have no personal direct experience with women being expected to do only certain activities. Children absorb what is around them, often without thinking. The lesson your children will absorb is that women can, and do, do everything. They are not too weak, too timid, or too out of their element to perform any activity. Your children will not learn from you that there are certain areas of life that are off-limits to them.

Men as Male Role Models

The fact is that most lesbian mothers do go out of their way to ensure that their children will have men in their lives. Some attribute this to their own personal experiences growing up. Margaret says, "Each of us [she and Sarah] have really important and strong relationships with our fathers. I respect my father almost more than anybody. He's really one of my favorite people in many ways. I could never begin to diminish the impact that he had on my life and who I became. So we found it important to bring in male role models. We weren't looking to say, 'Oh, who needs men, we don't need men.' That would be such a negation of these two people who helped to make us who we are."

Others base their desire to include men in their children's lives less on personal experience and more on a general belief that a male influence is crucial. Deirdre notes that the issue of male role models "is a concern. We want both of them [her son and daughter] to know what nice men are. We certainly have some friends that are very nice. I mean honestly, predominantly they're with women, there's no question about it." She feels that it's "very important for every boy and every girl, but especially" boys, to grow up with loving men in their lives.

Many lesbian mothers accomplish this by making a point of visiting their own family regularly, so that their children can develop a relationship with their grandfather, uncles, and male cousins. Rosita is typical in noting, "My kids have a lot of male role models. They have Gabriella's brother, they have my cousin, they have their male cousins, they have my sister's husband, they have all the men that I work with." There is clearly no shortage of male role models in Rosita's children's lives. For most of us, this is the case. Our families are full of men, eagerly awaiting the chance to spend time with our children.

In some cases, due to distance or some other reason, male members of our extended family are not around. If family members are not available to your child, there is no reason to panic. Especially as your child gets older there will be many opportunities for them to interact with men on a regular basis. In Joanne's opinion, her teenage son, Will, "has no lack of male role models at this point. He has a coach for EVERY-THING. He has a Big Brother that I chose and interviewed. There are just a lot of different men who are in his life, so he's not in a cocoon."

There are several things you can do to facilitate your child's involvement with male figures. Most communities offer organized activity groups for children, such as the Boy Scouts, sports leagues, camps, or after-school programs. Take advantage of these opportunities. Let the director or leader know that one of the reasons you are enrolling your child is so that he or she will have the opportunity to interact with a man. The point is not to force a close relationship between your child and the group leader (you couldn't force it, even if you tried). The point is to give your child a chance to get to know an adult male and to spend time with him. If they do develop a special relationship with each other, then great. If not, that is fine too; at least your child got to interact with him.

As your child gets older, you should be sensitive to his or her signals about this. If your child expresses an interest in seeing a particular person, be sure that he or she gets to spend time with that person. If you find most of your social outings as a family are done with other women, and your child begins to express discomfort with this, try to expand your social circle. Make a point of including some adult men in your own social lives. Your child is more likely to feel at ease with men if she or he sees you socializing comfortably with them.

Still No Father

There is a more subtle point related to the importance of men in your child's life that merits further consideration. No matter how many males are in your child's life, no matter how many grandfathers, uncles, godfathers, troop leaders, whatever, there is no adult male living in the house. Your children may have a genuinely close, loving relationship with your father, for example. But your child will not have the opportunity to develop the intimate kind of relationship that occurs when people live with each other, day after day for years. The type of attachment that forms between members of an immediate family who live together in no way compares to the more casual association between a child and another adult. Unless your child has a male parent who plays an active part in his or her life, your child is fatherless.

In some fundamental way, men may remain somewhat of a mystery to our children. Without the day-to-day closeness with a man, our children may grow up feeling that men are an unknown entity. Men may seem more appealing, more intriguing, or possibly more intimidating to our children than they otherwise might. This could play out in their lives in many ways. For example, your son might be prone to becoming more emotionally involved with sports or other male-only activities. Your daughter could go out of her way to find male approval. Tess recalls a period of time when her daughter, Caitlin, "would be really clingy to men whenever they visited, or if she saw another man she would be just really clingy." Tess felt this might be a reaction to Caitlin's not having a stable relationship with a man. Once Caitlin's visits with her father became more regular, this behavior went away.

We do not mean to imply that your son is doomed to be a jock, or your daughter promiscuous. Many children have been raised without fathers in their lives and do very well. This bears repeating. We are not saying that our children will be emotionally scarred by not having a father. We are saying that there could be subtle effects that all our love, support, and careful providing of male role models cannot erase. All we can do is to provide that love and care and ensure that our children have caring men in their lives.

One Last Issue: Are Lesbians Male-Bashers?

We all know the stereotype. A lesbian is a woman who has nothing kind to say to or about men. In fact, she dislikes men so much that she has turned to women for romantic relationships. The term "man-hater," in fact, is often used as a code word for "lesbian." Does this caricature bear any resemblance to real lesbians, and if so, what does this suggest about lesbian mothers?

We don't actually know any "man-hating" lesbians. We're not saying they couldn't be out there; we just don't know any. In fact, the only women we know who could even remotely be labeled as "man-haters" are some straight friends of ours who have been involved in miserable relationships with men. Nevertheless, let's explore the idea a little bit. Many lesbian mothers were once married to, or involved with, a man. Someone who leaves a relationship with a man for one with a woman is certainly expressing a preference. Proclaiming oneself as lesbian is, by definition, forswearing any future romantic involvement with men, at least for the foreseeable future. Those of us who came out as lesbians before having children made the decision long ago that we would not enter into intimate relationships with men. Being a lesbian necessarily involves rejection of men, at least as sexual romantic partners.

This rejection does not inevitably have to sink to the level of male-bashing. We know that men are not at the center of our decision to lead a lesbian life. We are lesbians because we love women, not because we hate men. It is a common misconception among straight people that lesbians are man-haters.

It seems to us that many women, both lesbian and straight, make occasional jokes or unkind remarks about men in general. (One of our current favorites: If a man says something in a forest and there is no woman there to hear him, is he still wrong?) We need to be very careful about making these types of remarks in the presence of our children. We do not want to give our sons, or our daughters, the impression that we hold men in low regard. This can be very damaging to our children who still have fathers in their lives. They may feel uncomfortable, torn between loyalty to their father and to us. Even if they don't show it, our children may resent these types of remarks, and ultimately may resent us for making them. In addition, we certainly don't want our sons to feel that we think poorly of them because of their gender. If you have a complaint to make about a particular situation, by all means make it, but be sure to do so in a way that makes it clear that you are not condemning all men.

In a way, our situation as lesbian mothers necessitates our holding to a higher standard in regard to our attitude toward men. The same remark that a straight woman could make without raising an eyebrow from anyone could easily be interpreted as "man-hating" if we make it.

What You Can Do to Handle Gender Issues Well

1. It is good for both girls and boys to have some experience in one-sex activities. Whether it is dance class or Brownies for your daughter, or soccer team and cub scouts for your son, try to let them have some regular involvement in boys-only or girls-only activities.

2. There are many popular books now on the perils of raising both boys and girls (boys are said to be at risk for denying their emotional side; girls at risk for denying their intellect and suffering poor self-esteem). These books are certainly worth looking at and often provide helpful suggestions. Take their more catastrophic predictions with a grain of salt, however. (Check our "Resources" for some suggestions.)

3. If you have a son, make special efforts to make him feel proud of being a boy. Make a big deal about taking him to the boys' and men's store to do his clothes shopping. Take him to a barbershop for haircuts, rather than to the same place you go.

4. Talk to your children about your own experiences of sexism. "When I was a child, my parents said I had to wash the dishes, and my brother had to shovel the snow. Even though it only snowed a

few times a year, and we had dirty dishes every day, they still thought that was the way it should be."

5. Young people tend to think that sexual discrimination and gender stereotypes are a thing of the past. Point out the subtle and not so subtle ways that it still goes on today. For example: "Do you notice how people talk about Janet Reno's appearance, or Madeleine Albright's wardrobe? Have you ever heard those things said about a male cabinet member?"

Resources

www.bbbsa.org

The Big Brothers Big Sisters of America organization offers one-on-one mentoring for boys and girls with an adult of their own gender. The child and the mentor decide what activities they do. The web site gives some general information about the program, and it does have a local chapter locator. However, the latter may not be useful if you do not live near a major city (you can locate the programs only by city, not by state or area). The National Office phone number is 215-567-7000; e-mail is national@bbbsa.org.

www.bgca.org

The Boys and Girls Clubs of America offers club membership, activities, and different programs for boys and girls. It does not offer one-on-one mentoring.

Reviving Ophelia: Saving the Selves of Adolescent Girls, by Mary Pipher (1995). New York, NY: Ballantine Books.

One of the first popular books written about the loss of self-esteem that so many adolescent girls experience and what we can do to prevent that.

Growing a Girl: Seven Strategies for Raising a Strong, Spirited Daughter, by Barbara Mackoff (1996). New York, NY: Bantam Doubleday Dell Publishing.

This book gives many concrete suggestions for raising a girl to be self-confident.

Great Books for Girls: More than 600 Books to Inspire Today's Girls and Tomorrow's Women, by Kathleen Odean (1997). New York, NY: Ballantine Books.

You will find books with strong heroines listed by reading level and type of book (for example, biographies, easy readers, short stories). A good resource to have when you go to the library or the bookstore.

Strong Mother, Strong Sons: Raising the Next Generation of Men, by Ann F. Caron (1995). New York, NY: HarperPerennial Library.

This book is especially helpful in terms of dealing with the adolescent years, and very empowering and encouraging to mothers.

Raising Cain: Protecting the Emotional Life of Boys, by Dan Kindlon and Michael Thompson (1999). New York, NY: Ballantine Books.

This book is not so much a parenting manual as a discussion of the negative effects of many common boyhood experiences, including non-supportive schooling, physical punishment, and rigid expectations for masculine behavior.

Real Boys: Rescuing Our Sons from the Myths of Boyhood, by William Pollack (1999). New York, NY: Owl Books.

This book talks about the "Boy Code" (the rules that boys feel they must follow in our society) and the powerful role that mothers play in helping their sons not lose themselves in the process of trying to follow it.

Great Books for Boys: More than 600 Books for Boys 2 to 14, by Kathleen Odean (1998). New York, NY: Ballantine Books.

Like its counterpart *Great Books for Girls*, this book offers titles by age level and book type (novel, nonfiction, adventure stories, and so on) that will appeal to boys and that feature good male characters.

Lesbians Raising Sons, edited by Jess Wells (1997). Boston, MA: Alyson Publications.

This is a collection of writings, including essays and poetry, by lesbians on their experiences of raising boys.

♦ CHAPTER 10 ♦

Sexuality and Our Children

It's here, it's real, and even though we knew it was coming, it can still come as somewhat of a shock: Our children are sexual beings. Of course they have been sexual beings all along, to a certain extent. Children show curiosity about their own bodies and about others' bodies, they enjoy exploring their bodies, and they take pleasure in touching themselves. Sexuality has always been part of our children's lives. Up until adolescence, it has been a fairly minor part of their lives. Once adolescence hits, however, sexuality begins to take on a larger role. We are no longer in the realm of the hypothetical when it comes to issues like our children's sexuality.

Sexuality can refer to several different concepts. Sometimes sexuality refers to someone's sexual orientation—whether they are gay, bisexual, or straight. Sometimes sexuality refers to someone's sexual behavior—the specific activities they engage in. And sometimes sexuality is referring to someone's general attitudes about his or her own and other people's sexual behavior—for example, whether someone is homophobic or repressed. These three aspects of sexuality are related, but they are not identical. Our children will need to accept themselves as sexual beings, become comfortable with sexual arousal and responsiveness within their bodies, and learn how to express these feelings respectfully, safely, and appropriately.

In addition to the universal concerns that all parents face as their children become adolescents, lesbian mothers have special concerns.

Given how difficult it was for so many of us to come to terms with our own sexuality, you might think we would be eager to discuss sexuality with our children and feel comfortable doing so. This is not always the case. Although many of us have found ways to become comfortable with ourselves as sexual beings, we are not necessarily comfortable talking about it, whether it is about ourselves or other people. As parents, though, we have a responsibility to our children to help them develop positive images of themselves as whole people, and this includes issues of sexuality.

Very few lesbians grew up in a home where their developing sexuality and identity were acknowledged, valued, and nurtured. We must provide this for our own children, even though we may not have experienced it ourselves and have no model upon which to base our actions. Lesbian mothers may have to deal with their children's fears that they will be gay, or be perceived as gay, because of our sexuality. As lesbian mothers, some of us have little or no sexual experience with men, and we may have difficulty advising our children on matters of birth control and safe heterosexual sex. We do face a different set of challenges from the average heterosexual parent, and we need to meet those challenges in the best way for our children.

Fostering Healthy Sexuality

Some people tend to view sexuality as a distinct issue, separate from other issues of childhood and adolescence. In contrast, as developmental psychologists, we view sexuality as one part of our children's lives that is inextricably bound to the rest of their lives. The choices our adolescents make about sex are related to the types of experiences they've had all their lives and how they feel about themselves. Children who feel generally good about themselves are more likely to grow into adolescents and adults who feel the same. When you feel good about yourself, you are likely to choose people to interact with who treat you well. All people make mistakes and, on occasion, make poor choices, but overall people with positive self-concept and esteem are able to learn from these mistakes more effectively and choose more wisely. Our adolescents will eventually be faced with important questions. Do I want to be sexually intimate with this person? Is now the right time? Do I have protection for the prevention of sexually transmitted diseases and/or pregnancy? When these questions arise we won't be there (thank goodness) to tell

◆ Did You Know...? ◆

Adolescents who have frank, open discussions with their parents about sexuality do not become sexually active any earlier than do adolescents who do not talk to their parents about sexuality.

Starr, C. (1997, April 15). Beyond the birds and the bees: Talking to teens about sex. *Patient Care*, 102–130.

them what to do. But the messages we have been giving them for years, about the type of person they are and what they deserve in life, will be. And that will help them feel confident about the decisions they make.

Will Our Children Be Gay or Lesbian?

One of the first objections that some social conservatives raise about gay and lesbian parents is that the children are more likely to grow up to be gay themselves. Putting aside for the moment the idiocy of raising that objection to us (first, we're lesbians ourselves—are we supposed to be horrified that our children could turn out like us? And what are we saying, that sexuality is like chicken pox or something—all that is required is exposure?), let's evaluate the issue. It is not entirely out of the realm of possibility that our children could grow up to be gay or lesbian, or even that there could be a greater chance that they will be. Some scientists argue that there is something biological or genetic that underlies homosexuality. By this reasoning, since we must have whatever that biological or genetic factor is ourselves, our children may indeed have inherited the tendency toward homosexuality from us. Other scientists would argue that social factors, not physiological ones, determine one's sexuality. According to this line of thinking, parents are the most powerful models for their children in terms of intimate relationships and sexuality. Our children have grown up watching us live in an intimate relationship with another woman. They have probably socialized on a regular basis with our gay and lesbian friends. These experiences may make them more likely to adopt a same-sex relationship themselves as adults.

There are other arguments as well. It has been suggested that lesbian and gay parents, perhaps unconsciously and perhaps not, discourage their children from becoming involved with members of the opposite sex. Our children may sense that we will be more supportive of them if they enter a same-sex relationship than if they enter a heterosexual one. This may be a way for them to get approval from us.

One could spin endless arguments and counterarguments about this topic, and believe us, many people have spent a great deal of time and wasted a lot of paper doing just that. A better way to approach the question is just to look at the data. Are children raised by lesbians more likely to grow up to be homosexual themselves?

The evidence is clear. Children raised by lesbians are no more likely to grow up to be gay or lesbian than are children raised by heterosexual parents.[1] Incidentally, studies of the children of gay fathers show the same results.[2] Most of our children will grow up to be heterosexual adults, just as most children in general grow up to be heterosexual adults. And children who have spent more time living with a gay or lesbian parent are not more likely to be gay than those children who have spent relatively less time with their gay or lesbian parent.

It is beyond the scope of this book to discuss the many physiological, sociological, and psychological factors involved in a person becoming heterosexual or homosexual; and in fact, all of the factors are not known. We do know that in every culture, in every type of family, in every era, most people are heterosexual and some people are homosexual. Scientists will continue to debate what factors, or what combination of factors, lead some people to homosexuality and lesbianism, but for now, we as lesbian mothers can confidently conclude that our children are probably going to grow up to be heterosexual.

Ironically, it may be easy for a lesbian mother to take pride in having raised a heterosexual child. After all, doesn't that prove that we're normal? If our children grow up to be heterosexual, doesn't that potentially demonstrate that sexual orientation is innate, not influenced by environment? And isn't that what we as lesbians have been saying all along? Deep down, we may have a lot riding on our children turning out straight. Some lesbian mothers may have a strong desire that their children not turn out to be gay. A group called Second Generation, which is now affiliated with COLAGE, is for children of lesbian, gay, bisexual, or transgender people who are themselves lesbian, gay, bisexual, or transgendered. Group founder Dan Cherubin told the *New York Times* (7 June 1988) that he had experienced some support from the gay and lesbian community as a whole, but also some very negative reactions. Some lesbian and gay parents fear that a group like Second Generation lends credence to right-wing extremists who claim that gay and lesbian parents will raise gay and lesbian children. One lesbian mother even told Dan that his group "is my worst nightmare."

We cannot be blamed for not wanting our own children to experience the discrimination and rejection that we did. It certainly is easier to be heterosexual in our society than it is to be gay or lesbian. But what we must keep in mind is that our children have no more control over their sexual orientation than we did. And society is changing. The next generation of gays and lesbians is going to have an easier time of it than we did. Many of us know what it is like to be rejected by our parents because of our sexual orientation; we owe it to our children not to do the same to them.

So, does having a lesbian mother have no effect whatsoever on our children's own developing sexual identity? Actually, here is where the answer becomes more complicated, and more interesting.

Will Our Children Wonder about Their Sexuality?

A very interesting study was done by Fiona Tasker and Susan Golombok comparing young adults who had been raised by lesbian mothers with some who had been raised by single heterosexual mothers.[3] There was no difference between the two groups in the rates of feeling attracted to members of the same sex. However, a different picture emerged when the young adults were asked if they had ever considered the possibility that they might be gay, or could conceivably find themselves in a relationship with someone of the same sex. The young adults with lesbian mothers were much more likely to say yes, they had considered the possibility for themselves. The young adults with heterosexual mothers had generally never given the issue any thought or consideration.

What this suggests is that our children may, at some point, wonder if they are lesbian or gay. They may, for example, question whether their feelings for their best friend are entirely platonic. They may find themselves admiring an older classmate or teacher, and then wondering whether their admiration is really a sign that they are not heterosexual. Joanne's son, Will, at fourteen, has expressed some of these concerns. "He wonders. He asks me, 'If you're gay and Rebecca's gay, does that mean I'm gay too?' "

By the time they reach adolescence, our children will certainly be as aware of same-sex relationships as they are of opposite-sex relationships. It makes perfect sense that many of them, when they have the type of strong emotional connections with people of the same gender that all adolescents do, will think about what that means for their own sexuality. It is not even uncommon for adolescents to experiment sexually with someone of the same gender. Some adolescents who engage in same-sex sexual experimentation are clear that they are just experimenting and that they are not going to become lifelong homosexuals or lesbians. Others may wonder about what this suggests about their own sexual orientation. Our children are particularly likely to wonder whether an incident of sexual contact with someone of the same gender "proves" that they are gay.

Clearly there is a difference between one's sexual experiences or behaviors with others and sexual orientation. Many lesbians have had sexual relations with men in their lives; many lesbian mothers were previously married. What you see in someone who is comfortable with his or her sexual orientation is a progression of congruent sexual behavior. In other words, a person who is comfortable with his or her homosexuality will, across time, have more homosexual and potentially exclusively homosexual intimate relationships. A person who is heterosexual will, across time, have more heterosexual and potentially exclusive heterosexual intimate relationships. To think that this happens in a day, however, is misleading.

Questioning and temporary confusion happen with most adolescents whether they have parents who are homosexual or heterosexual. It seems, though, that growing up in a household with parents who are gay makes open discussions between parent and child about sexual orientation more likely to happen. This is probably why we see that children who are raised by parents who are gay are more likely to say they questioned or "experimented" with their sexual orientation more than their counterparts raised by heterosexual parents.

Ultimately, what will happen is that most of them will decide, no, this does not mean I am gay or lesbian. It means I love my friend. They will find their emotional and physical attractions shifting to members of the opposite sex. In the long run, their having allowed themselves to consider all possibilities can only be beneficial to them. If they ultimately lead a heterosexual life, they will know that that is what they truly want. Their sense of self-awareness will increase.

The young adults who never give their sexuality any kind of thought whatsoever may initially have an easier time of it. They never question, wonder, or worry about themselves. This means they are not thinking about themselves and who they are, at least in this area. And while they may sail through adolescence without much difficulty, some psychologists believe that sailing through adolescence may not be the best course. Adolescents should be undergoing a kind of identity crisis. They should be trying to figure out who they are in many different arenas—religious beliefs, political values, occupational choices, as well as sexual identity. Adolescents who are actively trying to figure out who they are, are doing what adolescents are supposed to do. After thinking about their options and about their own values, older adolescents and young adults will fashion their own identities. They will ultimately become people who know who they are and are comfortable with themselves.

In the long run, you can see that a period of questioning is ultimately a good thing. As lesbian mothers we have shown our children an alternative. It is an alternative most of them will not choose for themselves, but we have shown them that ways of life other than the mainstream are possible. As our children develop intellectually and become more able to think about themselves, this can only be an advantage.

Joanne has explained this to Will. "I tell him that my sexual orientation has nothing to do with his sexual orientation. His grandparents are both straight, and he gets that. We talk about it. He's pretty much decided he's not, but he's still worried." Joanne feels that Will, at fourteen, is "worried" that other people will think he's gay because his mother is gay (and we address this in our next section). If you feel that your child is worried about "figuring out" her sexuality, there is much you can do to alleviate her anxiety.

If your child does start to question her own sexuality at some point, you should assure her that this is a very common thing for adolescents to go through, whether they have lesbian mothers or not. Intense feelings for friends, or even some sexual experimentation with someone of the same sex, do not necessarily mean that one is gay. Remind your child that you will love her whether she is gay or straight. She will figure out who she is, and she should not feel pressure to decide right now. And her sexuality is totally separate from ours.

Will Our Children Be Assumed to Be Gay?

Diane's daughter, Alyson, who knows she is not a lesbian, has already experienced a particular kind of teasing at school: other kids telling her she must be gay since her mother is. Diane says Alyson "feels that it's almost like an attack of racism." Joanne has noticed that her son Will is concerned that he will be perceived as gay by kids at school. "I think he's always afraid that people will see him as kind of a sissy boy. So sometimes he tends to overcompensate. It's pretty minimal—so he struts around a little bit more when he gets a foul called on him or something in basketball, that's the kind of thing he does."

Apart from whether our children ever wonder if they are gay, there is the issue that they may be perceived as gay by their peers. The impact this has will vary from child to child. For some, like Alyson, who at twelve years old has no doubts about herself, the effect will be feelings of disappointment in and surprise at her peers. For others, like Will, who is a little older and perhaps a bit more self-conscious, the effect may be a tendency to exaggerate his heterosexuality—in his case, macho displays during basketball games. For others, who may be questioning themselves and feeling particularly vulnerable to these kind of remarks, the teasing can be deeply felt and hurtful.

There are two important things you can do if your child is teased about being gay. First, reassure your child that there is nothing wrong with her, but there is definitely something wrong with the way the other kids are behaving. Second, contact the teacher, principal, or other parents and make sure that the message gets out that this behavior will not be tolerated.

The personality of the individual child involved is also a key factor in the child's response to teasing. Sometimes our children are quite capable of dealing with these problems on their own. Paula and Nancy's son Thomas experienced some teasing from kids at school and handled it in a unique fashion. "He and this friend of his would go around the school, and his friend would say to these people who were teasing him, 'Hey, I'm not gay, but I've got a friend who would like to meet you if you're still interested.' And at one point, this group of jocks was bugging him. They would go out in front of the school where people wait for their parents to pick them up. It rains a lot here, so it would be raining, and everybody would be kind of under this tree, waiting for their ride. And Thomas and his friends, they would put their arms around each other and they would go a couple of steps over toward these jocks, who would move away from them. And they'd wait a minute, and they'd move over again, and they eventually had these guys waiting out in the rain."

Talking to Our Children about Sexuality

Studies of parents and how they talk to their children about sex have shown some consistent results. Parents, in general, do not talk to their children very much about sex. In families where parents do discuss sexual topics, mothers are more likely to do so than fathers are. Young people tend to rely on their friends as their principal authority on sexual topics.[4]

There are not yet many studies done on how we, as lesbian mothers, educate our children about sex, but what studies there are have been encouraging. Tasker and Golombok found that the young adults raised by lesbian mothers felt more comfortable talking about sexuality and sexual issues with their mother or her partner than did the young adults raised by heterosexual mothers. Why would this be the case? The authors speculate that since lesbian mothers have already been open with their children about an important sexually related topic—their own lesbianism—their children feel comfortable broaching other sexually related topics with them. So again, we have an advantage that heterosexual parents do not. In a way, we have broken the ice by being open about our lesbianism. This is not to suggest that we have gone into great detail with our children about our sex life. But by being open about ourselves and our intimate relationships, we make it easier for our children to be open with us about their intimate relationships.

So the first step in encouraging our children to come to us with questions about sexuality is our own openness about ourselves. Openness, in fact, is a key in dealing with sexuality. Marie and Shirley were able to maintain this style of openness with their children, even though they were not open themselves about the nature of their own relationship at that time. Marie recalls, "Our kitchen table was an open discussion area, and of course with an age range from eighteen years old down to a year and a half, everything was discussed at that table. We didn't lie to them. When they came and asked about sex, we told them. If the one-and-a-half-year-old was sitting there, they sat there and listened to it too. There was nothing that they couldn't come and ask us about." Shirley adds, "They were never afraid to ask. I'm sure at one point we did discuss gays and lesbians. I know we talked about it. We never came out to them, but we did discuss it."

In talking about sexuality with children, starting early is better than starting late. Telling young children the correct names of body parts and explaining where babies come from are good things to do not only for the immediate benefit of teaching your child things she needs to know but also for establishing the type of relationship where these things can be discussed. Those of us who became pregnant via alternative insemination are fortunate, in a way, in that we are forced to discuss the logistics of reproduction with our children in a more detailed way than are parents who conceived the old-fashioned way. We can keep that style of being open and matter-of-fact as our children get older.

Usually by preschool age a child will have asked about where babies come from, and you should tell her. With Bailey, we read her *Heather Has Two Mommies*, which touches briefly on how the mommies got a baby started. For a while now, Bailey seems to think that this is how all babies get started—namely, that the mommy goes to a special doctor who puts sperm into her vagina so that the baby can start to grow. That is okay with us. That is how Bailey and her sister got started, and we felt that we should present that way first. There are, of course, other ways of getting babies started, and we will talk about those as our daughters get older and they become more interested in the subject. What is important is giving them the information they want when they want it.

At least as important as what you say is how you say it. You always want to convey that you are comfortable with the topic and you are willing to talk about anything. The conversations you have with your child when she is young are more important for giving her the message that you are amenable to talking about sexual topics than they are for any particular information you give her.

As children move into later childhood, they will become curious about the changes their bodies will soon be going through. Mothers of daughters have an automatic topic of conversation, in that we have to talk to our daughters about menstruation. There is certain information our daughters need to have—about when they will get their periods, how long they will last, whether they should use pads or tampons, whether they will get cramps, and so on. In talking to them, it is good to share your own experience. This helps them know what to expect and also shows them that they can turn to you for information and advice.

Mothers of sons face a different task. There is no single physiological development for boys, like the onset of menstruation in girls, to trigger a discussion. Boys are not going to need our help dealing with monthly hormonal fluctuations. And we have no experience as adolescent males to share with them or to fall back upon. It would be easy for us, as lesbian mothers of boys, to overlook how much our sons need us to talk to them about the changes their bodies are going through. Boys, no matter who their parents are, are at risk for being overlooked in the area of sex education. They need to know, for example, that wet dreams are normal, that masturbation is normal (girls need to know this as well), that erections can occur at inopportune moments. We need to help them feel proud of their physical maturation.

Last But Not Least: Talking to Our Children about Birth Control and Safe Sex

It goes without saying that part of our responsibility as parents is to talk to our children about birth control and about safe sex practices. We all know the appalling figures on teen pregnancy rates (currently, one out of every eleven sexually active teenage women in the United States becomes pregnant each year). We know that HIV infection among young people continues to be a great health concern. We know that, even though contraceptives are readily available, most sexually active adolescents in the United States do not use them regularly or correctly. In short, adolescents are in crisis when it comes to their use of contraceptives and practice of safe sex, and it could cost them their lives.

♦ Did You Know . . . ? ♦

Most adolescents are sexually active; that is, have had intercourse. By the time they are seniors in high school, one fifth of girls and one quarter of boys have had four or more sexual partners.

Seidman, S. N., & Rieder, R. (1994). A review of sexual behavior in the United States. *American Journal of Psychiatry, 151* (3), 330–341. *Sex and America's teenagers* (1994). New York, NY: The Alan Guttmacher Institute.

The existence of HIV, the virus that causes AIDS, is what poses the greatest danger to our sexually active adolescents. Most adolescents know how the AIDS virus is transmitted and how they can protect themselves. Despite this, most adolescents do not take the necessary precautions against the virus. In other words, they know that using condoms greatly reduces their chance of contracting the virus, yet they still choose, most of the time, not to use condoms. There are two reasons for this apparent contradiction. One is that most adolescents believe that AIDS is something that affects only other people—specifically, gay men and intravenous drug users. They do not view their own sexual activity as being a risk factor. The second reason is a more general characteristic of adolescent thinking—the belief that they are immortal and exempt from the consequences of dangerous behavior. This is what makes many adolescents do risky and potentially hazardous things. They often drive recklessly, drink too much, and engage in other unsafe behavior because they believe that nothing bad will happen to them. As they mature they will acquire a more adult understanding of risks and their consequences and realize that bad things can happen to them too. Until they reach that level of understanding, however, they are likely to behave in irresponsible, even sometimes dangerous, ways.

As lesbians who came of age in the 1970s through the 1990s, as most of us did, we have seen the effects of the AIDS epidemic at close range. Most of us have lost a friend, if not a number of friends, to AIDS. The virus decimated the gay male community, physically and emotionally, and we saw this taking place. Our heterosexual peers lived through this time as well, but most of them were somewhat more removed from AIDS—or at least they thought they were. They could afford to believe that HIV was generally someone else's problem and unlikely to affect them.

Now here we all are, parents at the beginning of the twenty-first century. The way in which we talk to our children about safe sex has to

---

♦ Did You Know . . . ? ♦

Knowledge about how AIDS is transmitted is not in itself enough to influence the practice of safe sex. Most sexually active adolescents know the basic facts about AIDS. Since they do not feel they themselves are at risk for contracting the disease, they do not take steps to avoid infection.

Sieving, R., Resnick, M., Bearinger, L., Remafedi, G., Taylor, B., & Harmon, B. (1997). Cognitive and behavioral predictors of sexually transmitted disease risk behavior among sexually active adolescents. *Archives of Pediatric and Adolescent Medicine, 151,* 243–252.

be influenced by our experiences and perceptions of the AIDS epidemic. As lesbians we are more aware than most parents that it would be a mistake to be cavalier about the virus and taking precautions against it. We should make it a point to talk to our children about AIDS and about the friends we have lost to it. We should tell them that there is no such thing as risk-free sex. Our friends who died never had a chance; the virus was infecting people long before anyone knew what it was or how it was transmitted. Our children are in a different situation. Now we know what it is and how you catch it. We must do all we can to make sure our adolescents do not fall into the group that thinks AIDS is not something they have to think about.

The specifics of safe sex practices, and birth control methods, do raise an interesting point for some lesbian mothers. Some lesbians have little or no sexual experience with men. For many of us, birth control has remained an academic topic as opposed to one we've actually had to deal with and be concerned about. How can we talk to our children about using condoms, for example, if we've never actually used them ourselves?

First, the specifics are not all that complicated. If you feel unprepared to get into the particulars of various birth control methods, educate yourself about them (see "Resources" at the end of this chapter for some good places to start). There are many books that do a good job of discussing various forms of birth control. If you still do not feel up to the job, consider using a professional. Planned Parenthood clinics provide information and birth control to adolescents. If you are worried that your child will be uncomfortable talking to you about these matters, you can find comfort in the fact that Tasker and Golombok found that adolescents of lesbian mothers were more comfortable talking to their mothers about sex and birth control than were adolescents of straight mothers.

If, despite your best efforts, your child is showing signs of being uncomfortable talking to you about sexual issues, don't despair. Your child may never initiate a conversation with you about sex, but that doesn't mean you shouldn't. Sometimes kids think they already know everything there is to know, and while they may know a lot, they certainly don't know everything. In addition, even today, adolescents often have a great deal of misinformation. Some children and adolescents are too embarrassed to bring up topics related to sex on their own. Before you sit down to talk to your child, make sure you know what you want to say. Whether you are planning on discussing the changes associated with puberty with your ten-year-old, or the importance of safe sex with your fifteen-year-old, you want to be prepared. Do your research (again, we refer you to the excellent resources at the end of this chapter) so you know what to say. If you feel uncomfortable, it is perfectly all right to acknowledge this to your child. You can say that your parents never talked to you about such things, and you don't want to make the same mistake. So this kind of talk is new to both of you.

Mothers of sons have an additional challenge. We don't have any experience as maturing boys, and that will be true regardless of how many books we read on the subject. If your child has a father in his life, you can ask him to assist you in talking to your son. This doesn't mean you don't have to talk to him as well. But it will probably be useful for your son to hear about puberty and sexuality from a male perspective. If your child does not have a father, perhaps you could enlist a relative or close friend to talk to your son. You should look on this male figure as a complement to your discussions with him. If there is just no one with whom you and your son feel comfortable, you must make a special effort to be as informed about male sexual development as you possibly can be.

What You Can Do to Foster Healthy Sexuality in Your Children

1. Show your child—don't just tell him—that you are open to discussing issues related to sexuality. You can do this in a number of ways. If you are watching television and a commercial comes on for tampons, remark that such things were never talked about on television when you were young, and how it is so much better now that menstruation is discussed openly. Point out newspaper articles on issues

like condom distribution in high schools, or falling teen pregnancy rates, and say how you feel about them. If it sparks a discussion about the issues with your child, great, but even if it doesn't, it gives him the message that you are willing to talk about sexually related issues.

2. Have books, and provide web sites, that your child can use to learn about sexuality and physical development, but don't just leave it at that. If you hand your child a book saying, "You might like to read this," and then never refer to it again, he may think that you don't want to talk about the subject. Instead, say, "I thought this book looked good. It gives a very clear description of what happens during puberty." Later, ask if he got a chance to look at the book. Talk about what an exciting time puberty is. Use resources as a springboard to discussions, not to replace them.

3. It is never too early to start thinking about how you want to talk to your child about sex. Begin as soon as your child starts to speak to use the correct terms for body parts. This sets the stage for later, open discussions.

4. You are entitled to some privacy regarding your own sexuality. You do not have to answer your child's questions about specifics of your own sexual history. One's personal sexual behavior is a private matter, and it is good for your child to learn that.

5. Find out about the sex education curriculum at your child's school. You may want to supplement it, if you feel it is lacking. Use the topics your child is learning in school to start discussions at home.

6. Do not be one-sided in your discussions about sexuality. Boys should know about women's menstrual cycles, just as girls should know about male physiology.

Resources

www.plannedparenthood.org

Planned Parenthood offers education about reproductive issues and birth control. The web site includes referrals to local health centers, answers to frequently asked questions, and legislative updates. Referrals can also be obtained by calling 1-800-230-PLAN.

www.teenwire.com

Planned Parenthood's web site specifically for adolescents. It contains answers to frequently asked questions, as well as an "Ask the Expert" column.

www.siecus.org

The Sexuality Information and Education Council of the United States, founded in 1964, promotes education about sexuality and responsible sexual choices. This is an excellent site, offering specific areas for parents and teens, as well as a library and bibliographies.

www.positive.org

The Coalition for Positive Sexuality was founded in 1992 by an alliance of grassroots organizations and Chicago high school students. Designed for adolescents, the site offers frank answers to questions on sexuality, sexually transmitted diseases, and birth control. The site is also very gay-friendly.

www.kidshealth.org

This site is maintained by the Nemours Foundation. It contains specific areas for parents, children, and adolescents on all kinds of medical topics. It covers everything from colic and immunization schedules to puberty and birth control. It has good general medical information, given in a relatively dry manner. The discussions about sex are straight-oriented; there is no mention of homosexuality.

www.goaskalice.columbia.edu

This site was originally designed for students at Columbia University, and is maintained by Columbia's Health Education program. There are areas for parents, teachers, and students. Topics covered include relationship, sexuality, sexual health, and general health.

It's a Girl Thing: How to Stay Healthy, Safe, and in Charge, by Mavis Jukes (1996). New York, NY: Knopf.

Written for younger girls (ages nine to twelve), this book covers topics like menstruation, buying a bra, dating, relationships, and sex.

The What's Happening to My Body Book for Girls, by Lynda Madaras (1987). New York, NY: Newmarket Press.

A book geared for young teens, this covers puberty, menstruation, sexuality, and birth control.

What's Going on Down There: Answers to Questions Boys Find Hard to Ask, by Karen Gravelle (1998). New York, NY: Walker and Company.

Written for boys heading into puberty (ages nine to twelve), this book talks about body changes associated with puberty (for both boys and girls), as well as sexuality.

The What's Happening to My Body Book for Boys, by Lynda Madaras (1987). New York, NY: Newmarket Press.

A book geared for boys in their early teens, this covers puberty, sexuality, and birth control.

Notes

1. Tasker, F., & Golombok, S. (1995). Adults raised as children in lesbian families. *American Journal of Orthopsychiatry, 65*(2), 203–215.
2. Bailey, J. M., Bobrow, D., Wolfe, M., & Mikach, S. (1995). Sexual orientation of adult sons of gay fathers. *Developmental Psychology, 31,* 124–129.
3. Tasker, F., & Golombok, S., op cit.
4. Coreil, J., & Parcel, G. (1983). Sociocultural determinants of parental involvement in sex education. *Journal of Sex Education and Therapy, 9,* 22–25; Miller, B., Norton, M., Fan, X., & Christopher, C. (1998). Pubertal development, parental communication, and sexual values in relationships to adolescent sexual behaviors. *Journal of Early Adolescence, 18,* 27–52.

◆ CHAPTER 11 ◆

Homophobia and Diversity

Why a special chapter devoted to homophobia? After all, in a way, this entire book is about dealing with homophobia. Whether we're talking about dealing with our children's schools or friends, religious organizations, our children's own sexuality, or some other issue, we are dealing with homophobia in one way or another. Right now, homophobia defines much of the relationship between lesbians and the rest of the world. It is the lens through which many institutions and individuals view us. As lesbians, we have to deal with homophobia all the time. As lesbian mothers, we have an additional opportunity to contribute to changing that reality. Through our example of being parents, we show the world that we are loving, caring people. Through our children, we show that we can raise loving, caring people. Our lives are a testament to the falseness of homophobia.

Right now, homophobia still exists, in sometimes shockingly brutal forms. In October 1998 college student Matthew Shepard was beaten and left for dead, tied to a fence by two young men who wanted to teach the "faggot" a lesson. Shepard died a few days later. The incident drew national attention to a phenomenon of which most gays and lesbians are already aware: violence against gays. From physical attacks such as the one Shepard endured, to verbal harassment to gay jokes, gay bashing is common and, some reports suggest, on the rise. As lesbian mothers we are in the position of having to allay our children's fears about our safety while acknowledging that incidents like the one involving Shepard do occur.

Homophobia exists in ways far more subtle than the attack on Matthew Shepard. We can be vigilant about slurs, epithets, and the like, and be careful to point out unfairness to our children when we see it. As lesbian mothers we are forced, by necessity, to discuss issues of tolerance and respect for diversity with our children. Since we are not in the mainstream of society ourselves, we must talk to our children about how others might perceive us as different, how this may make them feel uncomfortable, and so on. What many lesbian mothers try to do is to use this type of discussion, one that is about us, as a starting point for talking about how other people outside of the mainstream are treated too. This can lead to conversations about members of different ethnic and racial minority groups and the importance of showing others tolerance and respect. Many lesbian mothers feel strongly about inculcating a sense of social justice in the next generation.

Hate Crimes: What Do Our Children Think?

Hate crimes do happen. It is very difficult to get a precise figure on how many hate crimes occur, since it is generally accepted that these crimes are likely to go unreported. According to the latest available statistics from the Federal Bureau of Investigation, in 1998 1,260 hate crimes motivated by sexual orientation were reported. Of these, four were murders. Intimidation, which includes harassment, is the most frequent type of attack. Gay men, more so than lesbians, are targets of verbal and physical assaults, but lesbians are at risk for these experiences as well. Who can forget the chilling photographs of the fence in Wyoming where Matthew Shepard was left to die? His killing, and the images that accompanied the coverage of it, left most people of all orientations sickened. What effect, though, did this crime and knowledge that crimes like this happen have on our children?

The most important thing that we provide for our children, particularly when they are young, is safety. They need to know that they can come to us for protection, for comfort, for help. We teach them, from the time they are infants, that the world is a safe place and that we are there for them when they need us. When they are sick or hurt or frightened they come to us, and we make them feel better. We provide mostly physical comfort when they are young and then more psychological comfort as they get older. Even as adults, our children will turn to us for advice and consolation in difficult times.

What happens, then, when our children discover that we ourselves may not be physically safe? We need to assure them that we are as safe as we possibly can be. Fourteen-year-old Will expressed concern about his mother's safety after the Matthew Shepard incident. Joanne explained to Will that "there is a reason we live where we do. There's a reason we don't live someplace like Wyoming, and this is why. Because there are people who don't understand, and because they don't understand, they get crazed." Her emphasis was on reassuring him of her physical safety, while at the same time acknowledging that hate crimes do happen. In Will's case, this appeased him somewhat. However, he had his own way of dealing with his concern. "He has this really cool bat that he always uses when he plays baseball. And, he gave it to me, to put it next to my bed. So he feels much better now." Will needed to know that his mom would be safe, and for him, giving her a way to protect herself was his way of ensuring that. While we can feel sad that a child feels he has to give his mother a weapon as a means of self-defense, we should recognize the gesture for what it is. Will is helping his mother, and by making sure she is safe, he gets to feel safe too.

Marie and Shirley's adult children also expressed concern about their safety. "You know, they worried about it," says Marie. "I think the biggest thing they worry about, we travel a lot, and I think they worry about that. But we've basically taken the rainbows off the car, because we go into a lot of areas where I think that there would be problems if people realized." Even for grown children, their first concern is for our safety, and our first job is to reassure them that we are safe.

The next time a hate crime makes the headlines, do not make the mistake of launching into a discussion with your children of the necessity for laws against hate crimes, or the ignorance of some pockets of the general population, or the cruelty of some zealots who use tragedies like Shepard's death to put forth their own hate-filled agenda. These are all valid points, and you can bring them up later. What your children need to hear from you first is that you are safe, and that this is not going to happen to you. You can emphasize that you live in a safe area, that you surround yourself with accepting people, that you are cautious in strange places. Whatever you need to say to reassure your child, you should let him know that you are okay.

You can also emphasize that gay rights are stronger than they have ever been in this country. Many states (twenty-one as of this writing, plus the District of Columbia) have laws specifically prohibiting hate crimes based on sexual orientation. The federal government now monitors hate crimes, including those based on sexual orientation. Our society has been adding legal protections for gays and lesbians, just as it has a history of doing for other minority groups. We have every reason to believe that such legal safeguards will continue to increase in the future.

Once you have reassured your child, you can get into the reasons that hate crimes happen. You can tell him that ignorance breeds fear, and there are some very ignorant people out there. People who feel insecure about themselves sometimes strike out against others, either verbally or physically, to make themselves feel better. Sometimes people attack in others something they fear in themselves. Some people have never learned to think for themselves and so follow the negative, hateful things they have been taught. These people are to be pitied, but their behavior is still inexcusable.

Few of us grew up in families where homosexuality was seen as an acceptable option. None of us grew up in a society where homosexuality was applauded, welcomed, or celebrated. We were taught, explicitly or implicitly, that being gay is wrong, abnormal, and unnatural. We absorbed those lessons, which is why coming out to ourselves, our family, and the world at large was so difficult. Each of us has come a long way, in terms of accepting who we are and choosing to live our lives the way we want to. Whether we came out before or after having children, we have reached a point where we feel a degree of comfort with ourselves.

Tolerance as a Natural Consequence of Having a Lesbian Mother

Many lesbian mothers feel that our children will naturally be more tolerant because they are our children. Being raised in a family that is different from the norm will make them more sympathetic to others who are different as well. Becky feels that Samantha is "always going to be unique. She's going to be among the unique kids, because of the very obvious difference in her family makeup. I hope that what that does for her is give her a real appreciation for diversity, and for acceptance and for tolerance of things that are different from herself, and a greater acceptance for things that are different than what she knows."

Diane feels that twelve-year-old Alyson is "very open to being involved with different ethnic groups. Her school is very diverse anyway. I don't even think it's something obvious to her, you know, people's skin color or how the family makeup is, because she knows that there are a lot of different possibilities for how people grow up." Rosita also believes that her daughters will grow up to be more open to other people as a result of their experiences. "I think that one of the biggest differences that I see is that in our family we don't have the bias against people that some straight families have. And we're not sheltered. There are a lot of straight families that are very sheltered, who don't know anything beyond their bounds. I don't think we have that. And I think our children will be able to be much more open-minded, and I think that as a result their friends will be much more open-minded."

Kitty's children have not been in a lesbian family for very long. However, already Kitty sees effects on how they think about things. "I think it will make them more open to something, anybody, and they know that there are different ideas, and that we're still pretty normal people. Bradley asked us from the very beginning, why we don't get married. 'Well, because the law won't allow us to.' And he said, 'Well, that's stupid. If you love each other, why can't you get married?' So I think it's opened him up a little bit."

Our children are growing up in an unusual family. They will be members of a minority group, as we are. They will see that there are different kinds of families, and that one kind is not necessarily better than another kind. They will not have the kind of sheltered upbringing where everyone looks alike and all families have the same makeup. Even if we do nothing else to explicitly teach our children about diversity, they will absorb some lessons just from being our children. Most of us, though, want to go a step further and work to ensure that our children will not be prejudiced against others.

Teaching Tolerance:
Raising Children Who Don't Discriminate

It is the obvious next step. Our children know something about diversity already, at least in the area of sexual orientation. It will be relatively easy for us to expand their notion of diversity by talking about different races, religions, and ethnic groups. Many of us make the point of taking that next step with our children.

Karen talks to her daughter, Jessica, about diversity. "We talk about a variety of kinds of diversity. We have some very good friends who have kids who are from international adoptions, and we talk about the different skin colors kids have. And she tells me she wants to adopt a kid when she grows up. I think that's really important. We live in an area that also has a lot of economic diversity, as well as multicultural diversity. She knows about homeless people. I think that it's really important to talk about all the differences, and that it doesn't make anybody better or worse. The school has an annual Martin Luther King Day march, and that was a good time to talk about differences and how people were treated and what that means, but I think she gets a lot of that at school. And she gets a lot of that at home.

"I think she gets a lot more of that from me than she does from her dad. Her father is a gay, white, male physician, and there is a fair amount of classism and arrogance that goes along with being a gay, white male with that kind of privilege. So I think she doesn't get that sense from him in the way that I want her to have it. I think I put out much more effort in helping her to see the way the world is and to look at the way we would like the world to be."

Tara also believes her children will be more open-minded and tolerant, but "not necessarily because we're lesbians. I think it's because we're progressive; our politics, our attitudes, are progressive. My background is in social work, and so there's a lot of education that happens in my home around multiculturalism and diversity issues in general. I think they're going to be more tolerant of all of the 'isms,' and not necessarily just lesbians and gays."

Shirley and Marie were never out to their children while they were young, but they still made a point of teaching them to respect other people, including lesbians and gays. Marie remembers incidents where the kids were speculating that someone they knew was gay. "We'd say, 'Well, that's nice, that's his own business, it's not ours to judge him.'" The lessons seem to have paid off. "Once my youngest daughter at school walked in on a gym teacher embracing another teacher," recalls Shirley, "and thank goodness it was my daughter that walked in on them, because she just looked at it and turned around and walked out. She came home and told me and said, 'I haven't told anybody, Mom, and I'm not going to, because it's nobody's business.' And this was in junior high. I was really proud of her and I told her that."

We have noticed, now that our daughter Bailey is in kindergarten, that we too make a point of reinforcing the lessons she hears at school on tolerance and diversity. She has already had lessons on Martin Luther King Jr. and Rosa Parks, and she knows that in the southern part of our country African Americans were not allowed to vote or use the same bathrooms or drinking fountains as white people. We find ourselves automatically getting into long discussions with her when she tells us she has learned things like this in school, emphasizing how wrong it was for the white people to do this and how unfair it is to treat people badly because they are seen as different from us.

We think these are important lessons for Bailey to learn. We want her to be aware of injustice, to recognize it, and to know that it is wrong. We do this in part because we want to raise a socially conscious, unprejudiced child. But in all honesty, we do it out of a bit of self-interest as well. Although Bailey is aware of words like "gay" and "lesbian," she does not really understand how much of society views people who are gay or lesbian. Some day she will understand that there are people who don't like us, who don't think we should have the same rights as they do, because we are lesbians. She will realize that some people think we are unfit to be her parents. In short, there are people out there who would treat us badly because we are different from them. And when that day comes, we want her to already know about unfairness and prejudice. We have the same wish for Rowan as she gets older. That way, we hope, our daughters will recognize those things for what they are and not take them to heart. In a way, our emphasis on tolerance is as much for our family's benefit as for the greater good.

Living with Diversity

Our children are living with diversity. As the sons and daughters of lesbians, they are growing up in a family that is outside the mainstream. We feel that this will be an advantage to them as they get older, as we have discussed. We believe that living in an area where there is lots of diversity is also advantageous to our children. Giving them opportunities to see and relate to and interact with people from different racial, ethnic, and socioeconomic backgrounds will give them a broader outlook. Urban areas, where diversity thrives, are likely to be better places for lesbians to raise their children. It is not just because there are more lesbians and gays in big cities (although there are), it is that there is more of everything in big cities. If we want to provide exposure to all kinds of people, we should live where there are all kinds of people. Living in an urban area is not the only option, however. Even small towns with colleges are generally more diverse than the typical small town. If you live in the suburbs

---

♦ Advice from a Lesbian Mother ♦

"Where you live is important. I think it's really, really important to live somewhere where your kid is one of many, and not one of one. I guess that would be my biggest piece of advice: You want to live where there's diversity—I mean ethnic diversity, racial diversity, lesbian and gay diversity."

—Lisa

---

of a large city, you can make a point of visiting the larger city frequently so that your child can take advantage of what it has to offer.

Our Children as Adults: More Tolerant?

A few of the mothers we interviewed have children who are grown, or nearly so. If we can look at their children as models of how our children will turn out, then we have reason to be optimistic. Carla is nearly an adult at seventeen, and Gina sees a clear positive effect from her upbringing in terms of tolerance. "There is absolutely no prejudice in her whatsoever, toward anything or anybody, which also surprises me. It's amazing. It doesn't matter what color you are, what sexuality, what religion you are, my daughter will talk to you and want to be in your life, or just be kind to you." Shirley also sees the effects on her adult children. "I think they're more understanding and accepting and they're not prejudiced at all, against anybody, whether it's religion or their race or their sexual orientation. But they are very good about it, amazingly nonjudgmental. They are. I think it [having lesbian parents] has made them better people."

Who knows where such tolerance will lead? We think our children may grow up to be advocates for human rights. Our children probably have a better than average chance of becoming adults who will work toward social justice. We can look to the example of a young woman named Sol Kelley-Jones, a teenage daughter of two lesbian mothers. Like many other children of lesbians and gays, Sol was involved in COLAGE (Children of Lesbians and Gays Everywhere—see Chapter 4 "Resources"). In fact, at the age of eleven she became the youngest national board member of COLAGE. She has spoken in many public forums on the topic of gay and lesbian rights, including at the Millennium March on Washington for Equality in 2000. Concern about discrimination can start out being motivated by personal circumstances (say, being the child of a gay man or a lesbian) but can develop into a desire to work for justice and fairness for everyone. Our children can be the leaders of the future—just imagine how this will strike fear into the hearts of homophobes!

We do not have any guarantees that our children will grow up free from prejudice. In fact, it is unlikely that anyone in our society grows up entirely free of prejudice. It is just too pervasive to escape entirely. What we can guarantee is that our children will grow up in a family where respect for those who are different is explicitly taught and encouraged.

What You Can Do to Fight Homophobia and Celebrate Diversity

1. Expose your child to different cultures and different religions. This is especially important if you do not live in an area with much diversity.

2. Try preparing different ethnic foods as a way of exposing your children to other cultures. Most kids love Mexican food; try Chinese, Indian, Italian, Caribbean, and so on.

3. Look for books that show children of other cultures. Children's television programs, particularly those on PBS, are becoming more multicultural. Point out how unrealistic books or movies are that have only white characters.

4. Go to cultural events—exhibits, museums, and concerts—especially when they include cross-cultural themes.

5. Talk to your child about racism, sexism, and homophobia, emphasizing that they are all different versions of the same thing—fear and dislike of anyone who is different.

6. When there is another highly publicized homophobic attack on a gay man or a lesbian (and there will be), remember that your first responsibility is to assure your child of your safety.

Resources

www.aclu.org/issues/gay/hmgl.html

The American Civil Liberties Union (ACLU) has a web site specifically dedicated to the issue of lesbian and gay rights. It contains updates about recent and pending court cases on a host of issues relevant to gays and lesbians, including domestic partnerships, job discrimination, and parenting.

www.ngltf.org

The National Gay and Lesbian Task Force is a think tank concerned with monitoring and promoting legal and civil rights for members of the gay and lesbian community. Its web site has news about current legislation, as well as publications and books on relevant topics.

www.nclrights.org

The National Center for Lesbian Rights maintains a site that offers advice for lesbians on a host of legal issues. The site provides free legal information as well as local contacts.

◆ PART IV ◆

Special Circumstances

◆ CHAPTER 12 ◆

Divorce and Lesbian Breakup

Many families with children, whether headed by heterosexual or homo-sexual parents, undergo a marital breakup at some point in the child's life. Some families go through more than one marital breakup before their children reach adulthood. Lesbian mothers who have experienced the dissolution of their adult relationship, whether that relationship was with a man or with another woman, must help their children deal with their grief and uncertainty. Lesbian mothers in this circumstance must also come to terms with their own grief and uncertainty.

Heterosexual Divorce and Breakup

Marital breakups occur in many heterosexual-headed families; the latest statistics indicate that nearly half of all first marriages end in divorce (U.S. Bureau of the Census, 1992). Statistics also indicate that nearly thirty percent of children spend at least some portion of their lives in single-parent homes. In addition to the stresses that any child will experience following a divorce, children whose mothers have embraced lesbianism face a unique set of circumstances. They may have to adjust to their mother having a new partner who is another woman. They may even have to adjust to having another adult living with them, an adult who may wish to play a parental role in the children's lives. And, the children must come to terms with their mother's lesbianism and what that means to them while adjusting to the breakup of their first family.

Sometimes a woman who has assumed herself to be heterosexual all her life, who has even married and had children within that marriage, begins to recognize that she is not satisfied with her life. Sometimes a woman realizes that she is attracted to another woman; sometimes it is not a particular woman that she finds attractive, but more the idea of living a different kind of life, one that does not involve an intimate relationship with a man. Often, women who have ended a heterosexual relationship become aware that lifelong feelings of deep friendship with other women were more than friendships and were in fact love. While this development may seem natural to the woman involved, it can come as a complete shock to those around her, especially her children. The great irony is that the happiest time in the woman's life, when she feels she is finally truly happy, is also often the most difficult. She must explain her new life to her children while she may still be struggling to explain it to herself.

When Mom and Dad Break Up

The end of a committed relationship is like a death in the family; when children are involved, it signals the death *of* a family. Many adults, even many years after their own parents divorced, still identify the divorce as the most painful event of their lives. Numerous studies have found that divorce has a long-lasting impact on children, even lasting into adulthood.[1] We are not saying this to make you feel guilty or to make you question your decisions. You know, better than anyone, why the divorce WAS necessary and why you feel it will benefit everyone in the long run. We are saying this to remind you of what a monumental event your divorce is to your children as well as for you.

The first thing parents must do is to acknowledge that the end of their relationship will be perceived by their children as a kind of death. The children sense, correctly, that they are losing something and it is never coming back. This is true, even in cases where one parent was alcoholic, drug-abusing, or violent. Imagine that! Even if everyone in the family was miserable, with constant yelling and crying, your child may still say she wants things the way they were! It is natural to prefer to stay in the familiar situation, even if it was unhappy, than to go off into a totally new situation. And your child has no other point of reference. To her, this was family life. She will need time to learn that there is a better way.

Children experience grief at the end of their parents' relationship. They may express this grief in different ways. Some may appear obviously depressed, losing interest in school, friends, and favorite activities. Some may express it by acting out, defying parental rules and becoming rebellious. Some may try to become a parent's caretaker, even trying to be a confidante and adviser. Others may refuse to acknowledge or discuss the divorce at all. You can expect any of these responses, or a combination of them, depending on your own child's particular temperament and personality.

Boys and girls typically react differently to divorce. Boys tend to have more obvious behavioral problems. They are more likely to become disobedient, aggressive, and resistant to discipline. Girls are more likely to become more anxious and to have a particularly difficult time during adolescence.[2] These are group differences, and these differences are not true of all children whose parents have been divorced. Researchers in this area are careful to note that other factors play a role in children's problem behavior, not just their parents' marital status.

Children deserve an explanation as to the causes of the profound changes in their lives. They do not need, or want, a detailed, blow-by-blow description of the other parent's failings and faults. They need an explanation that they are able to understand, that does not dwell on the shortcomings of either parent, and that emphasizes that the children are blameless and both parents still love them very much. Older children are more able to appreciate that not everything has to do with them, and that there are not necessarily good guys and bad guys in every situation. You will be able to discuss the divorce in a more realistic way, now that they can understand concepts like differences of opinion, wanting different things in life, and no longer loving each other.

As with many issues, this is one that you will visit again and again with your children. You may feel you have discussed the divorce with them and they understand it well; then, years after you thought it was a settled issue, they may begin to ask questions again, as if the divorce had just happened. This is natural. As they become more mature they may ask more sophisticated questions about what precipitated the divorce. You should respond with as much information as you feel is appropriate. For example, you might say to a young child, "Daddy and I haven't been getting along, and we think it is better for everyone if we live apart from each other." An older child would be more ready to hear an explanation like, "Your dad and I came to realize that we really didn't belong together. He wanted the kind of wife that I just couldn't be. And I wanted the kind of life that he couldn't give me."

When discussing your divorce with your children, you should be as honest as possible. Answer your children's questions as they arise. Do not feel the need to give them more information than they asked for. They may continue to ask the same questions over and over. Be patient. It takes time for them to absorb the reality of the divorce. Resist the urge (if you have it) to criticize, blame, or insult their father. After all, he is their father and will be for the rest of their lives.

The children who fare the best after a divorce are those children whose parents find a way to get through this difficult period without abandoning their roles as parents and without involving their children in the marital conflict. This is easier said than done. The period after divorce is also extremely stressful for the parent. Even the woman who was in an unhappy marriage for years can find herself feeling anxious and sad immediately following the divorce. It often helps to remember that the first two years, and especially the first year following a divorce, are the most difficult. Things will get better. In the meantime, stay focused on your children. Maintain family rules and discipline. Resist the urge to treat your child as a confidante or adviser; your child is not your peer. Continue to give your children time and affection.

Coming Out to Yourself

Divorce is a difficult time for any woman. You have many stresses to deal with, from helping your children with their feelings to figuring out how you will live in your new circumstances to coming to a custody agreement with your children's father. In addition to all these pressures that any newly divorced woman has, you also have your own struggle to come to terms with your newly discovered or acknowledged lesbianism. This is quite a lot to deal with, and you may feel alone in your struggles.

You should keep in mind that you are not alone. Of course there are no statistics on how many women divorce their husbands and then begin lesbian relationships. But most experts who study lesbian mothers agree that the most common way for lesbians to become mothers is through heterosexual relationships. In other words, there are a lot of women out there who have done the same thing you have. Look at the "Resources" at the end of this chapter for web sites and books by and for women in your situation. Hearing from other women who have similar experiences to your own can be very comforting.

Try not to waste a lot of time feeling regret over choices you have made. Even if you now feel that you have been a lesbian all your life, you obviously were not at a point where you could allow yourself to accept that. You did what you were capable of doing at the time. You were raised in a very homophobic environment and you cannot blame yourself for having internalized a lot of that. You did your best, and even if your marriage was doomed from the start, it did have one good outcome: your children.

You need to remember to take care of yourself at this time. It would be easy to become so involved in worrying about and taking care of your children that you neglect your own needs. Be careful not to do this. If you have a new partner, be sure to have regular time with her alone. Your new relationship needs time and energy to flourish. Although both time and energy are in short supply for you right now, you must find a way to devote at least some of those things to yourself and your partner.

A new part of your life is beginning, and you should focus as much on the joy of that new life as on the difficulties. The lesbian community is a large and very diverse one. We have political activists, corporate lawyers, physicians, teachers, hippie earth mothers, butchy motorcycle riders, new-age pagans, and more. Explore the community to see where you feel most comfortable. A large part of the lesbian community is made up of mothers. You and your family will be welcomed by those who arrived before you. Take advantage of the support that is out there for you.

Coming out is like throwing a stone into a pond. The ripples just keep going and going. The primary people affected are your ex-husband and your children, of course. But there are also your parents, siblings, other relatives, and friends. These people may react with any combination of shock, grief, anger, or acceptance. You must remember that someone's initial reaction may not be his ultimate reaction. It took you a long time to come to terms with your sexuality; you must give other people some time to come to terms with it as well. We refer you to Chapter 5 for specifics on dealing with others. Try not to let other people's reactions make you feel that you have done something wrong. Do not let guilt or sympathy for someone else's unhappiness (even your own child's) make you second-guess your decisions.

Coming Out to Your Child

Your children are in a unique situation. They have been part of a heterosexual family for at least some part of their lives. Mothers who, after a heterosexual marriage, begin to identify themselves as lesbian need to decide how to address the issue with their children. We can give some general guidelines, but you know your children better than anyone. You are the best person to know how much information your child needs and can absorb. Obviously, it is more important to address this issue if you are involved with another woman. Those women who have come to identify themselves as lesbian but who are not currently involved with anyone may find themselves with a little time before they need to address the issue with their children. Single women can still tell their children that they do not see themselves being involved with a man in the future.

Preschool Children

Very young children, or preschoolers, tend to think of things in black and white and to see themselves as the center of everything. They will often think that the divorce is their fault and believe that their parents will get back together. Your explanation should emphasize that neither of those things is true. If you are still single, you may not need to bring up the issue of lesbianism at this time. If you are seeing someone, a simple explanation like "Kathy is my friend and I like spending time with her" is enough for now.

Sometimes our children know more than we think they do. Diane entered her first lesbian relationship when her daughter, Alyson, was four. One day Diane got a call from Alyson's preschool teacher, who said, "I think you might want to have a talk with your daughter. She's telling people that you're sleeping with your girlfriend." When Alyson got home from school she and Diane talked about it. "She was just so okay with it," Diane recalls. "We decided to sit down and talk about what love was and draw pictures about what love was. We love our grandparents, our siblings, our cousins, and we talked about what love means. And in each representation, there were people holding hands and hugging each other, and I explained to her that that's what the relationship was about. Caring for each other, and holding hands, and just being there for each other. She was fine with that; she understood it. She saw it in a very genuine way, so it just worked out really well."

Elementary-School-Age Children

Older children of school age will have begun hearing words like "gay" and "lesbian," and it is all right to start using them yourself. You should define the words for your child, even if your child thinks he or she knows the definition. Something like, "Kathy and I love each other, and we want to be together. Two women who love each other are called lesbians," would be all right. You should be open to any questions your child has and be prepared to answer them honestly.

Although Gina had been dating women since her daughter Carla was an infant, she did not use the word "lesbian" with Carla until she was seven. "When she was seven she asked me. She saw something on television, on Channel 13. It was a documentary on gays and lesbians, and she asked me a few questions. She came to me and asked me about my friends. 'What do you call it—a lesbian?' And I explained to her, yes, and she went down the line and said, 'Are you?' And I didn't want to, because all the books said don't tell them until they're ten. So I said, 'Well, would it matter if I was?' And she said, 'No, I don't care, I just want to know.' So I told her."

Irene waited a while before she told her children about her relationship with Kitty. "For a while, we really didn't tell them. We pretended we were roommates. It probably took a few months. We just sat them down and talked to them about how sometimes people just fall in love and it doesn't really matter what gender they are. Love is love, and we loved each other and we were a couple. We did use the word *lesbian* then, but I don't think they really understood, until not very long ago, what it really was."

Tess remembers how she came out to her oldest son, Evan. Evan had been living with his father immediately after the divorce. "At about the time that Barbara and I got together, he came and lived with us. About two months before he came to live with us, I explained to him what lesbianism was and that this is what I was and that I was happy. And he didn't care. Well, at first he did a little bit. But we've always been very open; we can talk about absolutely anything." Now, Tess adds, Evan says all the time that "he doesn't know what he'd ever do if Barbara left or if something happened to her or anything like that."

Adolescents

Adolescents are going through some monumental changes of their own. They are discovering their own sexuality and beginning to break away from family relationships while turning toward peers. Learning that your mother is a lesbian at this time can be difficult. Most experts agree that early adolescence is the most difficult time for a child to learn that his mother is a lesbian. If you are coming out at the same time as your child is beginning adolescence, your child may initially have a harder time with it than he would if he were younger or older. (Read Chapter 10 on sexuality for more specifics on adolescence.) Be sensitive to your child's situation. He is having to face his mother's sexuality while he is starting to come to terms with his own sexuality. Your young adolescent needs extra concern and reassurance.

Your adolescent may ask some difficult questions—ones you may not be able to answer entirely yourself. Were you a lesbian when you married Dad? Is that the real reason you got divorced? Do people just "turn" gay all of a sudden? Let him know your feelings about these issues. Some women, in looking back at their lives, feel that attraction to other women was something they always felt but did not label as "lesbian." Others were well aware of what types of feelings they had for other women and deliberately chose to ignore them. Still others did not have any romantic feelings for other women until relatively late in their lives. Whatever your experiences were, tell your child. You do not need to go into graphic details of your sex life (what adolescent wouldn't run screaming from the room if you did?), but do talk about the feelings you may have had for other women. If you are happier now as a lesbian than you ever were in any heterosexual relationship, tell your child this. If you feel your lesbianism was a contributing factor to the end of your marriage, you should acknowledge this to your child. It may sound strange, but in some marriages the woman's incipient lesbianism is the least of the problems in the marriage. Finally, explain to your child that scientists have studied sexuality for many years and no one knows exactly why someone is straight and someone else is gay and why that may change at some point in someone's life. All you can say for sure is what happened to you.

Ex-Husbands and Child Custody: Every Lesbian Mother's Fear

Many lesbians who were formerly married live in fear of their ex-husbands. We have all heard the horror stories of how vindictive ex-husbands have been able to use narrow-minded courts of law to deny lesbians custody of their children. There was a widely reported case in Florida where a man, who had killed his first wife, was given custody of his daughter after the child's mother began a lesbian relationship. The judge ruled that the father would be a better influence on the child. And, of course, there is the famous case involving Sharon Bottoms. A judge in Virginia took custody of Bottoms's son away from her and gave it to her mother because he felt that a lesbian household was not suitable for a young child. While not a custody dispute between parents, the case certainly illustrates the type of thinking that still goes on regarding lesbian mothers and the law.

These cases are, fortunately, rare. But they still strike terror into the hearts of lesbian mothers. The suggestion that we could conceivably lose our children because of who we love is horrifying. Mothers whose ex-husbands object to their lesbianism may feel themselves vulnerable to this type of threat, and with good reason.

Not all ex-husbands respond negatively when their ex-wives become involved in a lesbian relationship. Diane has been divorced from

Alyson's father since Alyson was a baby. Diane feels that her ex-husband was somewhat relieved when she told him that she was a lesbian. "He said, 'Well, I always kind of knew that there was something going on.' I think he'd probably rather have it be a woman than another man." Although Shirley had been living in a lesbian relationship for nearly twenty years after the end of her marriage, she never disclosed that fact to her ex-husband or anyone else for a long time. After she and her partner came out to their grown children, "one of the kids told him, and he said, 'Oh, I knew that a long time ago. I knew she was even when we were married.' Now I don't know if that was true or not."

In other cases, the ex-husband's response is quite negative. Irene's ex-husband did not take the news at all well. "Oh, he was mad," Irene recalls. "He had told Kitty that if she had been a guy, he would have killed her." Irene acknowledges that it was a difficult position for him. "I guess it was a hard thing to go through, to lose his wife to a woman." Irene's ex-husband went through a period of saying very derogatory things to the children about their mother. He also tried, unsuccessfully, to use Irene's lesbianism as a reason for her to lose custody of the children. That tactic did not work in court, as the judge did not view Irene's lesbianism as relevant. As grim as the situation between Irene and her ex-husband seemed to be, it has improved. "It took about a year and a half, two years, before he finally was not saying any hateful things anymore. He talks to Kitty occasionally, and he and Kitty have had a talk about her watching the kids while he's at work. So it's been a lot better."

Tess and Barbara faced a similar situation with Tess's ex-husband. They went through a legal battle for custody. Tess's ex-husband also brought up her lesbian relationship as a reason for her not to have custody of the children. In this case also, the strategy failed and Tess was awarded custody. Since then, Tess feels things have "gotten better. It's more of, now, the struggle of a normal divorce. He's remarried also, so we have the struggle between the stepparents that typically comes along with that. It's not an issue any longer of my being a lesbian."

Getting Legal Advice

What should a divorced woman who fears a custody fight with her children's father do? First, you must consult a lawyer. It is preferable to get a referral to a gay-friendly lawyer (see our "Resources" at the end of this chapter). This is best, because lawyers can be as homophobic and narrow-minded as anyone else. You are in a special situation and you need someone who is at least sympathetic toward you and preferably experienced in this area of law. If, after speaking to a lawyer, you get the feeling that he or she is in any way not comfortable with a lesbian mother as a client, go get yourself another lawyer. This person is working for you and you need to feel that he or she will be a strong advocate.

You should be completely honest with your attorney. Be aware of the fact that anything you say is completely confidential and protected. Your lawyer cannot tell anyone what you have said. Ask what the laws are in your state regarding child custody and homosexuality. In most cases, you will be relieved to find that lesbianism itself is NOT a reason to lose custody. If that is not the case where you live, discuss with your lawyer what your best options are. Your first and really only priority is your children.

It is beyond the scope of this book to give specific legal advice; we are not lawyers, and even if we were, the laws differ from state to state. Even within a particular state, the type of response you get in court can vary from county to county, or even from judge to judge. We can tell you that progress is being made on this front every day, with more jurisdictions siding with openly gay men and women in child custody cases. You have reason to be hopeful; at the same time, you have cause to be concerned.

Lesbian Breakup

It would be nice to say that all lesbian relationships that involve children last forever. That once two women have made the decision to become parents together, their love for each other and for their children overcome whatever problems may develop. It would also be nice to say that in those rare instances where lesbian parents do decide to end their relationship, both of them inevitably continue to keep their children's best interests at heart at all times. They work hard at maintaining their parental relationship, acknowledge that parenthood is forever even if marriage isn't, and make sincere efforts to support one another's parenting. It would be nice to say these things; unfortunately, they wouldn't be true.

Lesbian relationships do sometimes end, as do heterosexual relationships and gay male relationships. When any adult love relationship ends, it sometimes ends badly, with anger, bitterness, and hurt feelings all around. Lesbian relationships are not immune to these realities. Not only are they not immune, but the precarious legalities of lesbian parenthood can lead to even worse difficulties.

There is another aspect of lesbian relationships that can lead to difficulties in terms of custody decisions. In our society women still do most of the parenting and nurturing. When heterosexual couples divorce, most often the children reside with their mothers. So what happens when two mothers get divorced? It may well be that both mothers are equally involved in the care of their children. Both women are, after all, mothers, and both may feel that they should have custody of the children. Lesbian mothers may feel more equal in their claim on the children after their breakup than a man and a woman might.

Taken together, these two things—the lack of universal legal recognition for lesbian relationships and the strong desire of both mothers to be custodial parents to their children—suggest that lesbian couples who split up may be in for big, ugly custody fights.

There have been some well-publicized cases where, following a lesbian breakup, the biological mother goes to court to try to keep the nonbiological mother from having any contact with the child. An example is the case reported in no less a mainstream magazine than *Time* (21 June 1999) of Penny Kazmierazak. Penny and her partner, Pam Query, were in a committed relationship for several years. They decided to have a child and raise her together. Pam gave birth to a baby girl named Zoey and the three lived together as a family. After a few years, however, the couple broke up. Pam has argued in court that since Penny is not Zoey's biological or adoptive mother, she has no custody or visitation rights (the state in which they live, Florida, does not allow second-parent adoption). The case is being appealed. Meanwhile, Penny cannot see Zoey.

This sad story is not unique. Such cases have been brought in other states as well. The great irony of them, of course, is that these lesbians are using the laws that discriminate against them to try to delegitimize their former partner's standing as a parent. Put more simply, they are agreeing with the notion that we are not "real" families. We deplore this. Without denying the pain of a divorce, it is not acceptable to use the court system in this way. It gives homophobes ammunition to question our rights to have children, and it is certainly unfair to the nonbiological parent, but most of all it is grossly unfair to the child. Parenthood is a lifelong bond that should never be broken, unless there is abuse or neglect of the child by the parent. Even in the midst of a messy, bitter divorce, it is important to remember that.

Lisa recalls the effect on her sons of her breakup with their other mother. "It was very hard, and they were pretty traumatized. Well, they were very upset is really what I should say. We just basically said we couldn't live together anymore and just gave them lots and lots of reassurance that neither of us was ever going to leave their life. We went and saw a lesbian therapist who herself was a mother. She ended up basically saying that divorce really does not damage children, it's the fighting and the battling that does. We just have really, really left the kids out of any problems. We kept talking to them and seeing them and we would see them together. We would go to parent things together. We still do holidays together. And they've really done great." Lisa and her ex-partner, Robin, have basically stuck to the contract they had drawn up before they adopted the boys, with each of them having the children about half the time.

Joanne and her former partner, Rebecca, broke up when their son, Will, was four years old. Joanne says, "We work very hard to make ourselves friends for Will's sake. We talk to each other, and we go to his things together, so it's pretty amicable. She asks me when she wants to have him, which is about every week. I say yes, unless we've got something else going on. If I need her to take over for a weekend or something, I call her and ask her." While Joanne and Rebecca have no formal written custody agreement, they have been able to maintain an arrangement that allows both of them to have time with Will.

It IS possible (although it doesn't always seem like it is) for two parents who don't even like each other anymore to cooperate in raising their child. It may take involving an intermediary, such as an attorney or a divorce mediator, to work out custody arrangements. Lisa and Robin got help from their local lesbian mothers' group. It is best to get someone who has experience working with lesbians. Try to keep in mind that what you are doing is what is best for your child. If you are the biological parent who is tempted to try to keep your former partner away from your child, consider the fact that one day your child will no longer be a child. How will you explain to your adult child that you kept someone who loved her and wanted to be part of her life, someone who was instrumental in bringing her to life, away from her for all those years? You may find yourself having won the battle but having lost the bigger war. Remember that your partner is a mother too.

We recommend to all lesbian parents that they legalize the parental relationship in whatever way they can. Many states now allow so-called second-parent adoptions. If your state is one, get the adoption papers filed as soon as you can. You may feel that there is no need to get the adoption legalized, that you and your sweetie will never part and even if you did, you know you would never argue over your child. If this describes you, this is what we have to say: Good for you! Now file the papers. You may be right, you may never need the legalization. But you cannot predict the future, and this is too important to ignore. You might also want to consider that something could happen to your partner, and your child could be left without a legal parent. In that case, relatives could try to get custody, and child welfare could become involved. A nightmare could easily become a worse nightmare. File the papers.

If you live in a state where second-parent adoptions are not legal, then you must obtain all the legal protection that is available to you. This may mean drawing up wills, signing guardianship papers, and completing medical proxy forms. Again, you should consult a lawyer. These are routine matters and will not, in most cases, be expensive. We also recommend that you draft a joint letter, outlining your desire to be a family and that both of you be considered your child's parents. Keep two copies of the letter. Think of these things as protection for your child.

What You Can Do to Protect Your Children and Yourself in the Event of Divorce or Breakup

1. Maintain family traditions after a divorce. Keep birthday and holiday traditions as intact as you can. This will help give your children a sense of security.

2. If you have recently come out, take advantage of on-line resources and other supports. Look for resources that are specifically for lesbian mothers. Ones geared toward lesbians in general will probably be more about single life. Attend women's music festivals, gay pride marches, and gay establishments (bookstores, coffeehouses).

3. If you are neither your child's legal parent nor his biological parent, your status as a parent is shaky. Beyond drawing up whatever legal papers you can, keep documentation of your relationship with your child where you will always have access to it. (For example, keep a copy of the birth announcement you and your partner sent out together; keep copies of tuition bills; keep a record of doctor visits and school functions where you acted as a parent.)

4. Remember that your child is the priority through this transition. When and if you think it would be beneficial, seek the help of a mediator, lawyer, and/or therapist to assist with the transition for you and your child.

Resources

www.ssnetwk.org

The Straight Spouse Network offers support and education to ex-spouses of gays and lesbians. If your ex-husband is at all receptive, he may benefit from getting support from other men who are in the same situation.

www.pflag.org

Parents, Families and Friends of Lesbians and Gays is a large national organization for relatives and friends of gays and lesbians. The site gives information about local support groups, information about civil rights, and links to other sites. A great resource for any important people in your life who want to learn more, show support, or hear other people's stories.

www.lambdalegal.org

The Lambda Legal Defense and Education Fund is the national organization dedicated to promoting legal and civil rights to the gay and lesbian community. The site has updates on legal issues pertaining to us, as well as a state-by-state guide to laws and statutes regarding domestic partnership, antidiscrimination, and so on. (Nothing specifically on second-parent adoption yet.) The site lists regional telephone numbers, which you can call with particular concerns or for a reference to a lawyer. We found the wonderful lawyers who handled our second-parent adoption through Lambda.

From Wedded Wife to Lesbian Life: Stories of Transformation, by Deborah Abbott and Ellen Farmer (1995). Freedom, CA: Crossing Press.

The Other Side of the Closet: The Coming-Out Crisis for Straight Spouses and Families, by Amity Pierce Buxton (1994). New York, NY: Wiley Press.

Married Women Who Love Women, by Carren Strock (1998). New York, NY: Doubleday Press.

The Other Mother: A Lesbian's Fight for Her Daughter, by Nancy Abrams (1999). Madison, WI: University of Wisconsin Press.

Notes

1. Wallerstein, J., Lewis, J., & Blakeslee, S. (2000). *The unexpected legacy of divorce*. New York, NY: Hyperion Books.
2. Wallerstein, J., & Blakeslee, S. (1989). *Second chances: Men, women, and children a decade after divorce*. New York, NY: Ticknor & Fields; Hetherington, E., & Clingempeel, W. (1992). Coping with marital transitions: A family systems perspective. *Monographs of the Society for Research in Child Development, 57*(2–3, Serial No. 227).

◆ CHAPTER 13 ◆

Lesbian Stepfamilies

Several types of stepfamilies exist within the lesbian community. One type of family is one that originated within a heterosexual relationship. Following the end of that relationship, the mother embarks upon a lesbian relationship. Another type is one that originated with two women having a child together. They subsequently end their relationship, and one or both mothers begin a new lesbian relationship. There is also the case where a single woman became a parent on her own, and later during the child's life she takes a lesbian partner. In any case, the addition of a woman partner into the family changes the lives of everyone involved.

Often, when another partner enters the picture, she brings children of her own into the relationship. Sometimes the partners decide to have children of their own. These stepfamilies, or blended families, present new challenges to both the adults and the children. How well, or poorly, the family members adjust to the new circumstances depends on many things. The age of the children, the type of parental relationships they have had up until this time, the way the adults handle their new family, as well as the individual personalities involved, all play a role.

Biological Mothers Who Begin a New Relationship

There are certain key things to keep in mind while forming your new family. If you had children within a heterosexual marriage, you must make it very clear to your child that your new partner was not the cause of your divorce to their father. Even if you began a lesbian relationship while still married, you must make it clear to your children that your marriage was not making you happy and would have failed no matter what. Otherwise, you are setting your new partner up to be the "bad guy" who took Mommy away from Daddy. You should also make sure your children know that even if your new partner was not in your life, you still would not return to their father. Children often harbor the fantasy that their parents will reunite, sometimes for years. Naturally this can lead to resentment of your new partner.

Another important thing to do is to keep expectations about your new stepfamily realistic. Your children are not automatically going to love your partner as much as you do. They are certainly not going to start seeing her as their second mother immediately. Indeed, some older children may never see her as another mother. Your best bet is to have your partner go slowly with the children. She should start off trying to be a friend to your child, something like a typical aunt or a family friend. If possible, avoid having your partner play the disciplinarian role. You should be the one to enforce the rules. She should also stay out of any conflicts between you and your ex-husband. And she should not speak unkindly about him in front of the children. This can only backfire.

Allowing Your New Partner to Parent Your Child

Although biological mothers often say they want their partners to become equal parenting partners, when push comes to shove some may resist that. Allowing your partner to become a second mother means that you have to back off a bit at times and let her do it. It means that you have to let her read the bedtime stories, let her hold your child's hand when you cross the street, and let her be the one your child cries to when she hurts herself. This can be a hard thing to do, especially if you have been a single parent for a while. However, there is no way your partner will be able to become a parent to your children unless you let her. Resist the urge to take over when she is "mothering" your child. If your child hurts himself and runs to your partner for comfort, stay out of it and let her comfort him. If you run over and scoop your son from your partner's arms, you are sending a message to both of them that you are the only one capable of caring for him. After a while, your partner may stop trying.

Try to look at the benefits of having another parent, as opposed to another adult, in the house. You have someone who can actually share in the never-ending responsibilities of childcare. You have someone who can take over for you when you are exhausted, losing patience, or just need a break. You have someone with whom you can discuss ideas or problems. You have someone who can share in all the happy moments of family life. You may even have more time to pursue your own activities, or have a few minutes to yourself.

For Single Lesbian Non-Mothers:
When Your New Partner Is Also a Mother

Sometimes, a single lesbian without children finds herself in a relationship with a woman who already has children. So, in addition to all the usual negotiations that go on in a new relationship (Is this a committed, exclusive relationship? Should we move in together? How will we handle our finances?), you can add another huge area of negotiation: the children. If you began a relationship with a woman who has children, there are two issues that you face: how the children will affect your relationship with their mother, and what kind of relationship will you have with the children.

As you will discover almost immediately, the children will influence nearly every facet of your relationship with your new partner. How much time she has available to you and how much energy she has to devote to you depend in large part on how much her children require of her on any given day. Her children will be her first priority more often than not, and that is how it should be. Getting into a relationship with a woman with children means you are getting a package deal. You will not have the carefree days and nights that you would have if you were involved with a childless woman. This is just the way it has to be.

Joanne's partner, Denise, "never wanted children," says Joanne. "She and I are both very athletic, we like to climb mountains, we like to travel and do all those kind of things. Of course with a child you don't just pick up and go do those things. Denise also admits to having jealousy over the amount of time and attention that Will gets from me. If there's anything like a maternal instinct, she doesn't have it. But we talk about it. We've had therapy about it. She works hard at it, I work hard at it." It is just not possible for a childless woman to walk into a relationship with a woman who is already a mother without everyone having to make adjustments. It does take work, often a lot of work, to make all the relationships successful.

Despite these challenges, there are advantages to being involved with a woman who has children. You have the opportunity to gain a ready-made family. You may find that you become another mother to a child and are able to reap all the joys and satisfactions that come from that. You will be in a position to support your partner as she goes through the intense emotional experience of raising a child. You will also get to revisit many childhood events—when was the last time you went to the circus, built sandcastles on the beach, or played at the playground? There are many fun parts to raising children; don't lose sight of that.

When Both of You Have Children

Sometimes both partners already have children that they bring with them into the new relationship. This new family brings special challenges, as there are already two established households and two potentially different ways of doing things. Your task is to turn these two groups into one functioning family. At the beginning, try to have each parent discipline her own children. You will want to be as consistent as possible with house rules for all children. For example, if your children have been allowed to watch whatever they want to on television while your partner's children can only watch certain kinds of shows, the two of you will have to come to some sort of agreement as to what will now be allowed.

Jealousy can be an issue even when both partners bring children into the relationship. Marie recalls, "I really had a jealousy thing. I had a really hard time with it. It was true jealousy of the kids, because Shirley spent so much time with them. I felt like I was being left out of the circle, because she would work with them on homework and stuff like that, and I had PMS and I would get irritated at the littlest things. So nobody wanted to talk to me." It may take each of you some time to adjust to not being the only mother in the house.

Your children may find that their new stepsiblings are an additional source of support. Particularly if both you and your partner are coming out of heterosexual relationships, your children may benefit from living with another child who is going through the same thing. You will have the advantage of being in a relationship with someone who already knows how much time and energy being a mother takes. While you will have new children and their personalities to get to know, neither of you will be new at the job of being a mother.

The Big Negotiating Point for the Mother and Her New Partner: How Much Involvement with the Children?

Sometimes a biological mother gets the sense that her new partner may be more interested in her children than she is in her. Tara was previously involved with a woman who very much wanted to be part of her children's lives. So much so, in fact, that it made Tara uncomfortable. "Interestingly enough," says Tara, "that became a problem in that relationship. She wanted to sort of adopt my kids and become a stepparent before I felt ready to have her play that role. She became overly involved with my kids, which became unhealthy. That was eventually a big issue for why we split up. There were certainly other issues as well that led to that, but she couldn't accept the limited role that I felt was necessary. You'd think you'd want somebody who wanted to be involved with your children, but in a sense she was too involved. She became domineering and told me how I should parent my kids; so that became a problem."

If you are the new partner without children of your own, be honest with yourself about your reasons for becoming involved with your partner. If the most important one is that your relationship gives you a chance to be a parent, then you should reconsider. While becoming a

---

♦ Did You Know . . . ? ♦

Young children have the easiest time establishing a good relationship with a stepparent.

Wallerstein, J. S., & Kelly, J. B. (1980). *Surviving the breakup: How children actually cope with divorce.* New York, NY: Basic Books.

stepparent can be wonderful and fulfilling, it should never be your reason to be involved with another woman. It isn't fair to her or to you. You also risk hurting the children if your relationship with their mother doesn't work out.

Be careful not to move too fast into a parental role. Your partner has been her child's mother since day one and will quickly become alienated from you if you make a habit of criticizing her childrearing practices. Her children also need time to become acquainted with you and used to having another adult around. Let her handle the discipline. Turning yourself into the bad guy early on means you are digging yourself a hole that may be difficult to get out of later on. Irene recalls the early days of her relationship with Kitty. "At first, it was really hard. She had lived by herself for so long and wasn't around kids. She was raised more strictly than I was, and she had a lot of different rules she thought the kids should have to follow. That caused a lot of problems for a long time. I think we've been a lot better on that. If she disciplines them and I don't agree with it, I'll talk to her about it later on. Never in front of them. We have to negotiate a lot of the time. Sometimes we have come back and said to the kids, 'Well, this was wrong. Here's what we're going to do now.'"

Tara is now dating a woman who never had a desire to be a parent. "She actually wasn't sure she wanted to meet me when she heard I had kids. She never wanted children, and she never had dated anybody who had children. Later she changed her mind and said, 'Well, okay, I'll meet her.' She was still a little nervous about it, but we fell in love. While it poses some issues for us, neither of us wants her to be a stepparent at this point. She's very much involved in my kids' lives, but not in a parenting way. She's more of an aunt figure, or close friend. So it's worked out really well." Tara and her partner have no plans to live together any time soon. They are taking it slowly with Tara's children, not trying to force intimacy.

Some women never wish to develop a parental relationship with their partner's child. In Gina's case, her daughter Carla was ten when Gina's relationship with Kathy began. In the beginning, it was an adjustment for everyone. Kathy did not agree with how Gina handled some situations with Carla, and she resented the lack of freedom that came with having a child. "It's hard with a child, having a relationship. I guess it would be hard even in a heterosexual relationship." Even after all these

years of living in the same house, Gina characterizes Carla's relationship
with Kathy as "casual," not at all a parental relationship. "I'm basically
the mother, the father, everything."

Especially when the child is older when the relationship begins, the
mother's new partner may opt for a more friendly, less intimate role than
that of second parent. This may change over time, and a closer relationship may develop. In some cases, the relationship remains a friendly but
not very close one. When the mother is just dating a new woman, and
they have no serious commitment, a fairly casual, amiable relationship
between the new woman and the children is probably the best that
could be hoped for.

There are many factors influencing the relationship between a child
and his mother's new partner, not the least of which is the individual
child's personality. Tess sees a real difference in the type of relationship
her daughter, Caitlin, has with Barbara, in comparison to how Barbara
gets along with her sons. "The boys absolutely love her. To Evan, Barbara
is his world. They have little secret handshakes and little secret things that
they do. Barbara's just the 'go out in the yard and play ball with the
whole neighborhood' kind of parent and loves doing stuff with the kids.
My middle child, Caitlin—she's the difficult one. She's the most demanding child. It has taken them, Caitlin and Barbara, three years to
bond. I mean, they're very much alike, so it's kind of ironic. They're both
bull-headed, they're both overachievers, and just everything has to be
right down the line. So they butt heads a lot. It's taken three years of all
of us going to therapy and learning how to deal with Caitlin, and knowing that Caitlin's not the same as Evan and Sean, not as easygoing. So it
was not as easy for Barbara to bond with her."

Irene also sees a difference in the type of relationships her children
have with Kitty. "My little one totally loves her. She will go to her a lot
of times before she'll go to me for something. And she just adores her.

My older one really took to heart a lot of the things that my ex had said in the very beginning about us. He is closer to his dad in a lot of ways, and he thinks that it's Kitty's fault that we were divorced—Kitty took me from them. So he's not very close to her. There are a lot of times that he'll come ask me something and I'll tell him, 'Go ask Kitty, you need to ask Kitty about that.' He's doing better about that, I think. She's working part time, so she's here with the kids a lot more, and I think that's helping out a lot. They have to depend on her more often while I'm at work."

If your partner has more than one child, you may find that you have a different relationship with each child. Even biological parents have different types of relationships with different children. Some children are easier to get along with, some have interests that you can more readily share, some are a better match temperamentally to you. Your goal is to develop the best relationship with each child that you possibly can. In Denise's case, she found that she and Joanne's son, Will, share an interest in science. "Denise teaches hard sciences and she likes math and hard science and all of that. She found that that was a way that she could connect with Will. Will is in the honors program at school, so he has a lot of classes that require a lot of attention to science. So they work together on his projects. She helps him with his homework. We also try to include Will at least once a month in a family activity. We'll all go out and see a movie, or do things like that. We try to have dinner together every day." Finding a special way to connect with each child is an important step in establishing your relationship.

How Many Mothers Does a Child Need?

When a lesbian couple with children breaks up, the parents often enter new relationships. In these circumstances, a child could end up with four mother figures. This is Will's situation. Will tells people that he has "one mom, and he has a co-parent, and he has Denise and Elaine (his co-parent's new partner). He adores all of us and he wants us all to be there and to be part of his life," says Joanne. If when you become involved with a woman you are becoming the third or fourth woman in a child's life, you face many of the same challenges that any stepmother faces. There are two important distinctions, however. One is that you are not the child's mother's first female partner. The child is used to having a lesbian mother, or two, so you do not signify a radical change in his mother's lifestyle or his way of thinking about her. Your gender will not be an issue for the child in the way it might be if the child had been born into a heterosexual marriage. The other important distinction is that the child already has two mothers. You may feel that there is no room in the child's life for a third or fourth mother figure.

The truth is that a child who already has two involved mothers can still use another adult woman playing a role in his life. No matter how many mother figures he already has, he doesn't have you yet. With your own blend of experiences, interests, and personality, you have a unique contribution to make to a child's life. So how many mothers does a child need? The answer is, as many as he can get.

Lesbian Stepmother:
A Unique Creation

In all stepfamilies, the stepparent can take on a variety of levels of involvement. There is no model out there for what lesbian stepmothers should be like. None of us were raised with an idea of what such a person would act like, or what role she would play in an already established family. Each family creates its own version of a lesbian stepmother. That version may change across time, and it may differ from one child to another. It can remain fairly casual, or it can be just as close as a biological mother–child bond. You and your new family will have to decide what your role will be. As your relationship develops, you will need to keep reassessing your role in the family.

What You Can Do to Establish Healthy Stepfamilies

1. If you are the partner of a lesbian mother, try to establish an independent relationship with each of her children. Express an interest in whatever interests them, be it soccer, Harry Potter, or hip-hop music.

2. If you are the partner of a lesbian mother, do not disagree with her on how to deal with the children in front of the children. While this is good advice for any parent, it is particularly important for you. You are new to this family, and you do not want to make the child feel you are against her.

3. If you and your partner are having some sort of a commitment ceremony, make sure that the children are part of it. Include your mutual commitment to them in the service.

4. If you are the biological mother, make sure to put in writing that your partner has the right to pick up your child from school, be called for emergencies, and so on.

5. Do not insist that your child call your new partner "Mom" or any maternal-sounding name. Let him call her by her first name, or "Aunt Kate," if you prefer.

Resource

Lesbian Step Families: An Ethnography of Love, by Janet M. Wright (1998). Binghamton, NY: Haworth Press.

This book originated as the author's doctoral dissertation in social welfare. She interviews five different lesbian stepfamilies in depth and discusses the issues they all face.

◆ CHAPTER 14 ◆

Alternative Insemination and Adoption

Many lesbians created their families through alternative insemination (AI) or adoption. The process through which our children became our children is something that will continue to have an impact on our families as our children grow. The manner in which we became pregnant, or succeeded in adopting, is not just the prologue to our family's story. It is an ongoing facet of our children's lives, and it affects us as parents as well.

For example, many children of lesbians are conceived via an anonymous sperm donor, as were our daughters. Although we have a great deal of background information about the donor, which we will one day share with our daughters, they will very likely never meet this man or know his family. Some lesbians choose to use a known donor, to avoid this problem of the child never knowing his or her biological father. Both circumstances lead to some issues that we must deal with.

Some children of lesbians are adopted. Often adopted children are of a different ethnic or racial background from that of their adoptive parents. Some of these children will come to understand that they have two biological parents somewhere in the world whom they may never meet. Other children, products of the relatively recent phenomenon of open adoptions, will know their birth mother, if not their biological father, as well. Again, these different circumstances present somewhat different challenges to the lesbian mother.

AI Babies

Unknown Donors

It seems like such a simple process. You want to have a child, so you need to get pregnant. In order to do that, you need some sperm. For whatever reason, you don't want a father figure in your child's life. Maybe you'd like one but don't feel you know anyone who would fit the bill. You decide to go the route of the anonymous donor. Fortunately, there are sperm banks out there that do nothing except provide sperm from unknown donors to those women who require it. So you give them a call, order up some vials, and now here you are, a proud lesbian parent.

In our case we never seriously considered anything other than using an anonymous donor. We did not feel comfortable with having a third parent at the periphery of our family, and we were concerned about the potential legal ramifications if we did use someone we knew. Despite the best of intentions, people do change their minds, and we did not want there to be any possibility of a donor wanting more involvement in our child's life than we were comfortable with him having, which was none. So one night, over Chinese food, we pored over the printouts of medical and autobiographical backgrounds and chose our children's donor. Three months later, Beth was pregnant with Bailey. Rowan, conceived with the same donor, came along two-and-a-half years later.

There certainly are advantages to having used an anonymous donor. There is no parent in our daughters' lives other than the two of us. We have a very detailed report of the donor's history, with more information about his family's health than we know about our own family. Given the screening that the donor went through, we were quite confident that we were not passing on any problematic medical conditions. In our case, we banked extra sperm after Bailey was born. This is quite commonly done by families who use AI. We wanted our second child to be a full sibling to our first. We felt this would be an advantage, as they would be more likely to look alike (and they do). In addition, since we had gotten our

---

♦ Did You Know . . . ? ♦

While no one knows how many children are born to lesbians after they have come out, estimates from 1990 put the number at around ten thousand. Experts believe that the number is increasing.

Patterson, C. J. (1992). Children of lesbian and gay parents. *Child Development, 63,* 1025–1042.

---

first choice as a donor for Bailey, and we certainly liked the results, we wanted the same thing for our second child.

However, there are drawbacks to having used an anonymous donor. The obvious one is that our children, while having access to a great deal of information about the donor, will likely never actually see him or meet him or his family. As parents, we must help our children understand this reality as best we can.

Talking about AI to Our Children

Preschool-Age Children.   Most children do begin asking questions about where babies come from by the time they start kindergarten, if not before. Even children who don't show any particular curiosity about that will often ask about whether they have a father during the pre-

◆ Advice from a Lesbian Mother ◆

"Be open. Be open, and you've got to give up everything—your kids have to come first. Be honest and be there for them. It cost us $15,000 to get pregnant with Katya. Most [straight] couples take care of that with dinner and a glass of wine and a room afterwards, and it doesn't cost anything. When you are planning to become a parent, if you are a lesbian or a gay couple, you have to pay for it. You have to go through psychological testing, you have to go through physical testing—this is really a planning thing. Don't ever have children as a trophy or as a showcase; you've got to mean it. They have to, have to, have to be the center of your life, beyond anything."

—Rosita

school years. They will start to see that many of their friends do have fathers, and they may wonder why they are different. Deirdre and Meredith's daughter, Kelsey, started noticing that her family was different once she started nursery school. "Kelsey went through a period when she first started nursery school that she was asking about a daddy, because the other kids at school had daddies. We certainly talked to her about that, and got books about lesbian families and gay families and read those to her and talked about how special she is, that sort of thing." Preschool-age children who ask about having a father are not really asking for a biological explanation of procreation. They want to know why their family looks different from other kids' families. An explanation that focuses on how there are all different kinds of families, some with a mom and a dad, some with two moms, some with two dads, and so on, is the best approach to use here.

There will come a time when your child wants to know more about her beginnings. As with many topics, this is one you will visit over and over again as your child develops. Most lesbian moms find that a simple explanation works best for children who are starting to ask these kinds of questions. Katya, Rosita and Gabriella's six-year-old, asked her parents if she had a daddy. "And we said yes, and we said he's a very nice man, although we don't know who he is. He helped us out by letting Mommy Gabriella get pregnant with you." They went on to explain that Gabriella had gone to a special doctor who put the man's seeds into her uterus, and that is how Katya began growing. Katya seemed to understand and accept this explanation.

Elementary-School-Age Children.   As your child goes through the elementary school years, and certainly by the time she finishes elementary school, she will come to a more mature and complete understanding of how babies are conceived. (You will, of course, help her come to this more mature understanding—see our discussion in Chapter 10 on talking to your child about sex.) You will need to talk to her again about her biological father or donor, depending on how you refer to him. We suggest that, before you do this, you think back to your own decision-making process that led you to choose an anonymous donor in the first place. In addition to the mechanics of how pregnancy with an anonymous donor is achieved, your child should also know WHY you chose to become pregnant that way. The following might be a good way to approach the topic with your child.

"Your mother and I knew that we wanted to have children together, and your mother wanted to get pregnant and give birth. We decided that the best way for our family to have a baby would be to choose an anonymous donor from a sperm bank. We wanted to be sure the donor was healthy, we wanted one that looked kind of like me and my family [if that is the case]. We felt that you already were going to have two parents, and you didn't need another one. So Mama and I went to a special kind of doctor, one that helps women get pregnant. The doctor gave us a list of donors and what they were like, and we chose the one we wanted."

Emphasize that donors are men who want to help women have babies. It is not a question of your having "taken away" your child's father. The donor was anonymous and wants to remain so. His reasons could be his concern for the feelings of his future wife and their children; he might prefer not knowing for certain whether or not his donations resulted in any biological offspring; he may feel strongly about not wanting to intrude upon the family he helped create. Whatever his reasons, you are very grateful to the donor for allowing you to have a family. If you sense that your child needs to be reassured, stress that she began life the way all babies begin life. Many heterosexual couples use AI to start their families too. The sperm and the egg joined, and a new person started growing. You will also want to tell her about the two of you going to see the special doctor, about how much you wanted the process to work, and how excited you both were when it did work. Talk to her about your pregnancy, your preparations for her, and about her birth. It is a good idea to keep the focus on how much you wanted to have a baby.

Your child may want to return to the topic of the donor and want to talk more about him. This curiosity is only natural. We are, after all, talking about their beginnings in life. Be open, and show your child that you are comfortable talking about the donor. At this age, your child may actually be more fascinated with the mechanics of sperm donation than with the biological ramifications of having an unknown donor. For example, they may find the most intriguing aspect of the whole thing to be that some man actually agreed to masturbate into a paper cup! The idea of genetic influence may be much less important to them. Feel free to go into great detail about the process if this seems to be what your child is after. Talk about how sperm is donated over a period of time (usually several months), how it is then frozen, how the donor is tested to see whether he has any illnesses that would make him a bad risk to be a donor, and then how the sperm samples are released to prospective mothers. You can then get into how insemination works, if your child still wants to hear more. (It is likely that this will take a few separate conversations.) As far as the actual insemination, explain that you figured out when the best time of the month would be for you to do it (this may require some explanation of the menstrual cycle, if your child is not already familiar with it). When the time was right, you went to the doctor, or you and your partner got ready at home, and inserted the sperm into your vagina. Then you waited to see if you were pregnant. Finish by repeating how happy you both were when you found out the answer was yes.

Of course you will need to modify this basic outline, depending on your own personal circumstances. Not all lesbian mothers became pregnant while in a relationship; in that case you can emphasize how much you yourself wanted a child. Some women had to go through more complicated procedures to become pregnant. If *in vitro* fertilization or other more advanced reproductive techniques were necessary in order for you to get pregnant, you should feel free to discuss that with your child. Be prepared for reactions varying from indifference or disinterest, to revulsion ("Oh, yuck!"), to enthusiasm ("How cool!").

Adolescents. An adolescent understands more about biology and genetics than a younger child, and it is during adolescence that your child will probably start to wonder about what the donor is like or who the donor may be. Share whatever information you have with her. The amount of information that sperm banks provide varies widely. The trend is toward disclosing more personal information about donors, for example, their hobbies, talents, likes and dislikes, but not all banks provide this much detail. If you have very little data on your donor, other than basics like blood type, height, weight, and coloring, you can try telling your child about the "typical" donor. Typical donors are intelligent, have no health problems, are relatively open-minded, and willing to be inconvenienced in order to help someone they do not know have a child. They are also compensated for their efforts. If your child is unsatisfied with this amount of information, you do have an option. Some sperm banks are now asking for more personal information about donors than they used to, and the banks may be willing to try to get more information for you if you request it. It can't hurt to ask.

Adolescents are ultimately very self-focused, and you should view this as a normal, and thankfully brief, phase. Your child may proclaim, for example, that she must be academically gifted because her donor was. You, on the other hand, may feel that her gifts are more attributable to the hundreds of hours you have spent reading to her and encouraging her in academic pursuits, not to mention your own genetic contribution. Just let it go. She is still solidifying her own identity, as all adolescents are, and she is trying to put all the pieces of the puzzle together. It may be very important to her, for a while, to identify those traits that she shares with the donor. Let her do this, and do not feel hurt if she does not seem to be acknowledging your role in making her who she is. She will not be an adolescent forever.

We have noticed, in looking at the books written for parents who conceive children through donor insemination, that the bulk of the books deal with issues that just don't apply to our families. The big issues for straight couples who have used donor insemination are whether to disclose this fact to family and friends (not a problem for us; they know we didn't become pregnant by ourselves); and whether and when to disclose this fact to the child (again, not a problem for us; our children understood very early that our family is not like everyone else's and that they do not have a daddy). Children born to heterosexual couples who used donor insemination often react negatively to the news, particularly when they learn it as adolescents or adults. This is not surprising; something they have assumed to be true about themselves turns out not to be true. Their father is not their biological father. If you read any of these books for help in talking to your children about donor insemination, be sure to keep in mind that our families are very different from the ones they are talking about. There is no reason to think that our children will react with feelings of betrayal, shock, or anger when they hear about their conception, especially if the truth is discussed and not concealed from the start.

Known Donors

Some lesbians choose to become pregnant with known donors. Sometimes the donor is a relative of the nonbiological mother. Sometimes the donor is a good friend. Sometimes the donor is someone the mother does not know very well, but someone she feels would make a good biological father. The arrangements for how much involvement the known donor will have with the child vary as well. At one end of the spectrum are the families where the donor has no or virtually no contact with the child. These families do not differ much from those whose children were conceived with an anonymous donor. At the other end of the spectrum are families where the donor really is a father to the child, sharing fully in custody and all responsibilities.

Tara's family is an example of one where the children were conceived with a known donor, but this man plays little role in their lives. "He only sees them once or twice a year," says Tara. Cheryl and Jeanine also used a known donor, and while he does play a more active role in their son's life than does the donor in Tara's family, he does not play a parental role. "He's one of Adam's godparents, and he sees him at least on a weekly basis, if not more. He will babysit, he comes over, he's a good friend of ours. He is not a father in any specific sense of the word. He does not provide any kind of support, other than that of a friend."

Jeanine and Cheryl have given a lot of thought to how they will talk to Adam about the donor situation as he gets older. "We will probably use the term 'he gave us a gift,'" explains Cheryl. "Personally, I'm going to try to dissuade him from thinking of him in the role of father. When he starts asking questions, we're going to let Adam know that because of him, Adam exists."

Becky and Anne's daughter is biologically related to both of them. Their donor was a brother of the nonbiological mother (Becky and

Anne prefer not to make public which of them is Samantha's biological mother). They do plan on telling Samantha that her uncle is the one who fathered her, "eventually, when she asks. She hasn't asked," says Becky. In the meantime, her relationship with him is like that of any niece to her uncle.

Lauren and Julie share custody of their son, Nathaniel, with his father John. Lauren probably speaks for many women who chose to go with a known, as opposed to an unknown, donor. "The fact of totally not knowing, I thought, would be difficult. And the scary thing is you don't have any guarantees. The information that they give you—you don't know what the person really looks like, you don't know really. You know what they do for a living and supposedly what their personality is like, but there are so many unknowns."

In Lauren's case, "I had known John for a long time, and he really wanted to parent, not just donate. I thought that the more people that you have in a child's life who really love him, the better. Well, I grew up without a father, so that's part of the reason too, I guess. A father was one of the things, if at all possible, that I wanted for my child. And the other thing is that when I was making this decision, I wasn't in a relationship. It was going to be just me, and I thought for the child it would be nice for him to have at least two parents."

As things turned out, Nathaniel has three parents, and this too has its advantages and disadvantages. "I think we have been real lucky in a lot of ways—that we have breaks" when Nathaniel is with John. "We just had a nightmare flu one time, and it would have been horrible if we would have had to take care of him. John took him for a couple of days. So that has kind of lessened the pressure on both of us." On the other hand, with three parents and two households, tensions and disagreements invariably arise. "It's interesting because it's a three-way relationship, in that John also has his issues, and you want to make sure that things are consistent between the two homes." Strong commitment and open and frequent communication are especially important in these families.

When the Donor Changes His Mind

The biggest drawback to using a known donor, and one that keeps many lesbians from doing so, is the fear that the donor may at some point change his mind and not stick to the original agreement regarding contact with the child. This is what happened in Karen's case. "The major reason that I chose a known donor was because I was in a relationship with a woman who had two children by donor insemination that also had a known donor. So it was to try to keep things in a similar situation for all the children," explains Karen. "They [the donor and his partner] were supposed to be noncustodial dads." Things haven't worked out as Karen had planned. She and her partner split up when Jessica was still a baby, and around the same time Jessica's father decided he wanted to be more involved in her life. For most of Jessica's life, Karen, Jessica's father, and his partner have been waging legal battles over her custody. As it stands now, Karen and Jessica's father share joint legal and physical custody. "He certainly has her a whole lot more than I'd like him to. But in our state, if any dad wants to participate in his kids' lives, that's given a lot of credence. So even though we had a legal document spelling out how things would be, it doesn't matter. That got changed very easily."

Laws vary from state to state on the parental rights and responsibilities of known donors. You should know what the laws are in your state if you have used a known donor. Even if things seem to be working out

---

♦ **Did You Know . . . ?** ♦

In the majority of cases where a known donor is used, no legal problems result. Only in about ten percent of cases do the mother and the donor end up in legal battles.

Pepper, R. (1999). *The ultimate guide to pregnancy for lesbians.* San Francisco: Cleis Press.

---

well, you cannot be certain that the situation will not change in the future. It is best to find out what the legalities are concerning your specific situation.

Adoption: Special Pressures and Special Benefits

Lesbian Adoptive Mothers: Double the Pressure?

Lesbian mothers, in general, may feel extra pressure to be good parents, in order to prove themselves worthy. Adoptive parents, in general, often feel extra pressure to be good parents, because of all they have gone through to become parents. Imagine, then, how much pressure lesbian adoptive parents may be under when it comes to parenting.

Adoptive parents, whether they are heterosexual or homosexual, have to go through enormous hurdles to get a child that birth parents do not. The process is designed to protect the child, but it can still be arduous. Prospective parents must open up their homes to strangers, who come in and conduct the dreaded "home study" in order to determine whether they are fit to raise a child. They must undergo criminal background checks (which usually involve being fingerprinted). They must complete applications that ask about everything from parenting philosophy to bank accounts to one's social life and hobbies. And of course we're not even mentioning the tens of thousands of dollars it can cost to go through an adoption process. (Not all adoptions are this expensive. Adoptions that take place through state agencies, for example through the foster care system, can have minimal costs.) After all that, when they finally have a child in their arms, adoptive parents are often still held to higher standards—even by themselves.

As Margaret says, "Very often, adoptive parents think that they have to be perfect. You know, why would you adopt a kid and then put him in day care? I have a whole set of expectations for myself that other people don't have. For me, where it comes in, especially at first, is how could I ever complain about this child? It was like I couldn't say anything

---

♦ Did You Know . . . ? ♦

In the United States, adoption occurs in somewhere between two and four percent of all families.

Rosenberg, E. I. (1992). *The adoption life cycle: The children and their families through the years.* New York, NY: Free Press.

---

negative about her because we had had to work for her and prove ourselves differently. You have to prove yourself so much, and you get so scrutinized in advance that you feel like you have to live up to this whole other thing."

For lesbians, as for heterosexual women, adoption often follows years of infertility, and all the emotional heartache and financial burdens that entails. The decision to pursue adoption, rather than pregnancy, is often a very difficult and bittersweet one. Lesbians have often already been through an emotional wringer before they even begin the adoption process. It is common for them to wonder if they ever will hold a child in their arms whom they can call their own. When they finally do have their own child, they feel overwhelmingly grateful and blessed. Later, when ordinary life events occur, they remember how difficult it was to get this child and this may influence their decisions in negative ways. For example, a mother who really cannot afford it may give her three-year-old a lavish birthday party because she remembers the times when she wondered if she would ever have a child at all. Another mother may feel guilty expressing ambivalence or negative feelings about her adopted child—feelings that all parents have from time to time.

Adoptive lesbian mothers should acknowledge the double burden of pressure they may be carrying. It would be very easy for them to fall into a pattern of trying to be perfect mothers of perfect children. It would be very easy for them to deny that they have any feelings of doubt, resentment, or exhaustion. This is particularly true during the early years of their children's lives, when the situation is new and the demands are the greatest. Keep in mind that all parents have some ambivalent feelings about the demands of childcare from time to time. This does not make them, or you, unworthy of being parents. You may find it helpful to keep in touch with other adoptive parents—lesbian, gay, or straight.

Lesbian adoptive mothers may also have the extra pressure and worry that comes with adopting a child who may be at risk for developmental problems. It is not uncommon for there to be health issues surrounding the status of an adopted child. The possibility that the child's biological mother may have used drugs or alcohol, or been infected with a serious disease such as HIV, have to be considered. Children adopted internationally have often received substandard care, and this poses its own set of worries. The biological mother of Yvonne's son, Enrique, had a history of drug use, and this did cause her and her family some concern. "His biological parents are not very together, so I think they [her family] were concerned about what that meant in terms of the child I was bringing into my family. And, you know, there may be some truth there too. It's interesting. He's definitely had some learning problems and stuff. But as far as who he is, his personality, he's the most wonderful kid you could ever wish for. But he has some learning problems."

There is no doubt that children whose parents abused drugs or alcohol are at increased risk for developing physical, emotional, behavioral, or learning problems as they get older. Likewise for children who have spent their early months or years in an orphanage receiving poor care. But it is important to note that children are enormously resilient and can often overcome even the most seemingly damaging early circumstances. There are no guarantees with adopted children, just as there are no guarantees with biological children. The experiences we give our children should be designed to enable them to develop to their optimal level, and that is the best we can do.

Lisa is emphatic in her belief that adopted children are unfairly viewed as being problematic. "The one thing that I just feel really, really strongly is that it is not automatic that adopted kids are screwed up. Part of the adoption process suggests that your kids are going to be a mess. I never bought that, and neither did Robin." She remembers that at one point "we tried to give them counseling services and were turned down. And you know the school thinks it's a riot that these adopted Latino kids of Jewish lesbian parents really aren't messed up enough to qualify for counseling services."

Adoption as a First Choice

The stereotypical idea that many people hold is that adoption is a second choice, made mainly by those who, for medical reasons, were unable to bear their own children. This is not always the case. Many times, people who could have their own children choose to adopt. This is particularly true for lesbians. Two reasons often cited are the belief that there are many children in the world already who need love and care, and the desire to create a multiracial, multiethnic family.

Lisa is one example of a lesbian whose first choice was to create her family through adoption. "She [her former partner] and I both could have had children, but I've always wanted to adopt, even when I was straight." Lisa and her former partner wanted to have a diverse, interracial family. Lisa is white, her sons are Hispanic, and two former girlfriends were African Americans. "My son says we're just like any other family, except all mixed up." And that is just how he wants it. "Our family isn't like every other family, and we don't want to be."

Families like Lisa's are less prone to pressuring themselves to be the perfect, all-American family, whatever that means, since that was never their intention to begin with. Having a child of a different racial background, however, does create issues that don't exist in families where all the members are of the same race.

Interracial Lesbian Families

Often, lesbians who adopt a child are facing two hurdles: Not only are they raising a child in a lesbian-headed family, but they are also raising a child with a different ethnic or racial background from their own. Yvonne is white and her son, Enrique, is Hispanic. Yvonne feels the pressure to provide her son not only with a male role model, but with a Hispanic male role model in particular. "I guess I worry more about the Hispanic issue than I do about the male issue, because I want him to see that Hispanic men can be different things than what sometimes the example is here in the city. Because there's a lot of gang problems and all that kind of stuff here." She adds that she's not sure that she "would go out and search out a man to be in his life," whereas she does "go out somewhere specific and search out Hispanic culture for him to have." Yvonne feels fortunate that one of Enrique's biological siblings is being raised by a gay Hispanic man, and Enrique gets to see him regularly.

"Enrique is three-quarters Hispanic, and he looks very Hispanic, and he's always going to be recognized that way. So even though he lives in a family where his mom is white, his experience of the world is always going to be as a Hispanic man, because that's how kids are going to interact with him," explains Yvonne. Yvonne recently decided to have another child, this time by donor insemination. "I had specifically picked a Hispanic donor, and it was because of him." She wants her new baby to resemble his brother, so that Enrique will not be the only Hispanic child in his family.

Paula and Nancy's family includes a mixture of racial backgrounds as well. Nancy's two grown sons are hers from a previous marriage; their third son is an AI baby with a known donor; and their youngest son, C. J., is adopted. C. J., says Paula, is "adopted; he's African American. We decided that since our own boys had dads, he needed a dad too. So we put the word out in the community. This really nice, gay black man who is a banker and who was interested in becoming involved moved into our apartment, and then shortly after he moved in, his boyfriend moved in with him." Both men remain involved with C. J., even though they have since moved. This arrangement has allowed C. J. to have a male influence (in this case, two male influences) as well as an African American role model.

Lisa is another white mother of Hispanic sons. She has noticed how her sons' different personalities play into their own senses of racial identity. "My older son hangs out with a very multiracial group of kids. The one girl in the crowd is even a lesbian. My older son is very identified as a kid of color." She notes that "my other son is very mainstream identified, white rock music—all his friends are white, just about. He's much more concerned with being part of the status quo and, you know, image and money and all this kind of stuff." It is worth keeping in mind that children do play an active role in forming their own identity. It is important for adoptive mothers of children from another race to provide exposure to people of their child's background and to that culture. It is also important to allow your child the freedom to choose his or her own identity.

Open Adoptions

Increasingly, the traditional method of closed adoption, where the birth records are sealed and no exchange of information between birth and adoptive parents occurs, is giving way to open adoptions. With some variations, in an open adoption the birth mother chooses the parents who will adopt her baby. There is an agreement made prior to the birth of the baby about how much contact the birth mother will have with the child. The adoptive parents agree to send pictures periodically, in addition to having visits. Under this arrangement, the child will actually know his or her birth mother, and the birth mother will get to be a part of the child's life.

In his book *The Kid*, Dan Savage chronicles the open adoption process that he and his boyfriend went through for their son. As a gay male couple they experienced many of the same fears that a lesbian couple would in going through the process ("How open will the agency be in working with us? Will any birth mother pick a gay couple to be parents for her child? Will she be worried that the child will be teased?"). Happily for them, they were chosen by their son's birth mother very quickly, and the family is doing well.

There are no statistics on how many lesbians have done open adoptions, but the numbers are surely growing. There are birth mothers who choose lesbians as parents for their children, either because they think it doesn't matter or they think that it will benefit their child in some way—maybe it's the "two moms are better than one" idea. Lesbians who adopt their children in this manner do not have the task of explaining to their child that his biological family is out there somewhere but they don't know where. Instead, they must deal with the biological mother in the flesh. Their child may have three mothers in his life. As with most things, talking openly to the child from the very beginning about the circumstances of his adoption is the best thing to do. Having the biological mother around makes this task easier. Keep in mind, there are no strict models to guide adoptive parents as they go about forming a relationship with their child's birth mother. Every situation of this type will be unique, regarding the level of contact and involvement of the biological mother.

Lesbian Adoptive Mothers: Greater Acceptance?

Margaret feels that the fact that Alexa was adopted makes people more readily accept her and Sarah as lesbian parents. "I do think that it is easier and that we get a more positive response because she is adopted. People can process it differently, and I can see it in people's faces. People want to know who gave birth to her, so initially we say we're both her moms. When we say we adopted her from Russia, you can visibly see the change in people's faces. I think people are more comfortable with that. I think it makes sense to them. Even if they feel negative about lesbian parenting, I think the fact that she was a child in an orphanage and came to our house makes them feel less negative. So I do think it has served us. Should it be that way? No."

It seems that adopting children can make it easier for people to accept lesbian motherhood. Rescuing a child from an orphanage, or taking in a child with special needs or handicaps, is certainly a selfless and loving act. And even people with a negative attitude toward lesbian motherhood often have a difficult time faulting someone for adopting a child in need—even if that someone is a lesbian. So there may, in a strange way, be a social advantage for lesbians who adopt their children as compared to those who give birth to their children. This advantage is probably most pronounced when the children are young. As they get older, the circumstances of their birth generally are not discussed as often.

Of course this is a subtle example of prejudice against lesbian mothers. All lesbian mothers, no matter how they got their children, should receive the same level of respect from others. Adoptive mothers are no more, or less, selfless or virtuous than biological mothers. But the fact remains that people may be more at ease with lesbian adoptive mothers than with lesbian biological mothers. People who are uncomfortable with the idea of donor insemination or an anonymous donor may be more willing to embrace the idea of a lesbian taking in a child who has no parents. As Margaret and Sarah have found, being adoptive mothers can be an advantage in gaining approval from others.

Not a Secret

There are many books written for adoptive parents, as there are many books written for every conceivable type of parent and child. Once again, we have found, from looking at those aimed at helping heterosexual adoptive parents cope with the special situations and problems they uniquely face, that many of those problems simply do not apply to lesbians. As we saw with books written for parents who used donor insemination, the big issues are secrecy and when to tell the child she is adopted. Not to overstate the obvious, but no one is going to think that your children were born to two mothers. The books that are probably most useful to lesbian adoptive mothers are those written specifically on interracial adoption. Even if your child has the same racial background that you do, you may find these books speak more to your concerns: how to deal with having a family that looks different from others.

There are many complicated issues involved in creating our families (finding a reputable sperm bank, the legal issues involved in adoption, and so on), and we cannot possibly cover all of them fully here. If you are a lesbian who is thinking about creating a family, or adding to the one you already have, we refer you to the "Resources" section at the end of this chapter.

What You Can Do to Cement Your Family

1. Make baby albums for your children. If your child is an AI baby, include sonogram pictures and pictures of you while you were pregnant. If your child is adopted, include pictures of where he lived before you adopted him (if possible) and pictures of his homecoming.

2. If you had your child through anonymous AI, keep a copy of all the information about the donor and the sperm bank. Your child will want to see it at some point, probably adolescence.

3. If you have used a known donor, be sure you know the legalities in your state. You and the donor should have a written agreement outlining his rights and responsibilities toward the child.

4. If your child is adopted, celebrate two birthdays: his actual birthday and the day he entered your family.

Resources

Heather Has Two Mommies, by Lesléa Newman (1991). Boston, MA: Alyson Publications.

A children's book geared for preschoolers and early elementary-school-age children. It explains how a little girl with two mommies came to be, and how all families are special.

The Ultimate Guide to Pregnancy for Lesbians, by Rachel Pepper (1999). San Francisco, CA: Cleis Press.

This book contains lots of detailed information on how to get pregnant, including discussions of known versus anonymous donors and how to find a sperm bank. It also takes you through pregnancy, delivery, and life with a newborn. This is a great resource for lesbians who want to create or add to their families.

Considering Parenthood, by Cheri Pies (1988). Duluth, MN: Spinsters Ink.

Written by a therapist who works with lesbian parenthood groups, this book can guide lesbians who are considering parenthood through the decision-making process. It includes all the ramifications—legal, financial, and emotional—of this life-altering decision.

www.lesbian.org/moms/adopt.htm

This site contains a list of frequently asked questions, answered by gay and lesbian adoptive parents based on their own experiences. It contains some resources as well.

listserv@maelstrom.stjohns.edu

A list serve for gay and lesbian parents who adopted their children. Send an e-mail with "subscribe gay-aparent" in the body to get on the list.

Creating Ceremonies: Innovative Ways to Meet Adoption Challenges, by Cheryl A. Liebermand and Rhea K. Bufford (1998). Phoenix, AZ: Zeig, Tucker & Theisen.

This is one of the few books that addresses itself to older child adoptions and the ways parents can make their children feel like part of the family. It includes gay and lesbian adoptive families.

♦ PART V ♦

Conclusion

CHAPTER 15

Future Directions and Concluding Thoughts

Where Are Our Families Now?

Over the course of doing research for this book, we found ourselves on more than one occasion being pleasantly surprised by what we learned. For example, neither of us was aware of the many church-affiliated organizations that are advocating for acceptance and celebration of gays and lesbians into mainstream religions. We take this as a very good sign, considering the amount of publicity that the religious right gets.

We were often quite excited to find resources and supports that we didn't know about.

"I found that court decision, *Nabozny v. Podlesny*, that you were talking about."

"The one about the high-school student in Wisconsin, right? That's the one that really has school administrators running scared. It's amazing what a $900,000 settlement can do to one's sensibilities and sense of justice."

"And did you know that the federal government, that is *our* federal government, has issued guidelines on how to prevent harassment based on sexual orientation in schools? Can you believe this?"

"Let me see that. Oh, and take a look at this web site of gay and lesbian psychiatrists. I thought it looked pretty good."

And so it went. We found many more supports and resources than we had imagined and from more mainstream organizations than we would have guessed. And we didn't think of ourselves as uninformed when we began this book project.

As you are aware, we interviewed a number of lesbian mothers for this book. We have also done other research asking lesbian mothers and gay fathers about their experiences for another project. In both cases, we were struck by how positive the reports were, for the most part. Of course there was the occasional negative experience, but this was the exception. Most parents experience a few bumps on the road and some situations that require special care, but few people have reported experiencing any major problems.

So where are our families now? Overall, our families seem to be functioning very well and being accepted by the greater community.

We have made great strides in recent years. For example, the first second-parent adoption to a lesbian was granted in 1987. By 2000, seventeen states allow second-parent adoptions. More will certainly follow. Our families have more support out in the world than most of us realize, and these are increasing all the time. We are finding more legal recognition, based both on court decisions and legislation. We are being welcomed by more churches and synagogues. Our families are becoming part of the fabric of our communities.

Where Are Our Families Going?

What are the future directions for our families? We see two ways to look at that question. The first is to look at our families themselves and what changes might be ahead for us. The second is to look at the society as a whole and what changes might be ahead for it because of us.

In regard to both, we have some predictions. We predict that there will continue to be legislative advances in the areas of gay and lesbian adoption. These advances will bring some opposition by small groups of right-wing zealots. The zealots will likely win a battle or two here and there, but more and more cases (involving second-parent adoptions and single parents being able to adopt) are going our way. Our families are pushing for legal protections, and we are getting them. Ironically, even the sad occasions of lesbian mothers fighting for child custody may ultimately have a beneficial impact on our families. As more custody cases between lesbian mothers come to court, more jurisdictions will be forced to answer questions like What is a family? and Who is a mother? We expect those questions will be answered in such a way as to recognize our families as valid ones. Ultimately, just as divorce and single parenting within the heterosexual community have become commonplace, so too will parenting by people who are gay or lesbian.

Any minority group faces a challenge as it becomes more assimilated into part of a culture. The challenge is not to lose its identity as it moves and is integrated into the mainstream. The lesbian community has many characteristics that set us apart from mainstream society, beyond the obvious distinction of being comprised of women who love women. We are also a community that rejects sexual stereotypes; we favor egalitarian relationships; we value diversity; we do not accept patriarchal structures of authority as the best we can do. Our goal is to maintain what is special about our community and our families. As Lisa says, "We don't feel like we are 'just like everybody else,' and we don't want to be."

In the years ahead, our families may indeed become just like everybody else's, in terms of legal recognition. What we have to do is make sure that our families don't become like so many have become in the mainstream. Being overly materialistic, pushing our children to fit into some preordained role without regard for the child's needs or interests, and spending little time with them are not goals to strive for. We must work to maintain our own values even as we become more accepted by and part of mainstream society.

As our children grow up and enter the world, we predict that they will contribute to a greater understanding between the gay and straight worlds. There are children of lesbian mothers, such as Sol Kelley-Jones, whom we talked about in Chapter 11, who work as advocates for gay and lesbian families, making speeches, lobbying, and so forth. While this is an obvious way our children can make a difference, we certainly don't mean to imply that it is our goal to have our children work in this very public way. That is not our goal. What we are saying is that our children will inevitably have an impact upon other people's views. Through knowing our children and our families, other people—teachers, other children, neighbors, and so on—will get to see that lesbians are a lot like everyone else. In turn, those people will become a little more enlightened and a little less homophobic. Ironically, our children will play a large part in changing the world, even in these very private, subtle ways, more than we could have ever done ourselves.

Concluding Thoughts

We were upstairs in our office at our house, tying up the last loose ends for this book, when our daughters came in holding hands. They are now six and three. (They were four and one when we began.)

"Aren't you done with that book yet?" asked Bailey. "We want to play."

She and Rowan looked at us with hopeful, expectant faces.

We looked at each other. Are there any more perils facing lesbian mothers that we haven't covered yet? Have we thought of all the potential problems and challenges that face our families? Should we spend more time trying to imagine every possible difficulty that we or our children could conceivably run across?

Without even saying it aloud, we both came to the same conclusion. We may not have thought of every possible problem. But we know where all the likely problems are, and we have a plan on how to deal with them. We know our families face extra challenges, but we also have extra strengths. We need to go ahead and be the mothers we want to be, aware of the dangers but secure in our ability to handle them. Our desire, commitment, and ability to be parents will prevail.

"Yes, we're finished with the book now. Let's go play."

The girls jumped up and down excitedly. "Yippee!" shouted Bailey.

"Wippee!" shouted Rowan (the *y* sound still escapes her in excitement).

To quote a recent book: "Love really does make a family."

Appendix

Parenting Books

Here are some of the parenting books we have consulted and recommend. Some of them are fairly general, while others address a fairly specific group or issue.

Our favorite authors of parenting books are William and Martha Sears. He is a pediatrician, she is a nurse, and together they have raised eight children. We really like their approach, which emphasizes attachment parenting and positive discipline.

The Baby Book: Everything You Need to Know about Your Baby from Birth to Age Two, by William Sears and Martha Sears (1993). Boston, MA: Little, Brown and Company.

The topic is caring for your infant, both physically and emotionally.

The Discipline Book: Everything You Need to Know to Have a Better-Behaved Child from Birth to Age Ten, by William Sears and Martha Sears (1995). Boston, MA: Little, Brown and Company.

Beginning with establishing a strong bond with your child during infancy, the Searses discuss promoting desirable behavior, dealing with the undesirable, and advice on specific situations.

Parenting the Fussy Baby and High Need Child: Everything You Need to Know from Birth to Age Five, by William Sears and Martha Sears (1996). Boston, MA: Little, Brown and Company.

This book focuses on dealing with a child who is more demanding and intense than most. From soothing a colicky baby to disciplining a very active toddler, this book covers it (with lots of real-life examples and respect for parent and child).

The Family Nutrition Book: Everything You Need to Know about Feeding Your Children from Birth to Adolescence, by William Sears and Martha Sears (1999). Boston, MA: Little, Brown and Company.

The Searses cover the topic of nutrition this time. It includes everything from when to start solids to feeding picky toddlers to avoiding childhood obesity. The book is also a good general nutrition primer.

What to Expect the First Year, by Arlene Eisenberg, Heidi E. Murkoff, and Sandee E. Hathaway (1989). New York, NY: Workman Publishing.

A continuation of the wildly popular *What to Expect When You're Expecting,* this book follows the same format of giving month by month milestones. We found the "What Your Baby May Be Doing" feature, which lists specific abilities that babies should be able to do at each month, to be the best and most helpful part of the book. Provides good general babycare advice. We do not recommend trying the recipes.

Raising Low-Fat Kids in a High-Fat World, by Judith Shaw (1992). San Francisco, CA: Chronicle Books.

This book contains lots of information about helping your family break the high-fat habit. Includes recipes.

How to Raise an Adopted Child: A Guide to Help Your Child Flourish from Infancy through Adolescence, by Judith Schaffer and Christina Lindstrom (1989). New York, NY: Copestone Press, Inc., Crown Publishers.

Written by two of the cofounders of the Center for Adoptive Families, a facility in New York City, this book thoroughly discusses issues relevant to children of different ages, to special-needs adoptions and the multiracial family. There is very little on gay adoption in particular (less than one page), but a positive, warm approach to living in an adoptive family.

The Black Parenting Book: Caring for Our Children in the First Five Years, by Anne C. Beal, Linda Villarosa, and Allison Abner (1999). New York, NY: Broadway Books.

Written specifically for parents of young African American children, this book offers not only general development and pediatric advice, but also covers topics not found in general parenting books. Issues like cultural pride, self-esteem, and spirituality are discussed. Coincidentally, Villarosa is a lesbian mother, and she speaks of her own experiences parenting a biracial daughter with her partner.

Raising Lifelong Learners: A Parent's Guide, by Lucy Calkins (1997). Reading, MA: Addison-Wesley.

This book gives advice on choosing a school for your child, being an advocate for your child in the educational system, and promoting strong academic skills at home.

Perfect Parenting: The Dictionary of 1000 Parenting Tips, by Elizabeth Pantley (1998). Chicago, IL: Contemporary Books.

The author has busy parents in mind, so she lists common concerns alphabetically and provides concise, easy-to-follow suggestions.

The Queer Parent's Primer: A Lesbian and Gay Families' Guide to Navigating the Straight World, by Stephanie A. Brill (2001). Oakland, CA: New Harbinger Publications.

Brill's book offers many suggestions, along with interactive exercises and advice, on how to raise a family in a world that is not designed for us.

Families Like Mine: Children of Gay Parents Tell It Like It Is, by Abigail Garner (2004). New York, NY: HarperCollins.

Garner is a well-known advocate for children of LGBT parents (her own mother and father divorced when she was five and her father came out). Her book weaves her own experience of growing up with a gay dad with those of other young adults who grew up in similar families. Both parents and (older) children will benefit from reading this thoughtful book.

Out of the Ordinary: Essays on Growing Up with Gay, Lesbian, and Transgender Parents, edited by Noelle Howey and Ellen Samuels (2000). New York, NY: St. Martin's Press/Stonewall Inn Editions.

This is a collection of essays written by young adults who have grown up with GLBT parents. It includes a resource section as well as a foreword by Margarethe Cammermeyer, author of *Serving in Silence,* and a preface by Dan Savage, author of *The Kid.*

The Lesbian Parenting Book: A Guide to Creating Families and Raising Children, by D. Merilee Clunis and G. Dorsey Green (1995). Seattle, WA: Seal Press.

One of the first books written specifically for lesbian mothers, this covers all aspects of childrearing, from prenatal care to living with an adult child and everything in between.

The Lesbian and Gay Parenting Handbook: Creating and Raising Our Families, by April Martin (1993). New York, NY: HarperPerennial.

Martin was a pioneer in this book and, though some of the specifics are no longer current (for example, the legal landscape for gay and lesbian parents has changed quite a bit since this book was written), it is still a thoughtful, valuable resource.

Resources

Here are some selected resources of general interest to lesbian mothers and our children. Some of these have been included in earlier chapters.

Family Pride Coalition
P.O. Box 65327
Washington, DC 20035-5237
Telephone: 202-331-5015
Fax: 202-331-0080
www.familypride.org
e-mail: pride@familypride.org

A national group that offers advocacy and support for gay, lesbian, bisexual, and transgendered parents and their families (see page 70 for full details).

Children of Lesbians and Gays Everywhere
3543 18th Street #17
San Francisco, CA 94110
Telephone: 415-861-5437
Fax: 415-255-8345
www.colage.org
e-mail: colage@colage.org

A great on-line resource for children of gays and lesbians (see page 69 for full details).

National Gay and Lesbian Task Force
1325 Massachusetts Avenue NW, Suite 600
Washington, DC 20005
Telephone: 202-393-5177
Fax: 202-393-2241
www.ngltf.org
e-mail: ngltf@ngltf.org

A think tank concerned with monitoring and promoting legal and civil rights for members of the gay and lesbian community (see page 181 for full details).

National Center for Lesbian Rights
870 Market Street, Suite 370
San Francisco, CA 94102
Telephone: 415-392-6257
Fax: 415-392-8442
www.nclrights.org
e-mail: info@nclrights.org

The Center maintains a site that offers advice for lesbians on a host of legal issues (see page 181 for full details).

Parents, Families and Friends of Lesbians and Gays
1726 "M" Street, NW, Suite 400
Washington, DC 20036
Telephone: 202-467-8180
Fax: 202-467-8194
www.pflag.org
e-mail: infor@pflag.org

A large national organization for relatives and friends of gays and lesbians (see page 199 for full details).

Lambda Legal Defense and
    Education Fund
National Headquarters
120 Wall Street, Suite 1500
New York, NY 10005-3904
Telephone: 212-809-8585
Fax: 212-809-0055

Western Regional Office
3325 Wilshire Boulevard, Suite 1300
Los Angeles, CA 90010-1729
Telephone: 213-382-7600
Fax: 213-351-6050

Midwest Regional Office
11 East Adams, Suite 1008
Chicago, IL 60603-6303
Telephone: 312-663-4413
Fax: 312-663-4307

Southern Regional Office
1447 Peachtree Street, NE, Suite 1004
Atlanta, GA 30309-3027
Telephone: 404-897-1880
Fax: 404-897-1884

South Central Regional Office
3500 Oak Lawn Avenue, Suite 500
Dallas, TX 75219-6722
Telephone: 214-219-8585
Fax: 214-219-4455

www.lambdalegal.org
e-mail: lambdalegal@lambdalegal.org

The national organization dedicated to promoting legal and civil rights to the gay and lesbian community (see pages 199–200 for full details).

Gay and Lesbian Alliance Against Defamation
248 West 35th Street, 8th floor
New York, NY 10001
Telephone: 212-629-3322
Fax: 212-629-3225
www.Glaad.org
e-mail: glaad@glaad.org

GLAAD promotes fair, accurate, and inclusive portrayals of gays and lesbians in the media. You can keep up-to-date on the latest news and happenings about the media's depiction of our community.

Human Rights Campaign
1640 Rhode Island Avenue, NW
Washington, DC 20036-3278
Telephone: 202-628-4160
Fax: 202-347-5323
www.hrc.org
e-mail: hrc@hrc.org

The Human Rights Campaign is our country's largest gay and lesbian advocacy organization. HRC lobbies Congress, supports grassroots political activities, and works to educate the public about issues that affect the gay and lesbian community. Click on the "Family" link to get information about relationships, parenting, and family life issues.

In the Family: The Magazine for Queer People and Their Loved Ones
Publisher: Laura Markowitz
7850 North Silverbell, #114-188
Tucson, AZ 85743
Telephone: 520-579-8043
e-mail: lmarkowitz@aol.com

This mental health magazine focuses exclusively on lesbian, gay, bisexual, and transgendered families. It is published quarterly and has articles, book reviews, and fiction.

Gay Parent Magazine
P.O. Box 750852
Forest Hills, NY 11375-0852
www.gayparentmag.com
e-mail: acain@gis.net

A bimonthly magazine for gay men and women who are or wish to be parents. Both the magazine and web site provide a comprehensive listing of resources for gay parents and their children, as well as articles and book reviews.

And Baby Magazine
55 Washington Street, Suite 812
Brooklyn, NY 11201
Telephone: 1-866-ANDBABY
Fax: 718-422-7602
www.andbabymag.com
e-mail: info@andbabymag.com

A bimonthly publication for the lesbian, gay, bisexual, and transgendered community, covering issues from birth through adolescence. Both the magazine and web site include health/medical issues, legal issues, fashion, education, media topics, and a comprehensive national resource guide.

Local Parent Support Groups

A large number of lesbian parent support groups now exist throughout the United States and Canada. Because the contacts for these groups change frequently, you may want to call one of the national organizations listed above for the most current information. Alternatively, you can visit your favorite search engine and type in keywords such as "Lesbian Parents Support Groups" or "Gay Family Support Groups," which will provide you with a comprehensive listing.

As of the printing of this book, the web sites below provide contact information for many support groups and services for gay and lesbian parents:

www.gayparentmag.com   click on link for "Support Groups"

www.milepost1.com/~gaydad/Support.Groups.html

Index

About the Authors

SUZANNE M. JOHNSON received her PhD in developmental psychology from the State University of New York at Stony Brook. She is currently Associate Professor of Psychology at Dowling College, where she has taught for the past 13 years. Suzanne has been the recipient of several awards for her teaching and service to the college. She has presented research at the Society for Research in Child Development and at the American Academy of Child and Adolescent Psychiatry. Suzanne is currently conducting a national study of gay and lesbian parents with her partner, Elizabeth O'Connor. Suzanne and Elizabeth have two daughters.

ELIZABETH O'CONNOR also received her PhD in developmental psychology from the State University of New York at Stony Brook. She has held postdoctoral research assistantships at Stony Brook and at Harvard Medical School. Her research focusing on child development, adult relationships, and families has been presented at the Society for Research in Child Development and at the American Academy of Child and Adolescent Psychiatry. She is collaborating with her partner, Suzanne M. Johnson, on a national study of gay and lesbian parents. Elizabeth and Suzanne have been together for 16 years.